Korea's Occupied Cinemas, 1893–1948

Routledge Advances in Film Studies

Korea's Occupied Cinemas, 1893–1948

Brian Yecies and Ae-Gyung Shim

Routledge
Taylor & Francis Group
NEW YORK   LONDON

First published 2011
by Routledge
711 Third Avenue, New York, NY 10017

Simultaneously published in the UK
by Routledge
2 Park Square, Milton Park, Abingdon, Oxon OX14 4RN

*Routledge is an imprint of the Taylor & Francis Group,
an informa business*

© 2011 Taylor & Francis

Typeset in Sabon by IBT Global.
First issued in paperback in 2013

Library of Congress Cataloging-in-Publication Data
Yecies, Brian, 1967–
   Korea's occupied cinemas, 1893–1948 : the untold history of the film
industry / by Brian Yecies, with Ae-Gyung Shim.
      p. cm. — (Routledge advances in film studies ; 10)
   Includes bibliographical references and index.
   1. Motion picture industry—Korea—History—20th century.   2. Motion
pictures—Korea—History—20th century.   3. Motion pictures—Korea—
Foreign influences.   4. Korea—History—Japanese occupation, 1910–
1945.   I. Shim, Ae-Gyung, 1973–   II. Title.
   PN1993.5.K6Y43 2011
   791.4309519'09041—dc22
   2011000069

ISBN13: 978-0-415-74048-7 (pbk)
ISBN13: 978-0-415-99538-2 (hbk)
ISBN13: 978-0-203-80933-4 (ebk)

For Robert Shimhun and Alex Kangho. Carry forward what we have received from our mothers and fathers. Look up to the sky and feel the spirit of those who came before you.

This work was published with a publication subsidy awarded by The Academy of Korean Studies Grant, which is funded by the Korean Government (MEST, Basic Research Promotion Fund). (AKS-2010-AAD-4101).

Research for this book was made possible through an Advanced Research Grant (2008) and a Research Fellowship (2005) from the Korea Foundation.

Contents

Figures

Foreword

It is a pleasure and a privilege to celebrate the publication of this book, which has the potential to expand our understanding of cultural diversity. According to the Convention on the Protection and Promotion of the Diversity of Cultural Expressions accepted by UNESCO (United Nations Educational, Scientific and Cultural Organization) at its thirty-third session in Paris in October 2005: "Cultural diversity creates a rich and varied world, which increases the range of choices and nurtures human capacities and values, and therefore is a mainspring for sustainable development for communities, peoples and nations." Over the past eight years, I have watched Brian, whose mother tongue is English, and Ae-Gyung, whose mother tongue is Korean, working together to write this book. Their work reminds me of this phrase.

This book focuses on the Korean cinema, which of recent years has gained cultural independence as well as its own international influence on other countries' cinemas, while trying to maneuver away from the influences of American (mostly Hollywood) films and popular culture of which the spread was supported by the world power of the United States and its universally reaching language of English. I imagine Brian and Ae-Gyung, whose cultural backgrounds differ, would have discussed and debated long and hard to reach a consensus of understanding about the development of the Korean cinema. This would have involved an extensive process of analyzing diverse circumstantial variants surrounding the Korean cinema and comprehending the dynamic context of international politics, economics, and culture at the given time.

Brian and Ae-Gyung have traced the history of cinema in Korea painstakingly in countries such as South Korea, Australia, Japan, China, and the United States, whilst trying to understand the historiography of Korean cinema within the world cinema. As a former film-policy maker and now an analyst, I have observed the growth of Korean cinema since the 1980s and have experienced at first hand the issues surrounding the Screen Quota System, domination of screens by a few blockbuster films (lack of cultural diversity), and renewed sources of funding. While following their research outcome, which is based on empirical research of the years between 1893 and 1948, I have become certain that history repeats itself. Knowing the challenges of researching historical documents dating back to this period, I admire their hardworking attitude as researchers. They have cross-checked Korean cinema with Japanese cinema, American cinema and other Asian cinemas, and analyzed the relationship between industry people in different countries, while interpreting and re-evaluating these rare historical documents.

Seeing the commendable quality of completed work in this present book is certainly an encouragement for me to continue my own life-long research, and it is certain to inspire many other readers. In particular, their research that focuses on film and media (including advertisements) as an inter-cultural communication tool reminds us that the artistic achievements of an individual or a group cannot be separated by the world in which they live.

During the time that I worked for the Korean Film Council (1999–2008), I tried to make Korean cinema accessible not only as a product of consumption but also as a research objective. I helped to develop the policy support that built a Korean Film Library in several locations around the world with the hope of researchers using them as resource centers. I also helped to raise the future generations of creators and artists, and to enhance the freedom of expression of other Asian countries' cinemas. I recently have witnessed the dynamics and the potential of cinemas in Vietnam and Cambodia, as well as Laos, through my participation in the 1st Hanoi International Film Festival held in October 2010. I appreciate the continuous support from Brian and Ae-Gyung, which reminds me of the significance of cultural diversity, and I look forward to working with them well into the future on a range of under-evaluated topics regarding the Korean cinema since the mid-1980s and diversity in the production of more recent digital media and cultural contents.

I hope readers of this book will always think of this statement: "Cultural diversity is strengthened by the free flow of ideas, and that it is nurtured by constant exchanges and interaction between cultures."

Hyae-joon Kim.
Seoul, November 2010
Hyae-joon Kim has served as Coordinator, Screen Quota Watchdog
group; Vice Chief, Korean Film Institute; and
Secretary General, Korean Film Council (KOFIC).

Acknowledgments

This work in progress is the result of at least eight years of archive research and writing, which was made possible by the moral, financial, and practical support of friends, colleagues, and others too numerous to mention.

First and foremost, we are forever grateful for the inspiration and ongoing support that we have received from our families. Without unconditional love and encouragement from Robert ('Sheik') Yecies and Sandye Yecies, and Shim Sangdal and Hur Kwang Suk, we would not have realized our personal and professional accomplishments. We now aspire to 'pay it forward' to our own offspring.

A debt of sincere thanks is owed to a wide range of film industry people, scholars, and researchers who willingly shared their personal insights and experiences (and listened too). More often than not, it was humbling to be in the presence of such awe-inspiring individuals who made us acutely aware of the deep and complex emotions connected to filmmaking and of the lived experiences of the colonial, post colonial, and contemporary periods in Korea. Thank you, Lee Hyung-pyo, Cha Yun, Shin Chul (Korea's last surviving *byeonsa*); Kim Hyae-joon and Kim Mee-hyun (from the Korean Film Council); researchers Cho Jun-hyung, Chung Jong-hwa, and Oh Sung-ji (from the Korean Film Archive); and scholars Kim Soyoung, Yi Hyoin, Michael Robinson, Kim Kyung Hyun, Kitamura Hiroshi, Cho Hee-moon, Yi Young-jae, Jung Keun-sik, Chang Kyung-Sup, Roald Maliangkay, Mark McLelland, Mark Caprio, and Mark Morris. Our only hope is that their intellect, dedication, enthusiasm and persevering spirit regarding the national film industry and cultural diversity in Korea and Asia more generally will live on through our work.

Other wise friends and colleagues Bill Routt, Rick Thompson, Philip Kitley, Tom O'Regan, Ben Goldsmith, Adrian Mabbott Athique, Kate Bowles, Sue Turnbull, Richard Howson, Mary Beth Haralovich, Eileen Meehan, Darcy Paquet, Mark J. Russell, Jeong Hye-yeon, Matt Allen, and Fiona George deserve special mention for a range of reasons. Thank you for caring!

Librarians from across the United States, South Korea, Japan, and Australia eased our access to all of the rare archive documents that were read, collected, and cited in this manuscript. In particular, Ned Comstock at the USC Cinema/Television Library, Joy Kim at the USC Korean Heritage/East Asian Library, Barbara Hall at the Margaret Herrick Library–Academy of Motion Picture Arts and Sciences, and Lesley Smith from the UOW provided invaluable assistance with collections and materials. For their insights, special thanks goes to Genoa Caldwell (archivist, The Burton Holmes Historical Collection) and Michael Ward (a Holmes scholar, and director of the BurtonHolmes.org Web site). A plethora of other helpful librarians and archivists connected to the institutions listed in the bibliography have our deepest appreciation too, including Noel Broadhead (UOW) for copyright advice.

Along the way, the Centre for Asia Pacific Social Transformation Studies (CAPSTRANS) at the University of Wollongong, Korea Foundation, Asia Research Fund, Australia-Korea Foundation, and Academy of Korean Studies provided critical institutional and funding support for conducting numerous archive research trips in the United States and South Korea. Completing this study would not have been possible without their generosity.

Throughout the book, we have endeavored to present Korean and Japanese names with family name first, which is the conventional way of writing names in Korea and Japan. Also, Korean- and Japanese-language sources appear with the revised Korean Romanization and Japanese Romanization rules, except in cases where geographical locations are identified differently in specific names or titles of sources—as in the cases of 'Chosun,' 'Chosen,' 'Joseon,' 'Keijo,' 'Tokio,' or 'Busan' and 'Pusan.'

Introduction

In 2002, Wayne State University Press published one of the first collections of scholarly essays in English on South Korean cinema: *Im Kwon-Taek: The Making of a Korean National Cinema*, edited by David E. James and Kyung Hyun Kim. Until then, only a smattering of book chapters and journal articles had been published on the origins of Korean cinema and the ways in which the complexities of Korean culture were reflected by its filmmakers. Few other treatments of the subject have achieved a depth and breadth to rival this study of master filmmaker Im Kwon-taek, his films, and his audiences.[1] The insightful analyses and reference materials in *Im Kwon-Taek* provide a roadmap to take us beyond such milestones as Lee and Choe's *The History of Korean Cinema* (1998) and Hyangjin Lee's *Contemporary Korean Cinema: Identity, Culture, Politics* (2000), two important works which provide a historical overview with the latter offering close readings of films from both North and South Korea.

Prior to the publication of *Im Kwon-Taek*, the history of Korean cinema had received scant attention outside the peninsula. Indeed, there is almost no mention of Korea in Geoffrey Nowell-Smith's 'comprehensive' *Oxford History of World Cinema* (1996); and the second edition of Kristin Thompson and David Bordwell's *Film History: An Introduction* (2003) devotes a mere 900 or so words to Korea and its film pioneers.[2] This neglect is perhaps understandable given the known survival of only a handful of the estimated 160 Korean films made between 1919 and 1945, and the rash of poor-quality 'quota quickies' made in the 1960s and 1970s. In addition, only a small number of researchers has been working on the history of Korean cinema and the history of cinema in Korea—an important distinction that this book addresses. (Briefly, the former involves the direct agency of Koreans in the production process, while the latter often flourished with little or limited native agency.)

While there is a number of studies of this general subject in print (often written from a nationalistic perspective), few of them have seriously interrogated the dynamic linkages between foreign film culture, imported films, national cultural policy and audience reception, and the significant impact that all these elements had on the transformation of cinema in Korea. Most detailed historical accounts of Korea's modern history also exhibit this deficiency.[3] However, in this book, we explore such key historical subjects as the coming of sound technology and the impact of foreign cinema culture on Korea—areas which these books, as well as more recent scholarship, collectively brush over.[4] The gaps revealed by these well-regarded studies divulge a pressing need for more primary research in the field. Unlike the canonical histories of the well-known and well-documented national cinemas addressed by Nowell-Smith, Thompson and Bordwell, and others, there is still a great deal of work to be done by Korean studies researchers, historians, and translators, informed by rigorous scholarship and dedicated to investigating the cinema in Korea.

GOLDEN AGES: TODAY AND YESTERDAY

For the last decade, cinema in Korea has been a hot topic. After the South Korean Constitutional Court eliminated film censorship in 1996 under the government of Kim Young-sam, the first civilian president, the country has been developing one of the world's fastest-growing film and digital media industries.[5] New spaces for freedom of expression have opened and censorship is now considered a tool of the authoritarian governments of the past. Decades of military dictatorship, preceded by three years of occupation by the United States Army and thirty-five years of Japanese colonial rule, had kept the Korean 'Cinema Tiger' in a state of slumber.[6] Since the advent of democratic government, waves of popular Korean culture (aka 'the Korean Wave' or *Hanryu* or *Hallyu* in Korean), initially driven by the export of television soaps and K-pop (Korean popular) music, and then by the production of fresh and diverse screen genres, Korean narratives and aesthetic styles have reached out across the globe.

By the late 1990s, South Korean films were making their mark at home and abroad. Although the number of cinemas has declined from 507 in 1998 to 309 in 2008, the actual number of screens has risen from 507 in 1998 to slightly more than 2,000 in 2010. The number of cinemagoers occupying the 362,657 seats facing these screens has risen from 50 million for 1998 to more than 150 million today.[7] This surge, occurring in the wake of the 1997 International Monetary Fund (IMF) crisis, was fueled by the unexpected and extraordinary success of Kang Je-gyu's blockbuster *Shiri* (1999), which exceeded $US25 million at the box office and outsold *Titanic* (1997, released in South Korea in February 1998). Enhanced training opportunities for filmmakers at home and abroad and increased public and private funding have also contributed to the film industry's expansion. After 1996, conditions were ripe for the production and exhibition of an increasing number of domestic films by directors such as Lee Chang-dong, Kim Ki-duk, Lee Myung-se, Im Sang-soo, Park Chan-wook, Hong Sang-soo, Lim Soon-rye, and Kim Ji-woon, to name a few.

A bevy of rising stars and the proliferation of 'savvy' domestic film companies—largely thanks to the expanding promotional and publication efforts of the quasi-government agency the Korean Film Council (hereafter KOFIC)—have also helped the industry to win the lion's share of the domestic market. In 1991, 21.2 percent of all films screened in South Korea were locally made, but that figure had nearly tripled to 61.2 percent by the end of 2006. [8] In the first half of 2010, local film openings maintained almost half—47.5 percent—of market share.[9]

By global standards the dominance of Korean film in its own domestic market is an extraordinary cultural triumph, shared with only a few others—notably China, France, India, Japan, and the United States. Underlying this momentum is government support (in the form of a proactive film policy) and increasing ticket sales from local audiences. In terms of policy, the effectiveness of the Screen Quota System (SQS) cannot be underestimated, even though it was halved in mid-2006. Since 1966, the SQS has attempted to protect the domestic market from an onslaught of Hollywood films by requiring all cinemas to screen local films for a minimum of 146 days per year (73 days after July 2006).[10]

Between 2000 and 2005 this high-quality local product flowed outward to the export market, enabling aesthetically provocative filmmakers and their genre-bending commercial, art-house, and independent films to connect with international audiences at key festivals. The total value of Korean film exports in 2005 was almost $US76 million—185 times higher than in 1996.[11] During this period, the South Korean cinema rose on its tiger's paws to unprecedented heights, a phenomenon that was well documented in international trade headlines in *Variety* and *Hollywood Reporter*. By 2000, Hollywood distributors were reportedly learning lessons from the South Korean film industry and releasing American films at times that avoided vigorous competition from Korean blockbusters.[12] The Korean wave had come, but on Korean terms and in a Korean way. Henceforth, all the major film festivals—Berlin, Cannes, Hong Kong, Melbourne, Rotterdam, Tokyo, and Venice—could not get enough of South Korean films, inviting all the latest films and scheduling special retrospectives. Simply put, over the past decade it has been South Korea' s turn to ride the wave into the global spotlight, as the national cinemas of Japan, China, and Hong Kong have done in the past. In 2005 the South Korean film industry reached the zenith of its new golden age to become what we might call 'Planet Hallyuwood' (the fusing of *Hallyu* and Hollywood).[13]

However, since 2006 new pressures have been challenging the international stature and future development of the South Korean film industry. Extreme levels of competition between domestic art-house and commercial films, piracy and illegal downloading, and the halving of the Screen Quota System (as well as other government policy changes) have caused a significant loss of profits, paying viewers, and domestic and international DVD and cable-TV markets. The number of films exported has shrunk, too. In

2008, a total of 354 films was exported, but this figure slipped to 279 in 2009 (though, still much higher than the 38 films exported in 2000).[14] Hence, the South Korean film industry has been experiencing the ironic problem of increased global popularity alongside decreasing profits.

THE HISTORICAL NARRATIVE: OCCUPIED CINEMAS

The turning of the global spotlight on the South Korean cinema, since the remarkable success of *Shiri*, is just one of many chapters in Planet Hallyuwood's century-long history. Until now, most scholarship has focused on the industrial and creative periods, from the melodramas of the mid-to-late 1950s and 1960s to the new wave of critical realism films of the 1980s, as well as the post-*Shiri* period. For instance, Kim Kyung Hyun (2004) analyzes the masculine tropes in Korean films from the 1990s, while McHugh and Abelmann (2005) focus on melodramas from the 1950s, and the interplay between nation, gender, and genre. Shin and Stringer (2005) and Paquet (2009) focus on the formation of the so-called 'new Korean cinema' since 1993, when democratization began to take hold. While these previous studies show that Planet Hallyuwood did not emerge overnight out of thin air, they neglect deep insights regarding other critical and complex moments in the unfolding story of the national cinema, such as the Japanese colonial (1910–1945) and United States Army Military Government in Korea (USAMGIK, 1945–1948) periods.

Cinema has been alive in Korea in various ways dating back to the late 1890s. About half of this history has involved foreign occupation in one form or another. By 1893, Korea had well and truly begun opening up to foreign peoples and cultures, whereas only two decades earlier the country had been known as the 'Hermit Kingdom.' As part of Korea's opening up to foreign ideas and investment, the country's successive foreign occupiers—as well as other foreigners living in Korea and the Koreans themselves—contributed to the process of modernization, which included the exhibition and consumption of a mostly foreign cinema. Exposure to imported exotic images in public settings, as well as the simultaneous exoticization of images exported from Korea through novel technology, created 'modern spaces' for intellectual debate, shaping the growth of visual literacies and new ways of thinking and living in both the East and the West.

The preconditions for Japan's occupation of Korea had been developing for nearly thirty years before annexation was formally announced in 1910. After Korea had signed the Treaty of Ganghwa with Japan in 1876, Japan's influence over its national affairs increased steadily. The Eulsa Protectorate Treaty between Japan and Korea, signed illegally in 1905 by five senior Korean government officials without the approval of the head of state, King Gojong, brought diplomatic relations onto a new level and paved the way for the nation's annexation by Japan and its consequent loss of sovereignty.

Japan's stated aim in annexing an 'impoverished' Korea was to reform its 'corrupt maladministration' and to open up the 'Hermit Kingdom' with enlightened laws and ordinances. Japan had hoped to 'assimilate' Koreans in order to enable both countries to enjoy the 'advantages of modern civilization.' A speech given by Resident-General Prince Itō Hirobumi in July 1907 spoke directly to this issue: "The identity of Korean and Japanese interests in the Far East, and the paramount character of Japanese interests in Korea, will not permit Japan to leave Korea to the care of any other foreign country: she must assume charge herself."[15] It was in this complex political, social, and cultural milieu that Korea's cinematic history unfolded.

During the Japanese colonial and USAMGIK occupation periods, increased exposure to Japanese, American, and other foreign film cultures directly effected—or, at least, inspired—fundamental changes in the production, distribution, and exhibition of films in Korea. At the same time, Korean filmmakers were prevented from fully acting on these sources of inspiration—initially due to a lack of funding and, later, an oppressive government film policy. In this way, cinema in Korea was 'occupied' by economic, political, industrial, and cultural constraints brought to the peninsula by outsiders and then negotiated internally.

During the Japanese and U.S. occupation periods, the operation of multidirectional flows of power and agency left Korean audiences, filmmakers, and entertainment entrepreneurs with little choice but to cooperate with their occupiers. This involved embracing state-sponsored industrialization initiatives. Korean filmmakers responded by exploiting the state's assets in any way they could, while working, somewhat subversively, within the constraints (such as tighter film regulations) imposed by the Japanese and, later, American authorities.

Negotiating the often draconian measures promulgated by the state in each of these two occupation periods, Koreans did whatever they could to increase their training opportunities and their freedom to consume films—no matter which country they were sourced from. While Korean film pioneers may not have privately acquiesced in the state agendas promoted by the Japanese and USAMGIK, they found ways to exploit the opportunities that came their way. Hence, Koreans were not simply victims of occupation. And the Korean cinema did not simply wither away to nothing because of a lack of overt resistance.

With these factors in mind, this book adds to previous scholarship by presenting the results of new research that sheds light on the complexities and tensions that underpinned the development of cinema in Korea and the Korean cinema during these challenging times. Our research has uncovered many previously undocumented (in either English or Korean) aspects of foreign films exhibited for entertainment and educational purposes in Korea—all part of Korea's Occupied Cinemas.

As in the case of Japan,[16] early public film exhibition culture in Korea offered local audiences multiple pathways for engaging with Western culture and ideas, reaching a climax of activity in 1916, three years before Korean filmmakers began contributing to a local cinema of their own. By 1916, mass audiences had already acquired the power to escape into an ethereal space in which their imaginations could run free, unhindered by geo-spatial and geo-temporal constraints. The habitual viewing of foreign content introduced local audiences to modernity and Western mores—attitudes that incorporated not only economic and scientific developments but also the potential transformation of political, social, and traditional values.

Despite the claims made by most previous studies in this field,[17] we argue that the Korean cinema was not born overnight in 1919 with the production of Korea's 'first film,' *Righteous Revenge* (1919) (see chapter 2). By 1916, Japanese and foreign entrepreneurs had developed distribution and exhibition systems that resulted in the birth of an 'occupied' cinema in Korea—that is, a cinema predominantly controlled by non-Koreans. While these same industry systems and practices had developed in other countries across the globe in different ways, Korea's particular status as a Japanese-occupied territory makes the growth of cinema there a particularly complex and fascinating story.

In addition, this study acknowledges the significant differences between a 'Korean film industry' (or 'Korean cinema') and the 'film industry in Korea' under Japanese rule. Since about 1963 most Korean film scholars, film industry people, and even the Korean government have celebrated 27 October 1919—the original screening date of *Righteous Revenge* at the Danseongsa cinema in Seoul—as the birth of the Korean cinema. Thus, for most observers, the Korean cinema was born overnight in 1919 with the exhibition of this mixed-media production, which showcased live theater and filmed sequences on a single stage. Significantly, this was also the year of the March First Independence Movement, an outbreak of nationalism, which was violently quashed by the Korean Colonial Government.

METHODOLOGY AND SOURCES

The present book contemplates a different set of research questions with a wider view of the subject. Essentially, we have sought out new primary sources in North America, Asia (Korea and Japan), and the United Kingdom, which we have explored to develop new perspectives on the transformation of local and foreign cinema cultures in Korea and their impact on Korean society. The recent growth of communication technologies, and specifically digital databases, combined with rigorous detective work (the search for elusive information and evidence), have enabled us to extend the boundaries of our field.

Despite the ongoing efforts of a new generation of well-trained scholars—yet understandably, due to a perceived lack of primary materials—few events and developments occurring outside or between the four received phases or periods of Korean cinema history have received the attention they deserve. And, like other histories of national cinemas, the conventional history of film in Korea relies on a series of claims involving a myriad of 'firsts'—the first film, the first cinema, the first sound projector or traveling film exhibitor, and so on.[18] Unlike other national cinema histories, however, a lack of evidence, along with a dash of obduracy, has plagued the study of cinema in the peninsula until only recently. A new breed of studies has begun to offer a deeper understanding of film culture in Korea during the colonial period by illuminating the multifaceted ways in which Koreans negotiated hegemony with Japan—and more specifically censorship policies, which were at the center of the colonial venture.[19] Thanks to unprecedented access to previously rare and elusive archival materials, which in the last decade have become digitized, we are now able to gain a more rigorous understanding of the complex roles that the distribution and exhibition of foreign films and censorship regulations played in Japan's larger imperial project.

Augmenting this recent expansion of Korea's cinematic history, this book moves beyond the conventional and nationalist claims reiterated in many Korean- and English-language studies. In doing so, we are less concerned with 'firsts' and more concerned with mounting a rigorous investigation of cinema based on evidence collected from a variety of sources in English, Korean, and Japanese. We have conducted our research and synthesized these primary materials in a way similar to that of an archaeologist or forensic detective sifting through the evidence and then explaining the conclusions.

The research for this study was conducted over an eight-year period, primarily by targeting previously unexplored locations where we believed documents, periodicals, and personal historical accounts existed, in English and Japanese. We also made extensive use of online tools and resources. For instance, new information about foreign films exhibited during the Japanese colonial era was gathered by cross-referencing titles in key film databases such as the Internet Movie Database (www.imdb.com), Korean Movie Database (www.kmdb.or.kr), Complete Index to World Film Since 1895 (www.citwf.com/), and the BFI Film & TV Database (www.bfi.org.uk/filmtvinfo/ftvdb). Much of the data informing the book originated in news articles and regular opinion columns published in the *Maeil Shinbo*, one of three official gazettes published by the Korean Colonial Government along with the *Gyeongseong Ilbo* and *The Seoul Press*. Although it was a mouthpiece for government policy and agenda-setting campaigns, and managed by Japanese editors, the *Maeil Shinbo* had a primarily Korean readership. The newspaper aimed to educate Koreans about the 'benefits' that they were receiving from Japan; to remind them of their 'backwardness' as a nation; to imbue them with the government's assimilationist rhetoric; to discourage self-reliance and independent thought; and to promote Japan's modernization efforts on the Korean Peninsula. From the first days of Japan's occupation of Korea, the Japanese government had described

Korea as a 'backward nation where readers are easily influenced or incited by seditious comments, or where editors are often lacking in common sense and sound judgment,' concluding that the country's 'freedom is accompanied by certain disadvantages which far outweigh its merits.'[20] Thus the *Maeil Shinbo* was an important space for conceptualizing and for debating modern cinema culture, on which the newspaper frequently reported. Other local newspapers such as the *Chosun Ilbo* and *Donga Ilbo* supplemented the *Maeil Shinbo* after 1920, when Governor-General Saitō introduced a slight relaxation of cultural policy in Korea.

Throughout the colonial period, these and other periodicals exposed Koreans and foreign expatriates to regular press reports about developments in local cinema culture and the progress made by foreign film industries and entertainment culture more generally. For example, in early 1914, the advent of color motion pictures overseas was discussed, as well as their potential arrival in Korea.[21] Reports of this nature introduced local readers to various facets of modernity, creating curiosity and anticipation among both intellectuals and the general public as they experienced aspects of global change, first vicariously and then firsthand. For the Korean Colonial Government, the coming of cinema unleashed a set of novel and potentially uncontrollable factors that were dealt with in an unwieldy fashion, and on a province-by-province basis, until the systematization of film policy on a national level in 1926.

Other sources that have proven invaluable include missionary newspapers such as *The Morning Calm*—an Anglican monthly newspaper and the first English-language periodical in Korea—*The Korea Review* and *The Korea Methodist*, as well as other primary materials held in the David Allan Hubbard Library at the Fuller Theological Seminary in Pasadena, California. These sources have provided rare insights into the early entertainment culture that catered for the increasing number of Western missionaries, diplomats, and businessmen who had settled in Seoul and its outskirts in the 1880s and 1890s. The authors located a wealth of industry materials and publications dating back to the early 1920s at the Cinema/Television Library, Korean Heritage/East Asian Library, and the Warner Bros. Archives at the University of Southern California, as well as in the Arts Special Collections at the University of California–Los Angeles, and the Margaret Herrick Library–Academy of Motion Picture Arts and Sciences, also in Los Angeles. Additional industry materials relating to Hollywood's activities in the Asian region were found in the United Artists Collection located at the State Historical Society of Wisconsin in Madison, and also gleaned from correspondence with archivists in the manuscripts and special collections at Universal Studios.

Official publications such as the Annual Reports on the Reforms and Progress in Chosen, compiled by the Government-General of Korea (hereafter Korean Colonial Government), as well as the summation of the USAMGIK's activities, were perused at both the University of Maryland–

College Park and University of Wisconsin–Madison, while various United States government documents concerning Hollywood's export activities during World War II were examined in the National Archives (NARAII) in College Park, Maryland. Searches for both primary and secondary materials were also conducted in the Gordon W. Prange Collection held by the University of Maryland; the Papers of the Victor Animatograph Corp. in the Special Collections of the University of Iowa Library; and the Thomas A. Edison Papers and other motion picture catalogs in the Rutgers University Library, in conjunction with the New Jersey Digital Highway online archive and database. Finally, we consulted the James A. Thomas Papers and James B. Duke Papers from the Rare Book, Manuscript, and Special Collections Library at Duke University.

Investigating the history of cinema in Korea is a challenging task, due to the dearth of both primary and secondary materials in Korea's public libraries and archives. A simple database search for key words such as 'Korean cinema' and 'Korean film' in the National Assembly Library in Seoul, for instance, produces a despairingly short list of materials from the 1930s to the early 1970s. Issues of the entertainment magazine *Samcheolli* date back to 1929, yet this central library holds almost nothing from the 1950s, with the holdings from the 1960s only slightly larger.

Despite these major deficits, we were, however, able to source some important materials in Korea. These include industry materials in Korean and Japanese held by the National Library, National Assembly Library, KBS archive, Korean Film Archive (KOFA), Korean Film Council, Seoul National University Library, and Yonsei University Library; and miscellaneous copies of popular film magazines directed to a Korean readership, such as *Yeonghwa Sidae* (Motion Picture Age), *Munye Yeonghwa* (Literary Film) and *Nokseong*, from the archives of the late film historian Lee Young-il managed by the Korea National University of Arts. Rare film censorship materials were found among the holdings of the Ministry of Government Administration and Home Affairs, Government Archives and Records Service in Daejon. Various newspapers including *Hwangseong Shinmun*, *The Independent*, *Maeil Shinbo*, *Donga Ilbo* and *Chosun Ilbo*, some dating back to the late 1880s, were located in the aforementioned archives, as well as in the digital database provided by the Korean History Database (run by the National Institute of Korean History) and Mediagaon, run by the Korea Press Foundation.

Among the more valuable publications on the Korean cinema from the 1970s are the *Korean Film Collection* (1972), which contains an overview of the industry's sixty-year history to that time (beginning in 1919), and the *Korean Film Data Collection* (1978), which provides comprehensive industry statistics. These two government sources, along with *200 Representative Films From 70 Years of Korean Cinema* (1989), *Korean Film Index 1919–1989* (1990), Lee Young-il (1969, 2004), and master filmmaker Yu Hyun-mok's (1997) study of the cinema during the colonial period have formed a valuable starting point for this book.

Finally—although a few of its entries are slightly flawed due to human error—the Korean Film Archive's *Korean Cinema in Newspaper Articles: 1945–1957* (2004), *Chosun Cinema in Newspaper Articles 1911–1917* (2008), and *Chosun Cinema in Newspaper Articles 1918–1920* (2009) have provided near-comprehensive coverage of film-related news in the *Maeil Shinbo*, the only Korean-language daily newspaper published during these periods. These reference books, which were unavailable when we began the research for this project, now make it possible to investigate reportage of early cinema in Korea without having to visit Korean archives in person.

In Japan, articles from film magazines such as *Nihon Eiga*, *Eiga Hyōron*, *Eiga Junpō*, *Kinema Junpō*, *Shin Eiga*, and *Eiga no tomo* were sourced from the National Diet Library in Tokyo and the Waseda University Library. Although our study offered little scope for exploring many of the Japanese film titles exhibited in Korea during thirty-five years of colonial rule, we cite these materials, which date from around the time of the Second Sino-Japanese War (1937–1945), because they reveal the concerns that Japanese filmmakers shared with their Korean colleagues and their views about the various purposes of film production and distribution in Korea. Valuable insights have also been gleaned from a small number of Japanese scholars and experts on the Japanese cinema regarding details of film policy in colonial Korea, as well as Japanese filmmakers in Korea and vice versa.[22]

By combining and analyzing the information and insights gleaned from these rich sources in three countries, we hope in this book to offer a new understanding of the complex development of Korean cinema during the two occupation phases of Korea's history.

CHAPTER SUMMARIES

This book presents the findings resulting from our discovery of a small but diverse collection of Japanese-, Korean-, and English-language archival documents that, to our knowledge (and surprise), have never previously been discussed in any detail. We have drawn on these newfound materials to flesh out our understanding of the development of cinema culture and film regulations leading up to and including the Japanese colonial and USAMGIK occupation periods. Following previous work in this field, we have organized our discussion of the development of cinema culture in the peninsula into four distinct historical periods. However, this book differs from previous studies in the links it draws between the arrival in Korea of modern technology and ideas and the cultural, political, and social environment, as we follow the development of cinema, film exhibition, and filmmaking from 1893 to 1948. During this half century, Korean filmmakers seized every opportunity to learn production techniques and practice their skills, contributing to the growth of a national cinema despite the stultifying economic, cultural, political, and industrial conditions produced by their occupation by colonial and military powers. At the same time, Korea served as a highly important territory for the global expansion of the American and Japanese film industries, and, after the late 1930s, Koreans functioned as key figures in the co-production of feature-length propaganda films that were designed to glorify loyalty to the Japanese Empire. For these reasons, and as a result of the tensions created by divided loyalties, the history of cinema in Korea is a far more dynamic story than simply that of a national cinema struggling to develop its own narrative content and aesthetics under colonial conditions.

We begin our study by focusing on the earliest magic lantern shows brought to Korea by missionaries in 1893, and the first motion pictures exhibited in 1901 in the Royal Palace in Seoul. We then trace the coming of silent films before 1910 and the first attempts, in 1919, by Korean filmmakers to produce their own films with limited access to appropriate technology. The implementation of restrictive film policies under Japanese rule in the late 1920s and mid-to-late 1930s brought new challenges and opportunities for collaboration and study with more experienced (Japanese) filmmakers. Hollywood's market dominance in the early 1930s, and again in the mid-to-late 1940s prior to the Korean War, meant that the market was 'occupied' in a commercial sense. We also examine the effects on cinema of the presence of American occupying forces after World War II.

The beginnings of cinema in Korea are marked by the first public screenings (in a barn) of short French Pathé and Gaumont, and American Vitascope *actualité* films in 1897, possibly October (hypothesized to be this date because of a lack of evidence).[23] However, it should be noted that our own exhaustive examination of *The Times* of London through the Times Digital Archive, 1785–1985, reveals nothing about moving (or still) images being shown in Korea in October or at any other time near the end of 1897.[24] Chapter 1 therefore addresses the beginnings of cinema in Korea, between 1893 and 1905, charting the arrival of novel 'Western' pre-cinema technology, content, and ideas in the form of magic lanterns and slides brought to Korea by missionaries from the United States and United Kingdom. This chapter illustrates the powerful impact of this foreign technology on Korean society before the outbreak of the Russo-Japanese War, which ended with Japan's declaration of Korea as a protectorate and, subsequently, its occupation of Korea under the Eulsa Treaty.

The evidence presented here predates by a full decade all other known studies, including the comprehensive *Korean Cinema: From Origins to Renaissance* edited by Kim Mee-hyun (2007) on behalf of KOFIC, the foremost research, promotion, and development organization relating to the Korean cinema. Chapter 1 continues with an investigation of Korea and Koreans as both object of study and naïve audience in the work and activities of well-known American travelogue filmmaker Burton Holmes, the 'man who photographed the world.' It also introduces Korea's first real cinema entrepreneur, James A. Thomas, a well-traveled tobacco salesman who had come to Asia to promote smoking on behalf of the North Carolina–based American Tobacco Company. Thomas introduced public film exhibition to Korea before American businessmen and investors (and Seoul Electric Co. proprietors) Henry Collbran and Harry Rice Bostwick began entertaining tram crowds with moving pictures in June 1903.[25]

Unlike earlier studies based largely on oral history reports, our research reveals that Collbran and Bostwick had purchased a state-of-the-art magic lantern projector and film projector from Thomas. For about ninety minutes each night during June 1903, they entertained large crowds in the Seoul Electric Company's warehouse. A private cable-car box fitted with fluffy cushions was positioned close to the screen for the comfort of foreign guests. In less than a month, nightly audiences had grown to over eleven hundred people per sitting, generating healthy profits for the electric company only three and a half years after the American businessmen had launched Seoul's streetcar service. For the next four years—with the exception of reduced activities during the Russo-Japanese War (between February 1904 and September 1905)—these nightly film exhibitions fed customers' appetite for visual spectacle (and increased the company's monopoly on Seoul's electricity and streetcar systems). It also enabled the firm to build enough equity in its entertainment business to eventually expand. Undoubtedly, 1903 was a watershed year for public cinema culture in Korea.

Chapter 2 explores the impressive arrival in Korea of American, European, and Japanese entertainment films and newsreels; the establishment of temporary and permanent venues designated for screening moving pictures; and the rise of large-scale and rambunctious audiences. Here we focus on how the distribution and exhibition of foreign films stirred excitement in local film viewers in the lead-up to 1916, the real 'birth year' of the film industry in Korea. For the U.S. and Japanese film industries, this was the year in which film distribution and exhibition expanded into Korea in an organized way. However, we acknowledge that it was not until Korean-born filmmakers made the feature film *National Boundary* (*Gukgyeong*) in 1922 (released in mid-January 1923) that a genuine 'Korean cinema' was launched. Our analysis of this period provides new insights in the lead-up to the second phase of Korea's cinematic history that has conventionally been focused on the gradual rise of 'silent' film production after 1922. This led to a small production boom that began in 1926 with the release of *Arirang* and ended in 1934, just prior to the advent of local talkies. We also discuss the effects on the 'occupation' of the Korean cinema of the development of film laws and censorship guidelines in mid-1926, regulations that were tightened by the Korean Colonial Government shortly after the 1931 Mukden or Manchurian Incident.

Chapter 3 builds on the extensive research set out in an important study, *Korean Film Policy History* (Kim Dong-ho et al. 2005), by revealing how official film policy was used as a powerful tool to shape Korea's film industry, which nevertheless began to mature alongside advances in literature, painting, ceramics, and music. In particular, the cinema became a 'node of cultural construction' after Governor-General Saitō launched a new cultural policy designed to relax Japanese administrative control over Korean cultural and artistic activities. Allowing Koreans to gain film production training and experience (or, at least, not entirely preventing them from doing so) encouraged the creation of a local cinema, albeit one under occupation, to which Koreans contributed. The authors demonstrate that, from 1926 to 1936, cinema in colonial Korea was a vibrant business, involving the production of a relatively small number of domestic films and the distribution and exhibition of a much larger number of American films plus some British, Chinese, French, German, Italian, and Russian films. During this decade—the first golden age of Hollywood in Korea—American feature entertainment films overwhelmingly dominated the Korean market, a situation made possible with the assistance of Korean and Japanese film distribution agents. This chapter addresses how and why Korea—a small, occupied country—was seen as an important territory in Hollywood's campaign of global expansion and why the colonial authorities were slow to restrict Hollywood's domination of the market. In responses to the U.S. film industry's globalization operation, the Korean Colonial Government created a financially self-sustaining film censorship apparatus to control and to profit from an onslaught of films. It more than paid for its operation through application fees levied on more than six thousand American and five hundred feature and nonfeature films from other countries, the vast majority of which were approved with minor, if any, censorship changes. To this end, Hollywood 'collaborated' with the Korean colonial authorities by financially supporting its censorship infrastructure.

The third subdivision of Korean cinema history conventionally begins with the making and popular exhibition of *The Story of Chunhyang* (1935), the first 'successful' Korean talkie. We discuss how the collaborative pro-Japanese propaganda film projects made at this time both aided and constrained Korean filmmaking after the commencement of the Second Sino-Japanese War in 1937. This period ended in 1945 with the liberation of Korea from Japan and the arbitrary separation of the Korean Peninsula into a Soviet-friendly north and the south under the strong influence of the United States.

Chapter 4 charts the coming of sound to the Korean cinema during a period of hope for intellectuals and artists. This is the era when Korean filmmakers and live narrators (*byeonsa*) began to exercise greater agency in the film industry in Korea. It shows how exposure to a burgeoning radio broadcasting and foreign film exhibition culture inspired a new generation of Korean filmmakers to train with film studios in Japan, China, and the Soviet Union, as well as with Japanese filmmakers working in Korea. Koreans sought to legitimize their language and culture in a number of films and to embrace modernization by emulating Western production and exhibition practices. The first 'unsuccessful' talkie project in 1930, *Secret Story*, which aimed to synchronize a phonograph and silent film in the tradition of Warner Bros.' *The Jazz Singer* (1927), and *The Story of Chunhyang* (1935), the first 'successful' talkie, are presented as case studies which shed new insights on this remarkable technological changeover. The coming of sound was more than a simple 'transfer of modernity' to colonial Korea; it served as a powerful social, cultural, and industrial force that contested the traditional art of the *byeonsa*, the live film narrator, and enabled Koreans to contribute to a small but authentic cinema of their own.

Chapter 5 investigates how, following the outbreak of the Second Sino-Japanese War, the Korean Colonial Government—via the Japanese Department of Home Affairs—reacted to the cultural and ideological alarm bells sounded by the plethora of American films in Korea. During this time the censorship apparatus began discouraging 'Western' themes in the commercial entertainment cinema while simultaneously encouraging the co-production of pro-Japanese propaganda films. In this way the Japanese Department of Home Affairs, sometimes without the support of the Japanese film industry, politicized and intensified its use of film as a tool to make loyalty to the Japanese Empire (and volunteering for the war) an attractive option for its colonial subjects. Nearly all imported American and Allied films were banned (especially after the attack on Pearl Harbor in December 1941), and Korean film industry personnel, who numbered over a hundred by this time, had little choice but to 'collaborate' with Japanese filmmakers. Together they made films that promoted Asian unity and encouraged Koreans to protect the Japanese Empire from a Western invasion. As this propaganda filmmaking agenda was escalated under Japanese occupation, a slew of films from Nazi Germany and fascist Italy filled the gap previously dominated by Hollywood films. The chapter discusses some of the key colonial propaganda military genre films, including *Troop Train* (1938), *Volunteer* (1941), and *Straits of Chosun* (1943). These productions aimed to foster a reaction against Western imperialism in the name of the 'Greater East Asia Co-Prosperity Sphere' and were regularly churned out until Japan was forced to relinquish its control over Korea in August 1945.

A significant and exciting opportunity to gain new insights into the aesthetic and narrative conventions of the late colonial era arose in 2005, when seven propaganda films, previously thought to have been destroyed, were discovered outside Korea by Korean Film Archive staff. Scholars, archivists, and filmmakers around the world waited in eager anticipation to see these films, which were released on DVD in 2007 and 2008. In assessing the impact of these films, we refer to primary materials published by Japanese film critics and industry personnel, as well as newspaper articles and archival documents, in order to compare and contrast the evocative messages that they contained and the film policy that shaped them.

In chapter 6 we break new ground by exploring the impact on film culture of the primary goal of the United States during the USAMGIK period of military occupation—reorienting the southern half of the Korean Peninsula away from the former Japanese colonial government's antidemocratic, anti-American, and militaristic ideology and establishing an orderly government in its place. Functioning under the authority of General Douglas MacArthur, the Supreme Commander for the Allied Powers (SCAP), the Army Military Government in Korea governed the southern part of the peninsula from 1945 to 1948. To help achieve its goals on a wide front and as quickly as possible, USAMGIK's Motion Picture Section of the Department of Public Information arranged the exhibition of hundreds of Hollywood films in order to promote democracy, capitalism, gender equality, and popular American culture and values.

Most standard Korean film histories recognize this fourth period, that is, a postwar national cinema which existed between August 1945 and September 1948, which was divided along ideological lines. They explain how hardships and conflicts were endured by Korean filmmakers, and how Hollywood monopolized local screens, a situation which USAMGIK film policy—almost identical to the ordinances previously set in place by the Japanese—assisted. These previous studies are rightly critical of the stranglehold that Hollywood achieved after World War Two and of the United States' domination of Korean screens as a threat to local culture.[26]

However, we show in this chapter that while U.S. troops in the field enjoyed the increased availability and superior quality of American feature films, the Korean government-in-waiting was affronted by their perceived immorality. We also demonstrate that many of the Hollywood 'spectacle' films shown at this time, which have hitherto largely been unidentified, were used to inculcate Western notions of liberty among Koreans while distracting them from a tumultuous political scene. Nevertheless, the films exhibited did not always live up to this lofty purpose. Along with positive endings and positive portrayals of the 'American way of life,' representations of violent, antisocial, and misogynistic behavior were foreign to Korean cultural and aesthetic traditions, and often provoked negative responses from local audiences. While Hollywood attempted to reestablish its control over a historical regional stronghold that the Japanese had taken over from them in 1937, it exposed Korean audiences to a cultural milieu involving complex flows and interpretations of everyday American culture and ideals.

The book concludes by considering the complex dimensions of power and agency as they applied to both Korean nationals and their foreign occupiers during the Japanese occupation and USAMGIK periods. Our study aims to stand on the shoulders of both established and emerging scholars by offering new insights into the development and transformation of film culture and film policy in Korea both before and during the country's two major occupation periods. We hope that the journey we share with readers within these six chapters will shed new light on this remarkable and understudied subject.

1 Invasion from the West, 1893–1905

"Burton Holmes, the traveler, author, and lecturer, tells that while he was in Seoul, the capital of Corea, he asked an intelligent Corean what side his nation would take in the then impending war between Japan and Russia. 'You have seen two dogs fight over a bone?' asked the Corean. Mr. Holmes assented. 'Well,' continued the Corean, 'did you ever [see] the bone do any fighting?' " (*Chicago Daily Tribune*, 6 November 1904)

Up till now, our views of Korea's cinematic history have been informed by limited information and partial assertions about early cinema in precolonial and colonial Korea—an industry under the influence of occupation on multiple levels. Delving further back into the archives of Korean cinematic history, in this chapter we trace much earlier developments. By examining their social and cultural impact in the lead-up to the regularization of commercial distribution and exhibition of modern film in 1916, the birth year of cinema in Korea, we reveal how particular motion picture technologies and ideas were consumed in both local and foreign contexts. We also investigate individuals and groups who were key players in Korea's pre-cinema history.

In essence, those who were active in the formative stages of the industry were driven by the need to embrace modernity. Film first arrived in Korea as a by-product of Western-inspired commercial and cultural activities. Businessmen from the United States were preoccupied with gaining lucrative contracts for electrification, the expansion of transportation, mining, and the general modernization of the country. American missionaries were preoccupied with bringing their own versions of development to Korea and with helping the country rid itself of what they saw as 'heathen' traditions. Foreign photographers and cinematographers were obsessed with capturing some kind of ethnic or 'native essence' on film, developing collections of such material, and sharing this information with others interested in 'exotic' lands and cultures. Finally, and in a process that still continues, scholars have been preoccupied with reinscribing Korea's role in early film history, a process that involves unearthing fresh facts and addressing complex and unresolved research questions.

Although uncoordinated, the combined activities of all of these players have contributed significantly to the acquisition, exploitation, and recirculation of cinematic knowledge in and about Korea. Imaginations have been driven by the desire to consume and to possess mechanical representations of life and of foreign and local cultures. It is precisely the fascination of Korea's film pioneers with these representations that we seek to understand more fully today.

TRANSFORMATION OF THE 'HERMIT KINGDOM'

Previous studies have embraced the assertion that Korea's film history begins with the exhibition of foreign films, and not by local innovations in film technology and production techniques. While this is partly true, it oversimplifies the progressive impact of local business practices and censorship regulations on distribution, exhibition, and consumption patterns. There was a far more dynamic, two-way flow of culture and images in and out of Korea than has yet been acknowledged—a process which in turn facilitated cross-cultural exchanges, albeit mediated by Westerners, and expanded Koreans' views of the world.

Until the later part of the nineteenth century, Korea largely kept its geographical and geopolitical borders closed to foreigners and foreign cultures, thus earning it the nickname of the 'hermit kingdom.' However, responding to external pressures, in the mid-1870s King Gojong (1864–1907) and his government opened up the country and established diplomatic relations with the 'family of nations'; first with Japan, and then with countries such as France (in 1866) and the United States (1871), whose navies had visited Korea in the past. The government formalized these diplomatic ties by signing treaties of 'friendship and commerce' with Japan (1876) and with the United States (1882), the latter leading to the establishment of an official American diplomatic office (or legation) in Seoul in May 1883. Other, similar agreements followed with Germany and Britain (1883), Italy and Russia (1884), France (1886), and later Austria-Hungary (1892). As a result of these agreements, the government opened its ports and cities to commerce of various kinds, allowing an increasing number of foreign missionaries, along with diplomats and businessmen, to enter Korea and even settle there. Chemulpo (the old name for Incheon) became the site of a large foreign compound where missionaries from various denominations (mainly Catholic, Anglican, Presbyterian, and Methodist) began building and running schools and hospitals.

In tandem with this heightened foreign interest in the peninsula (or perhaps as a result of the challenges and uncertainties surrounding it), Korea underwent a series of fundamental structural transformations. King Gojong formed important links with several Western countries to aid the process of opening up and modernizing Korea. In November 1883, a handful of Korean diplomats completed an eight-week tour of the United States that included visits to textile factories, electricity plants, and railroad companies in California, Boston, and New York and high-level talks with United States President Chester A. Arthur. This diplomatic and trade mission began a long history of cross-cultural interactions in science and technology between Korea and the United States.[1] Not long after the delegation's return to Korea, the government began exploiting its trade relationships with Japan and the United States to facilitate economic development. Projects were initiated for advanced electrification, telephony, the development of a streetcar and railroad transportation infrastructure, and mining ventures, all operating from the capital city, Seoul. As the public voice of Korea, the king personally led the push for modernization.

Hence, beginning in the 1880s the modern technology of the West was gradually introduced into Korea, in many cases via Japan or Japanese trade routes. In 1883, Japanese underwater telegraphic cables were installed between Nagasaki and the Korean port of Busan. In September 1884, as a direct result of the Korean trade mission to the United States, King Gojong and Thomas Edison's Lamp Company struck a deal to build an electric power plant and install electric lights in the Gyeongbok Palace. The Edison connection would eventually prove valuable in the context of early film exhibition in the kingdom. Additional land-based telegraph lines were erected in 1885, connecting Chemulpo with the Chinese border and to the Chinese telegraph network via Seoul and Pyongyang. In early 1887 electric lights blazed out in Korea for the first time, illuminating the Gyeongbok Palace about two years before Japan's Mikado Palace and China's Forbidden City had installed such facilities.[2] In 1889, Seoul's telegraph lines were connected to Busan, reportedly totaling around 2,175 miles of cables.[3] While these changes were more complex to manage than King Gojong and some of his countrymen may have initially thought, these major advances in technology, communications, and engineering testify to the success of King Gojong's drive to open Korea to the world.

In spite of (or perhaps because of) these major changes, the country became embroiled in intermittent political, social, and cultural unrest, involving, among other things, assassinations of government figures, secret military agreements, and civic revolts. This turmoil formed the background to the first Sino-Japanese War (1894–1895), which was primarily fought on Korean soil over the combatants' right to claim vested interests in Korea. Prior to the outbreak of war, in mid-1894, local revolts had forced King Gojong to flee Korea and seek temporary refuge in Japan. At the time, reports of rebel threats against foreigners, and Americans in particular, frequently appeared in *The Washington Post* and *New York Times*.

In early 1898, after much of the unrest and instability had subsided, two American businessmen, Henry Collbran (from Denver, Colorado) and Harry R. Bostwick, received King Gojong's approval to electrify Seoul and developed the Seoul Electric Company. Electric trams, engineered and built by the Collbran and Bostwick Company, began operating in Seoul in 1898, linking it to the port city of Chemulpo, which was becoming an important gateway for trade.[4] By the end of 1901, the Seoul Electric Company, owned by the king, had taken the capital from kerosene lighting to incandescent and arc lighting—technology which was considered 'one of the most striking products of modern civilization.'[5] When the Seoul-Busan railway line was finally completed, it was claimed that it was the quickest and simplest way to reach Seoul from Japan, Shanghai, Hong Kong, the Philippines, Australia,

Vancouver, and San Francisco.[6] Korea was truly opening itself up to both East and West.

PICTURE THIS . . .

Building on their success with the Seoul Electric Company, and typical of a cohort of Western entrepreneurs operating in Asia, Collbran and Bostwick seized the opportunity to launch a new venture and bring a slice of the entertainment culture that was sweeping the Western world to Seoul. As an investment, they purchased an expensive, state-of-the-art combined magic lantern and film projector.[7] They acquired the projection equipment from James A. Thomas, a tobacco salesman from North Carolina and an overlooked pioneer of the cinema in Korea.

During June 1903, each night (except Sundays) between 8:00 and 10:00 pm, for the attractive price of around 3¢, large crowds were entertained with motion pictures depicting city life in Korea, Europe, and the United States. They gathered at the Seoul Electric Company's warehouse, a suitable venue because it was centrally located near the Dongdaemun (East) Gate and was large enough to accommodate the audiences that flocked to this novel form of entertainment.[8] In less than a month, these nightly audiences grew to over 1,100 people per sitting, generating healthy profits for the Seoul Electric Co., only three and a half years after Collbran and Bostwick had launched a streetcar service in Seoul. Over the next four years (with interruptions between February 1904 and September 1905 during the Russo-Japanese War), regular evening screenings enabled the company to expand its customer base and profits, which it plowed back into enhancing entertainment culture in Seoul.

In addition to these two American entrepreneurs, other major players with a hand in the development of Korea's early cinematic history included missionaries from the United States and the United Kingdom, who brought with them magic lanterns and slides depicting biblical paintings and, more specifically, the life of Christ (as seen in Figure 1.1). They also included Western travelogue photographers and documentary filmmakers such as J. B. Bernadou, Harrie Webster, and the better-known Elias Burton Holmes (1870–1958), who sought to capture images of 'authentic' Korean life and traditional culture.

A third group of cinematic invaders included a handful of Japanese entrepreneurs and an assortment of Japanese photographers and amateur filmmakers. They were drawn to Korea by the promise of new business opportunities and the desire to gain a better understanding of Japan's closest neighbor during and after Japan's wars with China (1894–95) and Russia (1904–05). During this time, Japanese photographers such as Fugita Giyokusendo, K. Murakami, and K. Iwata contributed to a growing photographic enterprise in the Chingokai (Jingogae in Korean) area of Seoul.

This is the area known today as Chungmuro, generally considered as the nexus of South Korea's contemporary film industry. These three Japanese photographers in particular took out half-page advertisements in local English-language newspapers such as *The Korea Review* to promote their studios and their large collections of local images portraying 'native manners and customs.'

Scholarship to date, including the comprehensive *Korean Cinema: From Origins to Renaissance*,[9] has overlooked—or, at best, underestimated—the remarkable contributions and dynamic linkages between these individuals and groups and their initiatives in Korea. And yet, through their involvement with photography, cinematography, and the subsequent formation of audience 'culture,' they contributed, either indirectly or directly, to the expansion of Western and Japanese imperialism. They shared a deep interest in exposing East Asia to various articulations of modernity. While each made formal and practical contributions to the rise of cinema in the region, as we now show, each of these players was motivated in its work by a different set of interests and assumptions about the recording and exhibiting of visual images as a spectacle.

The contributions of these cinema pioneers were made on two broad fronts. Firstly, they participated in the cross-cultural flow of media, information, and popular culture between Korea and the outside world, thus increasing awareness of Korean culture (both traditional and contemporary) and social practices. Secondly, they promoted Korea's increasing importance as a potential trading partner and commercial center, a country rich in minerals, raw materials, and labor, and as a strategic military location that separated Japan from its traditional adversary, China.

PROJECTING MODERNITY

By mid-1902, in addition to being the venue for a variety of Western missionary projects, Korea had become of increasing interest to the United States government and American industry as a result of its existing and potential commercial links. American expatriates outnumbered those from all other countries combined, and American capital invested in Korea had risen steadily since 1897—primarily with the opening of the Un-san mining and Standard Oil Company offices, but also supporting the development of the electric railway and electric lighting plant. These political and commercial connections brought with them a profoundly new and different set of social and cultural practices, technologies, and 'modern' ways of thinking, through which the West attempted to engage Korea.

Part of this thrust towards modernity was the exhibition of images and motion pictures from abroad, which further exposed Koreans to the outside world. The magic lantern (not to be confused with the Korean paper lantern), considered the ancestor of the modern slide and film projector, was introduced to Korea around the time when similar devices were reaching a peak of popularity in Europe and the United States. This device was a significant forerunner of modern cinematic technology, to the extent that it demonstrated a desire on the part of the operators to manipulate images and a matching desire on the part of audiences to see moving images.[10] The showman or practitioner was even able to create special effects or a sense of motion by dissolving between two images (projected on separate lanterns) or by moving multiple devices or images.

Following the development by Dutch inventors of the basic technology behind the magic lantern in the late 1650s, it gradually rose to popularity in the eighteenth and nineteenth centuries.[11] Itinerant projectionists, entertainment entrepreneurs, and public lecturers traveled throughout Europe and North America, showing collections of black-and-white and hand-colored glass slides and titillating spectators with images of local, regional and foreign peoples, cultures, and landscapes.

The projection apparatus consisted of a magnification lens and a light source which projected the images onto a large screen or white surface. It came in various shapes and sizes and was often illuminated from behind by candles or small kerosene lamps kept inside the cabinet—which explains the need for an exhaust pipe or chimney affixed at the top. The magic lantern was a novel way of exhibiting and experiencing images, primarily in a joint context of education and entertainment.

The earliest magic lanterns were brought to the region, beginning with Japan, shortly after the public optical illusion shows, known as Fantasmagoria or Phantasmagoria, held in Paris and London at the beginning of the nineteenth century.[12] Although their introduction is central to the cinema prehistory of the region, few Korean scholars agree about when the first magic lantern apparatus and shows came to Korea. Nearly all suppose that the technology was introduced *after* the first motion pictures were exhibited in Korea by Collbran and Bostwick in 1903. According to one of the earliest cinema histories written in Korea, *Stories behind the Korean Cinema*, published in 1962 by film director Ahn Jong-hwa, the Christian Youth Community in Seoul hosted magic lantern shows in 1907, depicting scenes from the life of Jesus Christ. While it is light on evidence, consisting mainly of a collection of personal memories and events, Ahn's book was one of the first to attempt a history of Korean cinema pioneers. In a later appendix to the book, which was republished in 1998, Kim Jong-wook presented evidence for a magic lantern show, in April 1905, of the landscapes and customs of India.

Since the publication of Ahn's book in the 1960s, film historians have uncovered little further evidence of pre-cinema culture in Korea. In 1977 the influential Korean Motion Picture Promotion Corporation (KMPPC), the predecessor of the Korean Film Council, announced that the first magic lantern showing had taken place in 1903 in the royal palace as part of celebrations commemorating the fortieth anniversary of King Gojong.

Notwithstanding these claimed 'firsts,' our findings demonstrate that the magic lantern was in fact brought to Korea in the early 1890s, a decade earlier than previously thought, by British Anglican missionaries, who used the apparatus to befriend, entertain, and educate Koreans, as well as Japanese and Chinese expatriates. They also sought to entertain themselves and other Britons and Americans living in Seoul and the foreign compound in Chemulpo.

Missionaries first came to Korea in 1893, inspired chiefly by their task of spreading the Gospel, but also keen to spread 'modern' ideas and to introduce new views of the world. They brought with them miniature cameras, like those used by detectives, which they used to record local culture. The missionaries then exported these 'exotic' images back to the United States and the United Kingdom, where they were used as fundraising tools to further their work in the Asia-Pacific region. These activities were described in detail in English-language newspapers and magazines such as *The Independent* (1896–99), *The Morning Calm* (1890–1910), *The Korean Repository* (1882, 1885–98), and *The Korea Review* (1901–06).[13]

The use of the magic lantern in Korea as a tool of religious instruction represents an important pre-cinema development. Spectators were reported as being awe-struck by the realism of the larger-than-life images projected onto the screen (usually a white canvas sheet).

After the signing of the 1882 Treaty of Amity and Commerce between the United States and Korea, Western missionaries began to influence Korean culture and society in new ways, particularly in the context of medical and educational work. For the most part, religious proselytizing was proscribed and was even punishable by death. Missionary activities were carefully controlled, as the following example indicates. According to an article in the Anglican magazine *The Morning Calm* in December 1891, in August that year the Korean government had permitted British Anglican missionaries to purchase a plot of land outside the foreign settlement area in Chemulpo in order to build a Western-style hospital that would care, in the first instance, for Koreans. The land, which overlooked the whole town, cost a mere $20 (or less than £4).

It is worthwhile tracing the background to this remarkable missionary initiative in some detail. The Anglican Bishop of Korea, Rev. Charles John Corfe (between 1889–1904), and other missionaries further contributed to Korea's social and cultural fabric by actively involving themselves in a particular form of media production and diffusion. This process involved two distinct but overlapping stages. First, they produced their own black-and-white and hand-colored magic lantern slides by recruiting amateur slide-makers to create materials at a fraction of the cost of purchasing professional collections—about eighteen pence per slide. Second, they set about expanding the market for the distribution and consumption of magic lantern slides, both inside and outside of Korea. By 1903 this religious-entertainment venture, aimed at students and others attending the mission's teaching sessions, was overlapping with the earliest known public film screenings in Korea.

In August 1892, Reverend Herbert Kelly, a British Anglican missionary who had first arrived in the region in 1913 but had remained in constant contact with Korean missionaries from London, was looking for suitable

Figure 1.1   Examples of the religious magic lantern slides that were exhibited in Korea in the 1890s. *Religieus, City* series images courtesy of Charles Barten, www.toverlantaarn.eu. Available at http://www.toverlantaarn.eu/8x8_religieus_City_series_1.html

people in both Korea and the United Kingdom to make magic lantern slides for him. Kelly was seeking to add new slides to his existing collection of negatives, many of which had been printed in various issues of *The Morning Calm* for the enjoyment of its readers. His mission (known as the Korean Missionary Brotherhood) was interested in creating a regular supply of slides, both to exhibit them in Korea and to show them back in the United Kingdom to generate a modest income stream to support the mission's work in Korea.

In November 1892, Kelly used an editorial article in *The Morning Calm* to promote the launch of his lantern slide project so that new images could be used to spread cheer over the Christmas period. According to an article in *The Morning Calm* in April 1893, these new images contained religious scenes similar to the 'Religieus, City' series (figure 1.1), other landscape scenes as well as covertly shot images, both public and private. The report also mentioned that Kelly was looking for a 'detective'-type still camera to take new candid shots without requiring the use of a heavy and cumbersome tripod. These small hand-held cameras could be taken almost anywhere, while concealed or disguised as everyday items such as a box or a book. Because they used rolls of film, these cameras enabled the taking of successive images without the need to change cumbersome plates or single sheets of film. Clearly, Reverend Kelly was eager to capture realistic and lively representations of Korean people and culture without drawing undue attention to himself.

As the various Christian missions were required to keep their evangelistic activities to a minimum, their employees had more time to study local customs, language, and traditions while developing medical clinics and educational programs and institutions. One outcome of these activities was the creation of a suite of new visual presentation materials and photography skills.

According to a report in *The Morning Calm* in July 1894 by M. M. Chambers-Hodgetts, general secretary to Bishop Corfe, a set of twenty-one black-and-white and colored magic lantern slides—which included sweeping views of Seoul, illustrations of daily life and stills of various missions working in Korea—was being used on a regular basis. These slides had been donated by an anonymous patron of the Anglican Church, who had spent time traveling in Korea, and had been acquired from an English officer in the Japanese Steamer Company. When added to their holdings of slides made from religious paintings (a practice which became popular in the United States after the 1870s) and images of exotic locales and foreign cultures, these new materials enabled Anglican missionaries to develop localized entertainment and educational programs for Korean audiences.

Gradually, the magic lantern became an indispensable educational tool for the missionaries—the showing of slides enabled them to overcome language barriers with their target audience. Hence, Korea became as much a locale for spreading foreign culture and new ideas through Western technology as it was a source of exotic imagery and foreign culture for export back to Britain for generating interest, awareness, and funds for continuing 'God's work.'

After the mid-1890s, and for the next fifteen or so years, magic lanterns were increasingly used for both indoor and outdoor 'education' and entertainment by missionaries and theater entrepreneurs alike. In the former case, they often served an unexpectedly larger purpose than their intended one of private enjoyment for a small group of (mostly male) missionary students. For example, in September 1897, Anglican missionaries from Seoul joined their colleagues in Chemulpo for an afternoon of celebration followed by a magic lantern show in the evening.[14] And according to *The Morning Calm*,[15] when the Chemulpo mission hosted an open-air magic lantern show at their compound for Christmas in 1898, the ostensibly private event became public after crowds of Koreans sought to catch glimpses of works by the French painter James Jacques-Joseph Tissot (1836–1902) and to listen to a live storyteller. Despite the bitter cold, these unruly eavesdroppers climbed trees and peered over the compound walls, and were eventually admitted to the presentation.

Apparently unfazed by this reaction, over Easter 1899 the Chemulpo mission hung a large canvas sheet outdoors to exhibit slides from the Tissot collection while a live narrator explained them. *The Morning Calm* gave a partial list of titles: *Hagar and the Angel in the Desert, Abraham Giving Counsel to Sarah, The Burning of Sodom, The Egyptians Admiring Sarah's Beauty, Ishmael the Archer, Isaac Bearing Wood for His Sacrifice, God Making Promises to Abraham, Abraham and the Three Angels*, and *The Offering of Abraham*. The crowd included a 'delighted and very reverent group of men and boys' and a group of women who were invited to gather behind the screen so as to remain separated from the males, a common cultural practice among Korea's traditional ruling class (*yangban*) at the time. (This became a controversial issue during early cinema screenings and is addressed in the next chapter.)

Few if any Koreans witnessing magic lantern shows in the late nineteenth century had experienced projected images of this kind and using this method. Accepting that the mechanical reproduction of realistic representations was foreign to the general population, some missionaries adopted a cautious approach. Anglican missionary F. R. Hillary believed that a lantern-lecture service showing images of the life of Christ would be neither comprehended nor appreciated by the 'ordinary heathen.' Rather, according to an article in *The Morning Calm*,[16] he saw the new technology as ideal for reaching out to 'inquirers and catechumens.'

In response to unruly behavior by Koreans at one or more slide shows, which surprised and possibly insulted the hosts, the missionaries decided to simplify the use of the magic lantern in public presentations—for example, by using only a single slide of the world map. However, the rowdy viewing atmosphere and the high level of audience participation generated during early magic lantern shows, as well as in early film screenings (discussed in the next chapter), proved difficult to moderate. It appears to have been similar to the rituals and practices that developed after 1905 among early nickelodeon audiences in small movie theaters in the United States.[17]

THE IMAGE AS EXPORT ENTERPRISE

As with the missionaries, the desire to exploit Korea's exoticism and natural beauty was shared by other Western photographers who had spent time in Korea and the wider region. These foreign travelers sought to capture images to educate and entertain members of the National Geographic Society, readers of the *National Geographic Magazine*, and others interested in learning more about an 'exotic' land and its peoples. For example, J. B. Bernadou, an ensign in the United States Navy and a researcher for the Smithsonian Institution's National Museum in Washington, DC, took a series of images of Korea and its people in 1883 while serving as an attaché at the U.S. legation in Seoul. He displayed his images during a public lecture in 1890 before the National Geographic Society. Bernadou's slide collection, as well as his written observations of Korean natural history, eventually became part of the Smithsonian's first ethnographic, zoological, and horticultural collection from Korea, portraying and documenting the social, cultural, industrial, and agricultural life of the country.[18]

Another American naval man, naval chief engineer Harrie Webster, who had worked in government service in Asia between 1894 and 1897, gave an illustrated public lecture in 1898 to the National Geographic Society in Washington, DC. His presentation included colorized images of the busy commercial life of Seoul and Chemulpo, as well as of historic royal tombs and schoolchildren at play.[19] Both Webster's images and those of Bernadou, published ten years earlier, pointed to the growing importance of Korea's geopolitical and trading relationships with the United States, including future prospects for mining gold and other minerals, and developing transportation franchises. The 'lure of the exotic' aside, the presentation of Korea through magic lantern slides gave viewers a privileged preview of an important emerging market for the United States. According to our own survey of local newspaper advertisements, this included a wide assortment of household and other consumer items such as alcohol, cheese, flour, linen and cotton goods, cigarettes, and sewing machines.[20]

Bernadou and Webster had shown only slides, and only in the United States. The pioneer of film screening in Korea was Burton Holmes (1870–1958), the first person to take moving pictures in the Philippines, the South Pacific, parts of Africa and, most probably, Japan and China. He is generally credited with coining the term *travelogue*. At the peak of his career, Holmes's portfolio included more than eight thousand travel lectures, all illustrated by his hand-painted, colorized, and photographed magic lantern slides and original motion picture footage.

His visit to Korea in 1901 (not in 1899 as some have claimed) occurred at the end of a world tour that also included Russia, China, and Japan. Holmes had been invited to visit Korea nearly ten years earlier, in 1892, by John L. Stoddard, a well-known travel lecturer and magic lantern show exhibitor twenty years Holmes's senior. (Between the 1870s and late 1890s, Stoddard was estimated to have made three thousand presentations to around four million people.[21]) However, at the time Holmes decided to remain in Japan, where he was visiting for several months.[22]

Few concrete details regarding Holmes's first short 1901 film of Korea exist outside of the advertisements and reviews of his talks in the United States in early 1902. What we know from *The Washington Post* (19 March 1902: 10), for example, is that his filmed crowded street and landscape scenes of the 'Hermit Kingdom' were 'unusually fine.' As the still images in figure 1.2 also suggest, Holmes mounted his camera on the inside of a trolley car in order to capture panoramic city views from the moving vehicle.

Yet, despite the fact that the only Burton Holmes footage of Korea on record, held in the Motion Picture Collection at George Eastman House (one of the major moving image archives in the United States), is clearly dated 1901, the myth of 1899 still persists.[23] Indeed, a blog[24] from late 2006 records the attempts of five contributors to solve the riddle surrounding what they believe to be this short film segment. Their postings make references to the film's inclusion of Seoul's electric streetcar system, the construction of the Namdaemun and Seodaemun gates, and outdoor advertisements for the Japanese Jintan medicine company.

Between the 1890s and the 1950s Holmes used his original magic lantern slides and motion pictures to titillate, entertain, and educate audiences. He was a master illustrator with words:

> On the screen a picture of a village at sunset—a river flows at the spectators' feet—misty mountains rise in the distance—the calmness of approaching night seems to hover in the golden twilight. All this simply an effect produced by the projection of a colored photograph and the utterance of a few suggestive words. (Cited from page 1 of the foreword to Volume 1 of *The Burton Holmes Lectures*, 1901).

Holmes's journey to Korea, detailed in the last of ten published volumes of *The Burton Holmes Lectures*,[25] took place during the first of many well-publicized round-the-world tours. The text and images reproduced in these volumes represent the narration for the public lectures that Holmes subsequently gave on each country he visited. The extraordinary extent of his travels is explained by the fact that he was a master organizer and a rapid writer, as evidenced by the numerous travelogue books, based on field notes, which formed the basis for his lectures. Indeed, with the exception of his autobiography, these volumes are our primary source of information about his numerous and wide-ranging trips.

This very full schedule required a well-planned routine. Holmes usually traveled abroad during the North American spring and summer, and then spent the autumn months writing lectures and books, and editing his photographs and films at his home in Chicago. He would then set off on his lecture circuit across the United States, presenting his illustrated lectures between November and the following spring. Holmes may not have been the first to give illustrated public lectures on Korea and elsewhere in Asia, and he may have been inspired by earlier presenters such as J. B. Bernadou. Nevertheless, Burton Holmes became one of the most prolific and successful travelogue lecturers of his day, building an enterprise that established him as a man ahead of his time.

Holmes usually traveled with a crew of two or three assistants, who looked after his photographic and cinematography equipment and helped him frame scenes. Numerous other local translators and temporary servants showed him around and transported his gear. The images in figure 1.2 show Holmes and his cameraman and assistant, Oscar B. Depue, a close friend and regular traveling companion, filming in the streets of Seoul. *The Averted Catastrophe* pictures the box-like film camera that Depue developed in 1899 and used during their 1901 tour of Russia, China, Japan, and Korea.[26] What is missing from these photos is the portable film developer that Depue also devised in 1900 for this trip.

It is interesting to speculate on the impact of Holmes and Depue on Korea and Korean culture. Certainly, they left an impression there at the highest level. During his stay in Korea, as he had done in many other places, Holmes had piqued the interest of influential people, ingratiating himself with one of the royal princes who in turn introduced him to the king and his family.

Through an invitation from Sir Jae-soon Lee, King Gojong's cousin and an influential government officer, Holmes and Depue were able to show their films to the king and Prince Youngchin, the baby crown prince. Holmes later recounted that the baby prince, the king's youngest son, was so fascinated by the projector that he wept violently when it was taken away and was left to fall asleep with the apparatus gripped tightly in his hands.[27] During the screenings, which included views of the royal palace and snippets of everyday life in Korea, the palace audience cheered as the moving images unfolded before them. These short films shown by Holmes on his portable projector, designed for showing 'miniature' motion pictures, were the earliest private film screenings made by a U.S. citizen in Korea. The king and the crown prince were so enamored of this novel technology that Holmes left the boxlike projector behind as a gift. In return, the king presented Holmes and Depue with gifts of fine silk, silver ornaments, hand-made fans embellished with exquisite calligraphy, and a rare (for Westerners) sitting in the royal court to watch the king's exotic cohort of eighty dancing and gyrating *gisaeng*.

Figure 1.2 A Trolley-Car, A Crowd, and *The Averted Catastrophe*, photos which feature Burton Holmes and members of his touring party in Korea circa 1901. The images appear on pages 59, 75, and 76 respectively in Holmes, E. Burton (1901).

In fact, in September 1901, shortly after Holmes's visit to Korea, and about twenty-one months before the first public recorded film screenings were held in Seoul, an anonymous writer in the local *Hwangseong Shinmun* declared himself impressed by the lively appearance of soldiers in a filmed military march, marveling at the realism of the figures on screen.[28] This commentator, who seems to have been Korean, had seen footage of the Boxer Rebellion in China (1898–1901) that was either shot by Holmes or brought to Korea by Holmes. Although we do not know where this screening took place, it signaled the coming of foreign film culture to Korea.

Holmes's demonstration of motion picture technology, albeit on a small projector and to a select crowd, reinforced the king's determination to introduce Western-style development and culture to Korea, and to continue the process of opening up the country to the outside world. For Holmes, the modernization process that Korea was experiencing made a deep impact on him. Spending time in Korea was an introspective experience, which led Holmes to speculate about the limits and potential of representational technology:

> Could cinematograph pictures be projected on the pages of this book, or exhibited by means of some simple little instrument that could be operated on the library-table (and this now bids fair to be soon accomplished), then one of our motion-pictures would at this juncture reproduce for the reader the sensations we enjoyed while dashing along the thoroughfares of Seoul on one of those swift trolleys, first toward the east gate from the straw-roofed suburbs,—the gate looming bigger and bigger, until at last we curve through a courtyard, and plunge into the tunnel-like arch from which we emerge to skim straight away up the main street of Seoul, scaring horses, and spreading dismay among the white-robed denizens of the Korean Capital. But pending the perfecting of the device that will bring the living illustrations produced by animated photography within the circle of the family reading-lamp, there revealing the very *life* of foreign lands, we must be content with pictures that suggest movement even if they do not reproduce it.[29]

Despite these speculations, Holmes may never have realized the full extent of the impact that he made in and on Korea. Along with his visit to the court, his ideas and filmmaking practices fuelled a modern, albeit nascent, cinematic consciousness in Korea. In our view, one might call Burton Holmes the forefather of cinema in Korea. Had he suspected it, then his 1953 autobiography, *The World is Mine*, might have contained more than a passing mention of Korea.

Like the magic lantern slides created and collected by the missionaries, Holmes's work shows how Korea was captured on film and brought to exotic life before foreign spectators. His extensive travels in the Asia-Pacific, Africa, and Europe, as well as North and South America, enabled him to capture the underdeveloped 'native' cultures that were worlds away from the environment in which he and his Western audiences had grown up. A pioneer of early film technology, he also envisaged motion-ride simulators and personal multimedia devices for use at home and the local library—a virtual reality multisensory interface in which users could navigate through still and moving images stored in giant databases and archives. In more practical terms, Holmes carved out a lucrative career from systematically making and exhibiting magic lantern slide shows and moving pictures as part of the demanding public lecture circuit. His sustained record of producing and exhibiting travelogues popularized the traveling multimedia show to such an extent that it still thrives today.

SMOKING PROJECTORS

At the start of this chapter, we noted that June 1903 was the date of the first public screening of commercial films in Korea. While most studies acknowledge the entrepreneurial roles of Collbran and Bostwick in these early screenings, the contribution of the man behind these two pioneers, James Augustus Thomas (1862–1940), has been consistently overlooked.

Hailing from North Carolina, Thomas was a tobacco salesman employed by the Liggett and Myers Tobacco Company of St. Louis, Missouri. Between 1888 and 1894 he was involved in surveying local tobacco trade practices, sourcing supplies, and promoting chewing tobacco throughout Australasia on behalf of the company. The instability of the region due to the outbreak of the Sino-Japanese War forced him to return to the United States in 1894. However, Thomas resumed his work in Asia in 1897, and in 1899 began working for the New York export offices of the giant American Tobacco Company, run by Washington Duke and his sons James Buchanan and Benjamin Newton, following its acquisition of Liggett and Myers.

In terms of business history, Thomas is probably best-known for revolutionizing the entry and diffusion of American brands of cigarettes into Australia, New Zealand, India, Japan, China, and other parts of the Asian region.[30] In Korea alone, he helped to increase the sales of imported tobacco, cigars, and cigarettes to an astounding value of $157,608—up from $85,000 in 1901.[31] However, sometime between 1902 and 1903, as a side business, Thomas initiated the first commercial film projection sales and training operation in North Asia and India. Like Burton Holmes, Thomas was a visionary. As we will see, he used his entrepreneurial acumen to jump-start the commercial motion picture industry in Korea, and possibly the wider Asian region, exploiting his connections with the American Tobacco Company's export office to procure the equipment he needed.

Thomas's primary business goal in Asia, working on behalf of the American Tobacco Company, was the creation of a commercial synergy involving the promotion, distribution, and consumption of tobacco and, inadvertently, other popular American leisure goods and services. At least in his early days, his job was simply to sell more cigarettes made in the United States. He had learned his trade from his father and grandfather, both tobacco farmers who had toured across the southern United States selling tobacco out of a covered wagon. Thomas was a consummate salesman who had developed extraordinary skills in the business of changing popular consumption habits.

While working in India between 1900 and 1905, Thomas would give away hand-operated sewing machines to anyone who brought him evidence of buying 55,000 cigarette packets, each containing a 'present ticket.' To promote this deal, he distributed one million advertisements in the Himalayan region alone. By giving away fewer than two hundred sewing machines at a mere cost of $12 each (a cost hidden in the sales price of the cigarettes), he enticed a new generation, and a whole new ethnic group, to smoke cigarettes made by the American Tobacco Company.[32] At other times, he gave away trinkets such as handkerchiefs, buttons, and small mirrors, items which he could never source as fast as smokers earned them with their present tickets. Throughout his travels, Thomas kept in frequent communication with the company's New York export office via cable messages. Given his solid financial backing in the United States, requesting more supplies, providing they were available, was as easy as sending another cable. Through such means, Thomas increased American tobacco sales in India from about $100,000 in 1900 to around $1,500,000 in 1905.[33]

Moving pictures were a key part of Thomas's marketing plan. In his autobiographical accounts, *A Pioneer Tobacco Merchant in the Orient* (1928) and *Trailing Trade a Million Miles* (1931), Thomas described how, around early 1903, he bought twelve projection systems ('outfits' of an unknown type) and a set of films for each projector for approximately $500 each. Into each film he spliced cigarette advertisements promoting brand names such as Richmond Gem and Admiral cigarettes (figure 1.3). This collection of equipment and accompanying films was divided up and shipped to China, India, Korea, and Japan, where it was used to develop local markets for American Tobacco Company products. Since Thomas could not be in four places at once, he planned to recruit and train local projectionists who could run these advertising campaigns on his behalf. It is unclear if he personally or the company paid the $6,000 required for these materials. Nevertheless, ordering more film projectors and other supplies was as easy as cabling New York.

At the turn of the century, a basic projector sold in the United States for less than $200. The images in figure 1.4 illustrate two of the handful of systems available in the United States at the time. The Thornward Optiscope was a combined magic lantern and film projector, and produced powerful limelight generated from oxyhydrogen tanks (at an additional cost of $48). When configured in this way (at a total cost of $166) and placed forty feet from the screen, the system promised to reproduce twenty-foot-tall images.

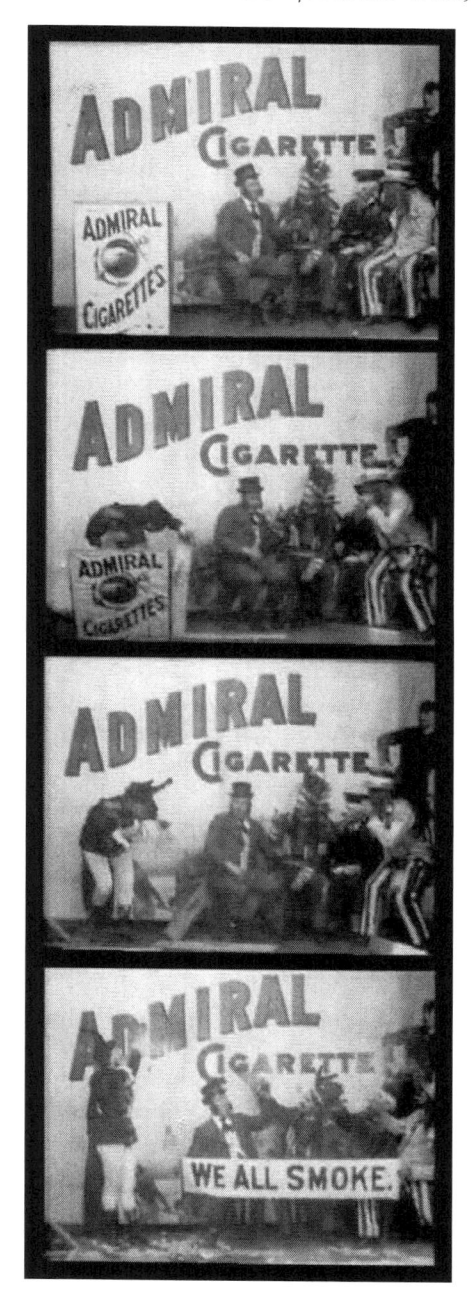

Figure 1.3 Still images from the short Edison promotional film *Admiral Cigarette* (1897). Thomas A. Edison, Inc., Edison Manufacturing Co. Courtesy of United States Library of Congress Motion Picture, Broadcasting and Recorded Sound Division, Washington, D.C. [34]

Naturally, this price did not include any supporting accessories or films. Alternatively, one could purchase the Thornward Exhibitor's Stereopticon, a portable system run on oxyhydrogen gas and fitted with two Thornward Universal [magic] Lanterns. This equipment enabled the operator to dissolve between still images, thus simulating a sense of motion and producing 'startling scenic effects.'

While other projectors sold for more than twice the price of the Thornward product line, available through the Montgomery Ward catalog, these were sold as package deals including films. For instance, according to the 1897 Maguire and Baucus summer catalogue of film and equipment, for $501.25 (or $465 cash price) one could purchase a hand-powered '97 Model Edison Projecting Kinetoscope (figure 1.5) as part of the 'No. 2 Standard' outfit. In addition to the projector, this package comprised an arc lamp for generating light, twenty-two Edison standard fifty-foot black-and-white films (worth $15 each), two Edison standard fifty-foot color films (worth $23 each), a film splicer/repairer, one hundred feet of blank film, one hundred extra carbon lamps, a twenty-foot lamp cord, and a magic lantern (stereopticon) attachment. Attachments for the oxyhydrogen gas-generated (calcium) limelight (also used with the Thornward) were available for an additional cost. Nearly 75 percent of the cost of this package (sold by Maguire and Baucus, one of Edison's few official sales agents) was for the films. Customers could select from a list of over two hundred fifty-foot films depicting rural and city life in the United States, as well as natural landscapes. A list of the Edison Projecting Kinetoscope films from this 1897 catalog is given in figure 1.6. [35]

As the American Tobacco Company's 'man on the ground,' Thomas could justify his company's investment in these film projectors because they augmented his advertising and promotional campaigns. In his memoirs, Thomas claims to have been the first person to arrange public screenings of advertising films in Korea, although details of these activities are unknown. [36] However, Thomas did note that these screenings did not produce the immediate results that he was expecting, because the import of the films with their scattered cigarette advertisements seemed lost on local audiences. At this stage, Thomas believed that his innovative promotional idea had failed, and he began looking for other ways of recouping his $6,000 investment, in the process developing a further entrepreneurial idea that would have a profound influence on the future of cinema in Korea.

Probably through mutual contacts in New York, and during his visit to Korea, Thomas befriended Collbran and Bostwick, who were busy operating and extending an electric railway in Seoul as well as building an electric lighting plant and complete waterworks. [37] In early 1903, Collbran invited Thomas and others to his home, where they enjoyed private screenings of some American films that Thomas had imported into Korea. It is unclear whether Thomas was using multiple Edison Projecting Kinetoscopes or a competing projector made or sold by either the American Mutoscope

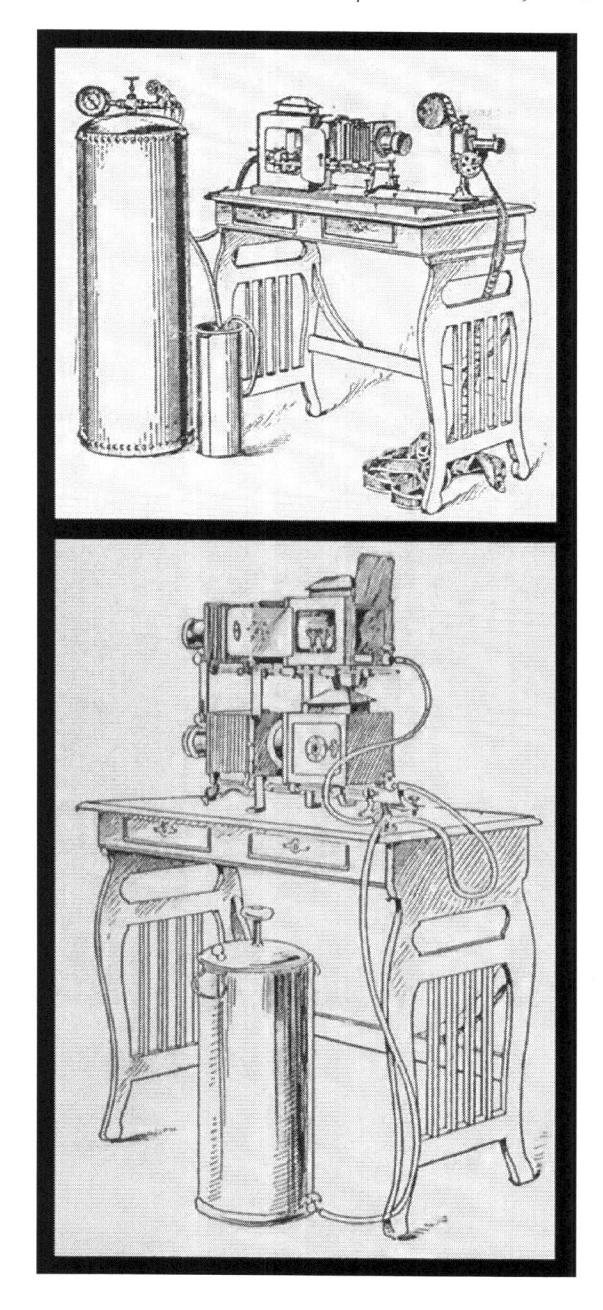

Figure 1.4 Thornward Optiscope and Thornward Exhibitor's Stereopticon images from the *Catalogue of Magic Lanterns Stereopticons and Moving Picture Machines*, Chicago: Montgomery Ward and Co., circa 1899. Images courtesy of the Internet Archive.

Company or the International Film Company. However, Thomas worked close to the business center of the United States film industry, which in the early 1900s was in New York. His office was only two miles from the International Film Company, which sold Edison films and others that they produced themselves. Thomas's office was also three miles from the main Edison sales offices, and a mere seven blocks from the American Mutoscope Company, which later became known as the Biograph Company.

The films screened at Collbran's home created such an impression that Thomas arranged to build a screening shed with two hundred seats at the end of the Seoul Tram Line, roughly six miles outside the city center. Each passenger buying a 5¢ tram ticket to the end of the line was rewarded with a packet of cigarettes and a complimentary pass to a screening of short American stop-motion, animated, and live action advertisements and

Figure 1.5 Newspaper advertisement for the Edison Projecting Kinetoscope, circa 1900–1910. Image courtesy of Wikimedia Commons.

actualité films and other movies featuring trick effects, which were commonly available in the United States at the time. The level of interest generated by this campaign was such that it disrupted the smooth running of the tram system while filling the screening shed to capacity. After a month of sold-out shows in June 1903, the film exhibition concept had proven itself not only profitable but ripe for expansion.

However, Thomas was not to be the chief beneficiary of his own innovation. In April 1903, after completing his assignment for the American Tobacco Company in Singapore, Thomas sold his entire business, with the complete projection systems and films, to Collbran, at a 10 percent markup. Thomas had proved that the concept was sound, and Collbran and his business partner, Bostwick, now sought to develop the business by exploiting Thomas's equipment and investing in new film exhibition technology. Thus, despite popular accounts, it was Thomas rather than Collbran and Bostwick who first screened commercial films in Korea, albeit as a cover for the promotion of American cigarettes.

MAGIC LANTERN NARRATION AND CINEMATIC PRECURSORS

Magic lantern shows continued periodically and remained popular in Korea well after the introduction of regular public film screenings, which began dominating the programs of the largest theaters in Seoul, Pyongyang, and Busan in the 1910s. In November 1905, Reverend W. D. Reynolds brought his modern lantern—which had been donated by the 'Korean Circle' of the Second Presbyterian Church of Norfolk, Virginia—to Presbyterian missions in Kunsan and Chunju (now Jeonju). His indoor evangelistic sermons and lectures, illustrated with a set of slides entitled 'Scripture Views,' attracted such large crowds that additional talks were held outside for the thousands of people who were keen to view Reynolds's realistic images of Christ. Reflecting on his use of the magic lantern in Korea, Reverend Reynolds noted in *The Korea Mission Field* (November 1905) that "as a means of drawing otherwise unreachable people and imparting religious teaching vividly and impressively, nothing can compare with the stereopticon" (illustrated in figure 1.4).

Missionaries did not have a monopoly of this projection technology. Magic lantern entertainment shows were also run in 1908 and 1909 by Collbran and Bostwick for company employees as well as the general public at the Seoul Electric Company Warehouse Theater.[38]

The appearance of magic lantern shows in Korea occurred at roughly the same time as the vogue for the 'projected picture,' or *utsushie*, reached is peak in Japan. This form of entertainment, which preceded the *benshi* in Japan, involved the simultaneous presentation of projected images and live narration. *Utsushie* had been performed in Japan since the early nineteenth century, but it reached a high point in the 1890s in vaudeville (*yose*) theaters.[39] At the same time, the combination of live narration with the exhibition of still images and motion pictures can be seen as part of a broader Western-inspired cultural innovation involving the institutionalization of recitation and elocution that flourished from the eighteenth century. Initially, this practice was part of the training received by lawyers, churchmen, and theater performers, as well as professional and hobbyist public speakers, in oratory skills and voice projection.[40]

Other entertainment forms also contained elements that acted as precursors of the cinema. In traditional Korean public storytelling performances, predominantly male practitioners wearing both male and female face masks entertained and interacted with audiences through witty and sarcastic dialogue and suggestive pantomime. Presentations often involved a large degree of audience participation, and by the end of performances it was common for the stage to be overrun by members of the audience singing and dancing with the actors.

This type of public celebration dates back to the late fourteenth century, where it was performed before common people in rural areas. As comic dramatization, this particular folk art form enabled commoners to escape the daily grind and enjoy a mixture of wit and laughter. Parodies were often directed at local traditions and rituals, criticizing class conditions that distinguished the country's large proportion of farmers and laborers from noblemen, religious figures (shamans and monks), and the middle class, which included doctors, translators, and tradesmen. Outdoor festivals were (and still are today) multiact improvisational performances, sometimes lasting from dusk until dawn, including enthusiastic musicians who often performed on the side of the stage.

Reaching a height of popularity in Korea in the nineteenth century, *pansori* theater performances, in which a singer and a drummer together perform satirical and romantic stories, engaged audiences through their emotive and often sentimental retelling of stories. *Pansori* performance appealed to the common person because of its basic emotive style, establishing a tradition, which was later adapted to make film more accessible to audiences through the role of an interlocutor, or *byeonsa*. The rowdy face-mask dance was another precursor of cinema culture.

One of the most significant developments to have grown out of the magic lantern shows that took place in Korea before 1900 was the live storyteller or locutor-man—one of the precursors of the *byeonsa*, who provided emotional interpretation and narration for silent and foreign films and made them more accessible to their audiences (see chapter 4 for more detail on the *byeonsa*).

These live storytellers also drew on Korean traditions of audience interaction with the story, leading to the loud and unruly viewing atmosphere at magic lanterns shows. This often disconcerted the missionary hosts, who may have failed to appreciate Korea's long history of lively and interactive outdoor performances and face-mask festivals. For the Korean spectators at these magic lantern shows, they were simply entering into the spirit of a new type of lively and colorful public exhibition. An obsession with modernity along with foreign goods and advances in Western technology and engineering, moving pictures and the apparatus needed to show them piqued the imagination of the royal family in particular. The crown prince's fascination with film technology had endured, too, eventually luring him to Japan, where he could learn more about film culture, among his other studies.

However, the spread of motion pictures was more than a one-way transfer of Western technology and engineering to Korea. As we have recounted in this chapter, Western slides and films were shown to locals in Korea while images of Korea were recorded and reported back to audiences around the world. For Korea and Koreans, motion pictures, as with electricity and the

Figure 1.6 Excerpt from the 1897 Maguire and Baucus catalog listing the Edison films available in the Edison Projecting Kinetoscope package. See Lumière Films, Edison Films, International Films, Maguire and Baucus, 1897. Series One, Producers and Sales Agents Active Before 1900. Motion Picture Catalogs Collection, Rutgers, The State University of New Jersey. (http://hdl.rutgers.edu/1782.2/rucore00000001079. Book.16837). Accessed 12 January 2010.

cable car, initially offered a spectacle of modernity. King Gojong's urge to bring the film camera and projector into the palace exemplified his desire for Korea to begin the process of transformation into a modern nation-state. Despite pockets of resistance to change, the king's desire to embrace this representational technology shows that he and those who shared his outlook were as preoccupied with the Western notion of spectacle as audiences around the world. It is likely that he was aware of the implications of Holmes's pioneering efforts and the potential benefits of the outside world seeing Korea on film. At the time, the illustrated travel lectures for which John L. Stoddard and Burton Holmes were becoming so well known were the ultimate means of promoting a foreign land and its peoples.

2 Foreign Cinematic Spaces and the Birth of the Film Industry, 1905–1916

In this chapter we explore how, before Korean filmmakers contributed to the development of a cinema of their own, cinema in Korea was 'occupied' by a foreign cinema culture. This occupation was literal in the case of the colonial government—although its attention had not yet turned seriously to regulating and controlling cinema in Korea—but is also an appropriate metaphor for the monopoly of film distribution and exhibition enjoyed by Japanese and Western (increasingly American) players.

This part of the book has three objectives. First, we outline how Korea became an exhibition market for films from Western Europe, the United States, and Japan for more than a decade before local filmmakers began producing their own films. Second, we explain how a nascent foreign film culture preceded a cohesive national film law and regulatory system. An influential expatriate community encouraged new audience behaviors that mixed traditional Korean performance culture with Western cinema-going habits. Throughout the early and mid-1910s, local audiences struggled to bridge the gap between domestic Confucian traditions and the mores associated with the new modern public spaces occupied by a foreign entertainment culture and new leisure activities. Foreign businessmen nurtured these activities and audiences with private investment, primarily from Japanese sources, without financial support from the state. Third, we show how the colonial authorities indirectly influenced the emergence of 'modern' cinema-going practices and examine the dynamic impact of these activities on Korean society. Indeed, as cinema grew in popularity and regularized industry practices began to take shape, it fell to local police first to censure and then to censor motion pictures. They focused their attention on films that they deemed harmful to public morality, in an ad hoc fashion and on a province-by-province basis. In the absence of a national film policy, the Press Law and the Security Law, both passed in 1907, served as preemptive measures for controlling 'movie-mad audiences'[1] and other potential 'disturbances' in Korea's colonized public sphere. Newspapers, journals, books, magazines, and other media enabling freedom of expression became easy targets for censorship.[2]

This period of Korea's 'occupied cinema' is best understood within these multiple contexts created by the pressures exerted by a variety of cultural forces—an authoritarian government, the market and the film industry, the self-fulfilling power of the audience and, standing behind all these, the underlying power of the text. These elements were all part of larger, dynamic cultural flows within the Japanese Empire.

HOSTING FOREIGNNESS: DISTRIBUTION AND EXHIBITION

For many Koreans, in both urban and rural settings, the turn of the century was a period of unremitting hardship and suffering. Conflicts such as the Sino-Japanese War (1894–95) and the Russo-Japanese War (1904–05) were fought on and over Korean soil. Korea had begun to lose its diplomatic sovereignty in 1905 after the signing of the Eulsa Treaty, which led to Korea becoming a 'protectorate' of Japan. In return, Japan now claimed the right to direct all diplomatic contact between Korea and the rest of the world, under the direction of the Japanese 'resident-general'—successively Prince Itō Hirobumi (1905–1909), Baron Sone Arasuke (1909), and Count Terauchi Masatake (1909–1910). A further complication occurred with the assassination of Queen Min, wife of King Gojong, by Japanese agents in 1907. Korea was fully annexed by Japan in 1910, and strict Japanese control continued under the new governor-general, Terauchi Masatake (1910–1916). Koreans were forced to accept their new civil status as colonial subjects and second-class citizens. Following annexation, sporadic nation-wide resistance and independence movements sprang up, attracting severe responses from the Japanese authorities. Suffering such hardships, there was little opportunity for local entrepreneurs to develop a local 'Korean' cinema. Korean filmmakers lacked the financial and technical means to express any form of 'resistance,' let alone Korean culture, on film—until the production of Korea's first 'kine-o-rama' (aka kino-drama), *Righteous Revenge*, in 1919.

Despite assertions by some scholars that Japanese interests dominated the film industry in Korea throughout the 1910s, at the beginning of the twentieth century the local film market was being shaped by a variety of individuals and groups.[3] The Korean Colonial Government and Japanese investors were only some of the parties who contributed to the development of a film market and industry in Korea during this tumultuous period. In fact, gradually, the film exhibition market was inundated by a variety of multinational players, mostly exhibitors and distributors, such as American entrepreneurs J. H. Morris and George R. Allen, Frenchman Alfred Martin, and Korean entrepreneur Park Seung-pil. As well, Japanese film studios such as Nikkatsu and Tenkatsu certainly wielded a powerful influence. Both local and international entrepreneurs targeted the Korean market, while others like them targeted other markets around the world.

The nascent distribution and exhibition market in Korea grew in similar ways to that of Japan and the United States, although naturally with local variations. In Japan, for instance, French Pathé films, acquired through various means, paved the way for new distribution practices after 1905. Entrepreneurs such as Umeya Shokichi, whose experience in China and Singapore had taught him how to profit from exhibiting films, used personal networks to obtain Pathé prints. Apparently unbeknownst to the original Pathé Company, Umeya created the 'M. Pathe Company,' rented large theaters in Tokyo to show films, and hired female usherettes to attract customers. Others, such as Yokota Einosuke, obtained an official license from the French Pathé Company. Competition between these and a handful of other exhibitors prompted new promotional ideas and the further expansion of distribution and exhibition networks.[4]

Meanwhile, in the United States, the exhibition market was dominated by a large number of local entrepreneurs aiming to make a quick profit from the burgeoning demand for motion pictures. The introduction of nickelodeons had already regularized the industry after 1905, with the establishment of nationwide distribution patterns. Although nickelodeons continued as late as 1914, they provided the first permanent home for motion pictures, attracting a rapidly expanding audience, which would continue supporting the American film industry over the following decades.[5]

Small-scale nickelodeon culture never latched on in Korea, despite the private screenings held for the royal family in 1901 by Burton Holmes. These royal viewings continued with the aid of the portable projector left behind by Holmes and Depue in 1901, as well as with other projection equipment likely to have been acquired from Japan. Film screenings in Korea throughout this period were directed at mass audiences, using large-screen projectors of various types. Conventional distribution networks were quickly established. Local agents purchased a supply of films from Japanese film producers and foreign film importers based either in Japan or Korea (and then rented the films out, taking a percentage of the profits). Producers and importers most likely sold the marketing rights to films in Korea as part of a larger territorial marketing strategy. In turn, local agents or buyers, including entrepreneurs, smaller distributors, and theater owners, re-rented the films for a flat fee and for a limited time.[6] While operating on a much smaller scale than in Japan, the United States, or Europe, exhibitors in Korea rented foreign films rather than purchasing them, particularly after the exhibition market grew and exhibitors became more organized. (This method, however, presented little opportunity for the importer to capitalize on an unexpected 'hit.')

The arrival of the cinema in Korea raised a number of cultural issues, notably the use of indoor venues for mass entertainment. Historically, traditional Korean performance arts, such as mask dances, *sadangpae* (itinerant troupes that performed folk and dance songs), and *pungmul* (folk music performances that included drumming, dancing, and singing), occurred mainly in outdoor settings. These were open spaces in which people from all walks of life and social classes, ranging from *yangban* (nobleman) to common men and women, could share a public space and remain at an appropriate distance from one another. (The missionaries' magic lantern shows usually took place outdoors, as well.) Koreans had no experience of an indoor exhibition sphere apart from private performances held in the royal palace and in other provincial government buildings. Indoor theaters, along with churches, trams, and department stores, were part of a newly formed and modern public sphere in which people came in unusually close contact with one another.

Koreans looked to Confucianism to provide their foundational social, moral, cultural, and legal mores. Most Koreans had grown up with long-standing Confucian traditions that required physical separation between noblemen and commoners on the one hand, and men and women on the other. Thus these novel indoor spaces—which enabled people from all walks of life to mingle freely and without discrimination—were greeted with alarm by traditionalists.

Korea's first indoor theater—not yet a permanent cinema, as it alternated between film exhibition and live performances—was the Hyeobryulsa Theater, built in 1902 by the royal family in the North Village (Bukchon) area of Seoul, better known today as Jongno. The Hyeobryulsa was built to commemorate the fortieth anniversary of King Gojong's accession to the throne. The theater had two levels with a seating capacity of five hundred, and films were shown there from mid-1903 after it had acquired a projector.[7] This projection system was probably acquired from James Thomas, the North Carolinian tobacco salesman who had sold state-of-the-art projection equipment to Henry Collbran and Harry R. Bostwick (see chapter 1). Around this time, Collbran and Bostwick also entered the market with film and magic lantern shows in their Seoul Electric Company warehouse (with a hiatus during the Russo-Japanese War, but resuming screenings in 1906).[8] In 1907, this venue became known as the Gwangmudae Theater.[9] Also in 1907, a third theater, the Danseongsa, opened in the North Village district of Seoul.

In mid-1907, in an attempt to further the royal family's interest in modernizing Seoul, French national Alfred Martin established a small cinema near the West Gate. Martin introduced the public to popular Pathé films imported from Paris in a regular series of evening screenings. He cleverly provided the royal family with private previews to gain their approval, and then followed this up with advertisements in local newspapers stating that the films had received the royal family's endorsement. To attract a wide variety of patrons across gender and ethnic boundaries, and to compete with the Seoul Electric Company's cinema, Martin offered two classes of seating—basic and premium, costing between fifteen and fifty *jeon* (or between approximately 4.5¢ and 15¢). He also offered reduced rates of 3¢ for children, thus creating an additional market and differentiating his programs from those showing in the Seoul Electric Company warehouse. Films were exhibited as the main attraction but, since they were short single reelers, live dancing and singing acts were included as preshow entertainment.[10] Given that most venues at this time had originally been purpose-built for legitimate theater, film screenings continued to share the stage for several years with magic lantern slide shows, live theater, and dancing and singing performances.

At the end of 1907, the use of *byeonsa* or live narrators began to appear as an experimental practice within this larger entertainment context, sporadically at first, but more regularly after 1910.[11] While performing off to one side of the screen, *byeonsa* aimed to give audiences a heightened understanding of the film by imitating human voices across a range of ages, classes, and regional backgrounds. *Byeonsa* eventually became an important art form and method of cultural expression, as these live narrators offered a 'Korean' experience—a traditional performance presented in Korean, for Koreans. In the mid-1910s, when films began to expand from one-reelers to two- and three-reelers (or 'volumes,' as they were advertised in Korea), *byeonsa* performers became a valued asset to cinemas and their operating and marketing strategies. Some became well-known personalities. *Byeonsa* such as Kim Duk-kyeong, Seo Sang-ho, Lee Byeong-ju, and Lee Han-gyeong were identified by the *Maeil Shinbo* as important Korean entertainers of the early 1910s.[12] Gradually, the colonial authorities expressed increasing concerns about *byeonsa* and their potential to weave spontaneous political or social commentary into their performances. Interestingly, the existence of *byeonsa* retarded the advent of sound films in Korea, a topic covered in chapter 4.

While drawing on traditional forms, cinema culture in Korea was being influenced from the outside by the colonizer as well. In 1908, the Japanese resident-general, Prince Itō Hirobumi, contributed to the popularization of cinema in Korea by hiring Yokota Brothers and Company, one of Japan's pioneering film companies, to make a film of Korea's Crown Prince Youngchin on a state visit to Japan. Director Makino Shōzō accompanied the Korean Prince, filming him at school, playing sports, and visiting the Imperial palace—attention which reportedly boosted the Prince's ego.[13] These short one-reel *actualité* films—which Makino probably sold to the Yokota Company for $15 each, as he did with his other films at the time[14]—were then sent to Korea for private exhibition at the royal palace as well as in public cinemas. These happy images of the crown prince were intended to assure Koreans of the prince's well-being under Japan's care. This celluloid public relations campaign, which played on the love of cinema that the crown prince had developed as a child during his time with Burton Holmes, exploited the prince as if he were an advertising product. All the same, through this royal initiative, the resident-general had created an important opportunity for the Japanese film industry in Korea.

THE NEW COMPETITION

Between 1908 and 1916, there were at least fifteen cinemas in Korea competing for audiences. Some were purpose-built cinemas, such as the Gyeongseong Godeung Yeonyegwan (hereafter Godeung), built in 1910 close to both the Korean and Japanese residential areas in Seoul; others, such as the Wongaksa (formerly the Hyeobyulsa) and the Jangansa, were traditional theaters adapted for screenings. As a greater number of films and variety of film genres became available, these venues responded by installing projectors and screens in their main seating halls or in adjoining purpose-built spaces.

As one would expect, most cinemas were located centrally within the biggest cities. Among the largest and most popular cinemas in Seoul was the Godeung, which could accommodate audiences of up to two thousand, and was being promoted as Korea's first regular and permanent cinema venue. Other popular cinemas included the Danseongsa and Umigwan, each of which had the capacity for around one thousand spectators. Instead of individual seats, many of these early venues seated people on long wooden benches (or bench-like stairs), tatami mats, in standing-room-only areas, or a combination of all three seating types. A large proportion of the audience probably saw films while standing, as a result of which theaters were frequently filled beyond their notional seating capacity. Tickets were often priced according to how close the seating was to the stage.

Due to their size, the Godeung, Danseongsa and Umigwan exhibited by far the largest number of films and ran the most film advertisements in the newspapers. Smaller cinemas, such as the Eoseongjwa, Daejeonggwan, and Yurakgwan, could accommodate between two hundred and one thousand patrons, again through a combination of seats and standing areas. In addition, organizations such as the Seoul YMCA frequently ran film-screening nights for various purposes, including religious and entertainment events.

In response to the great social and cultural upheaval created by the Japanese occupation, exhibitors began focusing on creating more luxurious venues and promoting a better screening experience for people who were willing to pay more for entertainment and leisure activities. Watanabe Tatsuzo, the Godeung's Japanese owner-operator, used an aggressive strategy to stand out among his competitors. Advertisements for the Godeung's grand opening—which showcased French Pathé films of world landscapes, magic lantern slides about good hygiene, live comedy and performances by Japanese dancers, and Korean *gisaeng*—claimed that the Godeung was one of the world's best motion-picture cinemas.[15] As if to emphasize its exclusive character, the Godeung offered two seating levels with long benches and standing-room-only areas on the first floor, and highly decorated Japanese tatami mats for wealthier patrons on the second floor. Watanabe had acquired a regular supply of French Pathé films from the Japanese Yoshizawa Co. These Japanese connections enabled the Godeung to gain a competitive edge among the Japanese living and working in Seoul.

Although the Godeung's admission prices were higher than at other cinemas, it offered a range of prices from one won (about 30¢) for the VIP seating to lower-priced seats of 3¢, 6¢, 9¢, and 15¢. It followed a strategy similar to that of the new 'flagship' cinemas in the United States in the early 1900s that were characterized by a downtown location, larger size, and higher admission fees—successfully positioning them as 'luxury' cinemas and signaling the American film industry's 'prosperity and presumed permanence.'[16] At the same time, in Britain, exhibitors were putting up large new permanent buildings that were dedicated to screening regular (and eventually longer) film programs as a way of differentiating themselves from the penny arcades and other itinerant venues that appealed to the masses. From around 1910, these prestigious, purpose-built urban exhibition venues were catering to more sophisticated audiences by promoting an ambience of 'prominent and permanent entertainment.'[17] These new cinemas strove to create an atmosphere of elegance and good taste, notably represented by ornate decorations and plush materials.[18]

The Godeung building showed that Korea's exhibition market was following a similar path, while at the same time offering cheaper admission prices to mass audiences. Like Frenchman Alfred Martin, Watanabe ingratiated himself with the palace, and used local newspapers to publicize his royal invitation to visit King Gojong, armed with a selection of Pathé films and a projectionist.[19] Clearly, the palace was equipped with sophisticated projection equipment of its own.

The Godeung's success—measured in terms of large paying crowds on a repeat basis—inspired other cinemas such as the Daejeonggwan to pursue a similar strategy of promoting itself as a 'luxury' cinema. In 1912, the Daejeonggwan I, run by Japanese brothers Nitta Kōichi and Nitta Matahei, was attracting wealthier, mostly Japanese, patrons (including soldiers) with its elegant décor. It developed a reputation for hosting a mix of material—live Japanese plays preceded by foreign films, both comedies and dramas. And, in order to steal a march on competing cinemas such as the Yugwanggwan and Jimansa, the Nitta brothers installed luxury amenities at the Daejeonggwan—such as heating and fan cooling, a smoking room, tearoom, bathroom, and usherettes.[20] One reason for wanting these flagship cinemas to appear modern was that their Japanese owners presumably wanted expatriates to experience similar levels of comfort in Korea as they would back home in Japan. In 1913, cinemas such as the Hwanggeum Yuwon further differentiated themselves from rivals by specializing in female *byeonsa*.[21]

Japanese studios and film entrepreneurs understood that cinema was likely to be as popular in Korea as elsewhere in the world. They approached the film market in Korea with gusto, because it provided a potentially important base from which to develop the Japanese film industry over the long term. Of course, it also enabled them to make a profit in the short term. In fact, for major film companies such as Nikkatsu and Tenkatsu, Korea was seen as a crucial market in terms of expanding their business and developing efficient production and distribution systems. Unlike some Western entrepreneurs, who were limited to operating as either exhibitors or distributors, Japanese players adopted multiple strategies. Some operated as cinema owners and exhibitors who plowed their profits back into their local operations; at a later stage, cinematographers, editors, and engineers used their advanced technical expertise and training to make Korea a second base from which to make films. Although they collectively 'occupied' the film industry in Korea, few of the Japanese film companies involved acted in concert with one other and none successfully dominated the Korean market by themselves. Rather, foreign companies and entrepreneurs adopted multiple and competing strategies for the distribution and exhibition of short and feature films in Korea between 1906 and 1916—all feeding off the public's seemingly insatiable desire for new entertainment media.

The impact of these foreign players on the early development of the film industry in Korea can be reduced to three central themes: the expansion of local cinemas, with assistance from major Japanese studios; the adoption of a variety of promotional and marketing strategies; and a considerable flexibility in the film genres, programs, and formats adopted, a process driven by both commercial and cultural factors. The methods adopted to nurture the nascent film industry in Korea were far from monolithic.

EXPANDING PROGRAMS

For the United States and Japanese film industries, film distribution and exhibition expanded in Korea in a recognizable way in the early 1910s. Serialized films first became popular in the West in 1912, a peak year for Western film exhibition, particularly in the United States.[22] This was a significant time in Korea, too, and saw the introduction of programming changes that lasted nearly a decade. Foreign film companies embraced this moment as a significant opportunity to transform the occasional cinema-going experience into a ritual.

Two major Japanese film companies, Yoshizawa Co. and Yokota Co., first made their mark in the Korean exhibition market in 1910, when they supported the opening of the Godeung. Yoshizawa even imported a projectionist from Japan. Watanabe's strong connections to the Japanese film industry suggest that Yoshizawa had its eye on expanding into the Korean market, a factor that no doubt weighed with the Nippon Katsudō Shashin (Nikkatsu or Japan Cinematograph Company) Trust, formed in 1912 as a partnership between Yoshizawa Shōten, Yokota Shōkai, Fukuhōdō, and M. Pathé.

Between 1910 and 1912, the Godeung continued to exhibit a combination of Pathé films and magic lantern slides along with live stage performances.[23] Other exhibitors also began competing for patronage in Seoul. In

April 1911, the Eoseongjwa Theater, located outside the Namdaemun Gate (Southern Gate) near the electric tram line, hosted the 'Heuksam Motion Picture Screening Event.' This mixed-media program comprised a colored magic lantern slide show of India and Arctic landscapes; the screening of the eighty-meter (quarter-reel) Pathé Frères film *La Chasse aux Phoques dans la Mer de Tasmanie* (1910, *Hunting Sea Lions in Tasmania*); a film about New York (probably either Edison's *Fire Dept. of New York City* or *The Police Force of New York City*, released in early 1911 and 1910, respectively); and Selig Polyscope's *Lost in the Jungle* (1911) and *The Ocean Harnessed* (1911). All the films shown were distributed by the General Film Company in the United States. Like the Godeung's programs, the Eoseongjwa also offered audiences a variety of non-film entertainment, including magic shows and multiact educational plays.[24] The weekly screening programs shown at these theaters—which were imported as packages from the United States, Japan, France, and China (Shanghai and Tensin), either directly or through Japan—included a variety of silent shorts, series, and newsreels such as *Pathé Animated Gazette*, the *Vitagraph Monthly of Current Events*, and *Gaumont Weekly,* as well as educational documentaries and cultural films. Daily programs advertised in the *Maeil Shinbo* around this time featured between ten and fifteen titles of short films. These films, which appeared regularly in theaters from late 1911, stimulated audiences and delivered the world to Korea's doorstep.

Outside the major cinemas, small organizations with limited budgets continued to operate itinerant magic lantern shows in and around Seoul. In March 1911, the Korean Doctors' Study Group staged nightly magic lantern shows at the Gwangmudae Theater and also at a nearby primary school in order to promote sanitary habits. These showings illustrate how the technology was being used for educational and public service purposes, with the aim of improving health and living standards in Korea. The shows are said to have attracted thousands of intrigued spectators.[25] Because the number of venues holding film screenings was small at this time, magic lantern shows maintained their charm and novelty, attracting people with diverse subjects. Yet, as we will see, magic lantern shows were gradually being replaced by film screenings.

In 1912, cinema-goers in Korea had access to hundreds and hundreds of film screenings of exotic places and fantastic adventures, as well as numerous current events documentaries. About half of all films seem to have been imported from the United States, while the other half came from Britain, Europe, Japan, and a few from China. It was also about this time that interest in film screenings began to surpass live theater. The impact of these images on Korean society and culture must have been considerable, particularly given that these were the early days of the Japanese occupation. One possible explanation is that entertainment cinema was being facilitated (or at least not prevented from growing in size and scope) in order to distract urban audiences from the realities of the colonial situation. Whatever the case, Korean entrepreneurs maintained only a small degree of agency in these developments.

At the center of this newly forming cinema culture were the Godeung and Umigwan.[26] Perhaps more importantly, the program changes implemented by the Godeung at the beginning of 1912 signaled a gradually increasing flow of Japanese funding coming into the film industry in Korea, helping Japanese entrepreneurs to gain a foothold in what was an entertainment novelty in Korea, just as it was in Japan.

This flow of investment enabled the Godeung to not only hold more regular screenings than before, but also to update its programs on a biweekly basis. Permanent staff, including a full-time projectionist and a live band, helped build a loyal customer base.[27] The Godeung remained popular despite being more expensive than other cinemas. Within two short years, profits from screenings enabled it to renovate and enlarge its premises into a more prestigious and exclusive 'flagship' cinema.[28] In 1914, the Godeung was purchased by the owners of the Daejeonggwan and renamed the Daejeonggwan II, specifically targeting Korean audiences.

The Umigwan, erected as a purpose-built cinema by Japanese entrepreneur Hayashida Kinjirō in 1912, differentiated itself from the Godeung by aiming to attract Korean patrons with foreign films. Park Jeong-hyun, a Korean who had been trained at Nikkatsu as a projectionist, was hired as a manager in 1913, strengthening the Umigwan's connection with Nikkatsu. Park's assistant was Lee Pil-wu, one of Korea's first cinematographers (see chapter 4 for his story).[29] Park and Lee's job was to create an appetite for foreign films in Korean audiences. At this time, the number of titles began to fluctuate and entrepreneurs such as Park and Lee began to promote specific film genres. Again, *byeonsa*, which were also promoted in newspaper advertisements, played an important role in this strategy by performing live in Korean. After mid-1913, the Umigwan stood out from other cinemas (such as the Daejeonggwan II) with its popular performances by *byeonsa* like Seo Sang-ho and Lee Byeong-jo, who were able to draw repeat customers by creating local interpretations of these foreign texts.[30]

Eventually, the Umigwan was able to secure exclusive distribution contracts with Universal Pictures, which began producing serials in 1914. Among the Universal screenings that excited local audiences was *Broken Coin* (1915), Francis Ford's well-known adventure-mystery serial.[31] Universal Pictures firmly established itself as a leading supplier of films in Korea by negotiating through Universal Harima, its Tokyo partner. After 1917, newspaper advertisements for the Umigwan made great play of the fact that it was exhibiting 'great pictures' from Universal.[32] Until the Danseongsa and Chosun Cinema began focusing exclusively on attracting Korean audiences in 1918 and 1922, respectively, the Umigwan was the premier cinema of its kind. Given the popularity of its serials, and the fact that serialized films returned the greatest profit for Universal during the 1910s,[33] the Umigwan played a significant role in the company's international business success.

These American pictures were popular because of their superior production values and cliff-hanging narratives. Again, we may wonder about the impact these films had on Korean society, other than to feed demand.

By 1913, other Japanese exhibitors such as Hayakawa Koshū entered the scene. Well aware of the popularity of motion pictures, Hayakawa traded in his junior high school teaching job in Seoul to develop a career in Korea's burgeoning film business. He created the Hayakawa Entertainment Bureau, a local amusement business, which imported films from Nikkatsu and initially showed them at the Hirakgwan cinema on a trial basis.[34] Here, Hayakawa's connections with Nikkatsu established him as a successful entertainment pioneer who went on to make a significant contribution to the development of the early film industry in Korea. In 1913, on Nikkatsu's behalf, he purchased and managed the Hwanggeumgwan (*Ōgonza* in Japanese) cinema in Seoul, and then the Haenggwan in Busan in 1917 and the Chosun Geukjang in 1924, where he distributed and screened foreign films on a permanent basis.[35] Ten years later, in 1923, Hayakawa formed the Donga Cultural Association through which he produced and directed the silent film *The Story of Chunhyang*, made with an almost all-Korean production crew. He showed the film at his own cinema in December 1923 and then at the Chosun Geukjang in September 1924—an early example of vertical integration in the local film industry. Hayakawa continued to develop this strategy in Korea until his death in 1926.[36]

It has been observed elsewhere that, in the late 1910s, the Nikkatsu and Tenkatsu groups controlled large theatre chains in Japan.[37] The important point is not the size of their holdings, but the fact that these two integrated studios were able to manage cinema chains under a variety of distribution and exhibition contracts. Instead of owning the venues outright, they either operated them directly (*chokuei*), under special license (*tokuyaku*), or engaged them on a percentage basis (*buai*). The special-license option was by far the most common type of relationship between Nikkatsu and the theater chains in Japan.[38] Cinema owners who opted to share a percentage of the box-office takings with a major Japanese film company incurred the burden of day-to-day operating expenses while gaining access to the studio's film catalog. As in Japan, the special-license option arrangement was the one favored by Japanese film companies operating in Korea, seeking an opportunity to expand their markets into Japanese-occupied territories.

While Japanese film studios continued to manage and control cinemas in Korea in this way, the exhibition market also experienced occupation under their economic hegemony. Nikkatsu and Tenkatsu covered all running costs and also received all the box-office revenues. Even when they were owned by separate investors, temporary film-screening venues as well as the permanent theaters and cinemas generally entered into a 'special contract' with either Nikkatsu, Tenkatsu, or the Shōchiku group. This committed them to exclusive screenings of the studio's films, in a 'block booking' arrangement. While these agreements provided a group of films to a cinema from the nominated studio, it was often done under coercion and without inspection or appraisal, leaving the exhibitor with a potentially small number of popular films in amongst many box-office duds. The Korean exhibitor paid an agreed monthly fee for an ongoing supply of films, and the Japanese studio provided a projectionist (or, at least, a projectionist's salary) and a manager to oversee day-to-day operations, as well as a live narrator and projection equipment, and an engineer as required to service and repair it. After 1926, this included wiring cinemas for sound; that is, installing either a sound-on-film or a sound-on-disc attachment to a silent projector and speakers (see chapter 4). This arrangement facilitated the diffusion of Japanese sound technology and the exhibition of Japanese, Korean, and foreign sound films.[39]

As part of their 'special licenses,' the Daejeonggwan and Hirakgwan cinemas paid a commission to Shōchiku or Nikkatsu for each film they screened.[40] Each print was rented from their Japanese partner, and shown first in Seoul and then in provincial cinemas, before being returned to Japan. By 1916, the Nikkatsu group, with Matsuda Masao as its local manager, owned the Hirakgwan outright, while the Tenkatsu group set up a distribution relationship with Danseongsa. In 1921, Shōchiku made a larger investment in the Korean market after it gained control of the Hwanggeumgwan in Seoul, formerly owned by Nangō Kimitoshi. Eventually, the Teikine group (owned by Fukuzaki Hamanosuke) purchased the Daejeonggwan; and the Makino group, an early and prolific independent production company founded by pioneer Makino Shōzō, purchased the Junganggwan, previously owned by a Matsuki-san. In 1920, Tokunaga Kumaichiro opened the Tokunaga Motion Picture Co., distributing Warner Bros. and FBO films from the United States, as well as Japanese films from Toa Kinema and Tōkatsu.[41]

Later, Korean nationals also came to play a role in the exhibition industry, although they were less well-funded than many of their Japanese counterparts. Park Seung-pil was one of the earliest Korean entrepreneurs to make a mark on cinema in Korea. Park, who came from a theatrical background, rented the Gwangmudae Theater from the Seoul Electric Co. in 1908 and transformed it into a traditional performing arts center.[42] As we show in chapter 3, Park's contacts with the Japanese film industry would prove invaluable when he began producing Korea's first 'kine-o-rama,' *Righteous Revenge*, and a documentary with panoramic views of Seoul in 1919. Lee Gi-se is another name that stands out. Lee, whose contributions are also discussed in detail in chapter 3, was owner of the Gaeseongjwa cinema in Gyeonggi Province, built in 1912.

Eventually, the larger number of exhibition venues enabled local importers to 'road-show' a film. This meant that they were able to exhibit a picture on their own account, booking a venue on a film-by-film basis and pocketing a percentage of the ticket sales. This strategy worked best with the larger cinemas and theaters, and with popular pictures. All the entrepreneurial exhibitors active in Korea during the mid-1910s set out to train audience habits by cultivating repeat business. As discussed in chapter 5, this strategy of building an audience base played into the hands of the Japanese propaganda machine, particularly after the state clamped down on the industry after 1937 and increased the number of 'educational' and 'military' films produced and distributed by the Chosun Film Production Corporation, which was established in 1942 (see chapter 5).[43]

By the mid-1910s, the main cinemas in Seoul had developed loyal Japanese, Korean, or foreign audiences, or a mixture of the three. Cinemas continued to cater to these three audience groups depending on which quarter the cinema was located in, rather than on the origin of its films. Cinemas such as the Godeung, Daejeonggwan, Eoseongjwa, Hwanggeumgwan, and Hirakgwan, all located near the Japanese neighborhoods in Seoul and Namchon, preferred to screen Japanese films for local Japanese businessmen, military personnel, government officials, and expatriates and their families. Programs included both Japanese and foreign films accompanied by performances by live Japanese narrators (*benshi*). The cinemas found in Korean neighborhoods like Bukchon, including the Umigwan and the Danseongsa, screened Western (primarily American) films for their predominantly Korean audiences, which also included members of the traditional ruling class (known as *yangban* before the Japanese annexation), aristocrats, noblemen, and scholarly officials.

By 1916, middle-class urban patrons and even members of the lower class such as farmers and laborers had begun frequenting the cinema. New cinemas were being built with comfort in mind as audiences began going to the pictures several times a week. New cinemas attracted families and children, too, as exhibitors reached out to different social classes and both genders. People from all walks of life and every age group had their interest whetted by this foreign phenomenon brought to Korea as part of a larger wave of modernity.

MARKETING NEW HORIZONS

In order to exploit further the 'occupied' market and to reach an expanding audience base, exhibitors began devising strategies to build their businesses and generate new profits. The use of marketing tie-ins was already established as a key method for increasing awareness of particular kinds of merchandise, brands, film titles, and stars, and, of course, for promoting cinema attendance. As we saw in chapter 1, in the late 1890s James Thomas promoted tobacco consumption in Korea using giveaways and product tie-ins as well as on-screen cigarette advertisements. Japanese exhibitors followed in Thomas's footsteps. For example, in 1913, anyone who had purchased the Lion toothpaste product (imported from Japan) could show the container in exchange for a free ticket to the Umigwan, where the program included a short documentary on the Lion toothpaste factory in Japan.[44] Following the success of the Lion tie-in campaign, the Chosun Tobacco Company invited customers to exchange fifteen empty tobacco packets for a ticket to either the Umigwan, the Daejeonggwan I and II, or the Hwanggeumgwan in Seoul, all of which were owned by Japanese.[45]

Devising screening programs with creative and seasonal themes was also a common promotional technique employed in the 1910s. Instead of simply showing whatever arrived on its doorstep, during the summer of 1914 the Daejeonggwan II promoted a 'cool' theme to its predominantly Korean patrons by screening a short documentary about Niagara Falls, a *Gaumont Weekly* film about winter in Europe, and four two-reel serialized social dramas, plus the three-reel *Beauty and the Beast* (1913) directed by Harry C. Mathews for Rex Motion Picture Company, which was distributed by Universal.[46] These promotional ideas were part of a new wave of foreign advertising novelties designed to develop new consumer markets.

Like many other countries—with the exception of France and the United States—Korea became a site of image consumption rather than of image production. Until mid-1914, as World War I was beginning and about four years after studios and cinemas in Europe began moving toward feature-length productions, nearly all films exhibited in Korea were one and two reels long. However, within a relatively short period, the average length of screenings jumped from two or three reels to about ten reels. Program diversity also expanded among newly established cinemas as a competitive strategy, thus giving better value to an increasingly discerning audience. Judging by newspaper reports, serialized romantic tragedies and dramas, adventure films, detective and mystery stories, comedies and action-packed Westerns (most of which exploited suspenseful cliff-hangers), and travelogues from the United States, United Kingdom, Denmark, France, Germany, Italy, Norway, Russia, and Spain were filling Korean cinemas to capacity.

While audiences in Korea could not get enough of these travelogues and fiction genres, they also developed an appetite for newsreels and educational documentaries about war, trains, and landscape themes. Local representatives from Biograph, Edison Studios, Selig, and Essanay, as well as Universal Pictures (Bluebird, Nester, Butterfly, Thanhouser), arranged the distribution of films from the United States. European films were imported from Pathé Frères, whose films were among the earliest exhibited in Korea, Bioscope (UK), British and Colonial Cosmopolitan, and Milano Films and Società Anonima Ambrosio (S.A. Ambrosio) from Italy. Films from the pioneering Japanese film companies Yoshizawa Co., Yokota Co. and M. Pathé—before they joined together under the Nikkatsu banner—also appeared on Korean screens. 'Sensation'[47] films were very popular in Korea at this time, and the Umigwan and Daejeonggwan II exhibited American and European detective and action-adventure films such as the eight-reel Stuart Webbs detective serial (made by the German Continental Kunstfilm

GmbH, directed by Joe May and starring *femme fatale* Mia May, his wife in real life).[48] These were stirring stories involving secret societies, double agents, seedy underworld figures, secret messages, and striking locales—all the while engaging with modern gadgetry and ideas. Genre and country of origin were key selling points for these films. Many of them were imported into Korea within eighteen to twenty-four months of release in their country of origin—reinforcing the international or 'global' flavor of the early motion picture experience in Korea.

Serials, which were as popular in Korea as they were throughout the rest of the world at this time, were usually presented as two-reel chapters (approximately 20–25 minutes long). Single reels were ten to twelve minutes (1,000 feet) long—a projector's common holding capacity. This type of film was cheaper to produce and import than full features, which generally became available in the United States after 1912.[49] More importantly, they were easier to understand than feature films for non-English-speaking audiences, in spite of the fact that some serials were created from segments of feature-length films that were cut and distributed separately over several months. Serials exploited simple narratives and characters, and utilized frequent action and stunt sequences. Their episodic nature (each week's offering was part of an extended narrative) and their use of the cliff-hanger ending held audiences' interest over several weeks. While other filmed series contained episodes, they comprised discrete stories with shared characters.

The emergence of longer-running films, which were becoming standard in the United States and Europe, soon exercised a profound effect on exhibition in Korea as elsewhere in the world. By mid-1914, serialized films—with two or more reels—had begun to appear in Korea. Newspaper advertisements also began to promote more details about each film (including studio names). This was a major transition that occurred only a few years later than in the United States itself.[50] This new kind of movie proved enormously popular. Sellout crowds were not uncommon, and sold-out shows were promoted in the popular press as a way of generating even higher levels of interest and excitement.[51]

As the frequency of cinema attendance increased, so too did people's desire to watch new films rather than re-runs of older ones. Audience members criticized the showing of older films at the Umigwan in 1915, for example, comparing its program of 'scrap' films unfavorably with the newer offerings being exhibited at the Daejeonggwan and Hwanggeumgwan.[52] (In fact, 'newer' films here meant the screening of relatively current newsreels and documentary footage. At the time, both the Daejeonggwan and Hwanggeumgwan had been showing short films of Emperor Taishō's coronation ceremony. Audiences were thirsty for almost anything new.)

When choice of films, or genre, became an important factor for audiences, as in other parts of the world, exhibitors began using newspaper advertisements as a key method of promoting their program changes. On the basis of the regular flow of film advertisements appearing in local newspapers after 1913, the larger cinemas changed their programs of between five and twelve films on a weekly basis, while smaller cinemas—such as the Wongaksa's Yugwanggwan and the Jangansa's Jimansa cinemas—rotated programs about every ten to twelve days. The Umigwan and Daejeong-gwan II, which seem to have had the largest newspaper promotion budgets of all the permanent cinemas in Seoul, changed their programs weekly. This became a necessity later on, after the two cinemas had begun sharing film prints. (In 1915, cinemas began showing three to four longer action and adventure feature films and several other shorts that were shared.) Sometimes on the same day, in a process called *kakemochi* in Japanese, a man on a bike was used to transport films between screening locations.[53] The appearance of the same program in the advertisements run by these two cinemas clearly shows the strategy employed by the Japanese owners to become more efficient by sharing prints—or perhaps as a way of overcoming the challenge of limited supplies.

Exhibitors in this period did everything they could to feed foreign culture to local audiences. As a way of differentiating their cinema from its competitors, the managers of the Yugwanggwan promoted it as a truly sophisticated venue—advertising the fact that they enabled the local consumption of global culture by screening films depicting the daily life, customs, and landscapes of developed countries. Titles of films screened at the Yugwanggwan include: the one-reel Pathé Frères comedies (made in the United States) *How Rastus Gets His Turkey* (1910), *German Lakes*, *Danish Painter's Dream*, and *French President's Visit to UK*; the one-reel *A Sixteenth Century Russian Wedding* (1908) from the Soviet Union; and *Italian Ships*.[54] Advertisements promoting these types of films attempted to create awareness of and interest in modern life, especially in the West, suggesting that Koreans were interested in developments in the world around them.

It is worthwhile here to trace the program changes that gradually occurred to give us a better understanding of local exhibition patterns. In 1912, a typical screening at the Godeung and other city cinemas included *Enemy of Electricity*, *The Uncle's Fortune* (1908), Spanish filmmaker Ricardo de Banos's series *The Moroccan War* (1909), *Enemy on the Train*, Pathé Frères' *Marriage of Princess Ena and Alphonse XIII, King of Spain* (1906), a variety of Pathé weekly films, pioneering Spanish film director Segundo de Chomón's sixty-meter short *The Magical Roses* (1906), and other non-fiction *actualités* and magic lantern slide shows depicting Japanese landscapes and various artists at work. Other films covered an eclectic range of topics including airplane and car races; Latin-style weddings; mythological stories about Pan; dancing girls in caves and daydreaming train conductors; the British Royal Horse Guards; sword fights; Turkish soldiers in World War I; children ice skating; beaches and ports; romance stories; various musical performances; and the Pathé Frères' biblical story *Cain and Abel*

(1911, directed by Henri Andreani) and Italian S. A. Ambrosio's *Arabian Infamy* (1912, directed by Mario Caserini).

Between 1913 and 1914, a typical screening at the Umigwan or Daejeong-gwan II included aspects of American political life in *Theodore Roosevelt in Africa* (1909), *Theodore Roosevelt at Fargo, North Dakota, During Progressive Campaign* (1912), and Edison's *The Declaration of Independence* (1911), as well as the Vitagraph Studios' film *Barbara Fritchie: The Story of a Patriotic American Woman* (1908), directed by J. Stuart Blackton and starring Julia Arthur. Audiences also enjoyed D. W. Griffith's *The Telephone Girl and the Lady* (1913), Edison's *The Battle of Trafalgar* (1911), and one-reel British Pathé films of the crowning of Edward Prince of Wales as well as biweekly *Pathé Animated Gazette* newsreels (featuring London city life, British and Italian troops in World War I, fishermen in the Solomon Islands, and segments about climate change); as well as the British and Colonial Kinematograph Company's (British and Colonial Films) *Under the Union Jack* (1911) and *Tragedy in the Alps* (1913, directed by Charles Weston). Newsreels in daily programs showcased footage of King George V returning from India; Luna Amusement Park and the zoo in Paris; city life in New York; snow-covered mountains in the Alps; Spanish bullfights; scenic views of Bulgaria, Budapest, and Tunisia; and Niagara Falls. The first color film screened in Korea may have been the 1913 screening of Pathé Frères' tinted *Unveiling of the Queen Victoria Memorial* (1911, directed by G. A. Smith and projected with Charles Urban's Kinemacolor projector made by his Natural Color Kinematograph Company).

The sum of these films was significant. Collectively, they brought a tremendous diversity of images to Korea at a time when Koreans (and Japanese, and Chinese, as well as American and European expatriates living in Korea) seemed thirsty for new things. In fact, it seems there was little critical faculty applied to the consumption of these movies, because *anything* was fascinating.

By mid-1913, the average length of films shown in Korea began increasing gradually, enabling exhibitors to provide a range of short films and serials and to move away from magic lantern slide shows to fill out their screenings. Showing at this time were *Pearl as a Detective* (1913, directed by Phillips Smalley and starring serial movie queen Pearl White), shown in Korea as part of a collection of 'Pearl' films produced by New York–based Crystal Studios; the five-reel French crime-fiction serial *Zigomar* (1911, *Zigomar the Eelskin* in the United States) directed by French film pioneer Victorin-Hippolyte Jasset; and S. A. Ambrosio's *Il cavallo fedele* (1914, *Faithful Horse* in Britain), *Un'avventura in treno* (1914, *A Railroad Experience* in Britain), the three-reel drama *La torre dei vampiri* (1913, *The Vampire's Tower* in the United States), and the five-reel film *La stanza segreta (Milleottocentotrenta [1830])* (1910, *The Secret Room* in Britain). Another Italian epic feature film, 2,200 meters in length, showcased the life of Napoleon. Other films screened at this time included a two-reel Biograph military action film about a hostage; Pathé three-reel films about a hometown tragedy and an action-detective story; and three reels of *Les amours de la reine Élisabeth* (1912, *Queen Elizabeth*), starring Sarah Bernhardt in a portrayal of the life of Elizabeth I (1533–1603) and her relationship with Robert Devereux, Earl of Essex.

Normally, these and other serialized films would be released twice a week, with screenings repeated twice daily. However, the occupying administration had an agenda for cinema in Korea that went beyond mere 'distraction by entertainment.' Early audiences were regularly exposed to specific types of ideological or 'message' films, particularly as part of the drive to propagate Japanese nationalism, in special screenings organized by the Korean Colonial Government. The *Maeil Shinbo*—one of the government's primary mouthpieces—sponsored screenings in Seoul, Incheon, Busan, Daegu, and Pyongyang, distributing either free or discounted film tickets for subscribers to its newspaper. To celebrate the opening of its Daegu branch in 1912, for example, the *Maeil Shinbo* offered half-priced tickets to the local cinema. In Pyongyang, the newspaper ran free screenings for subscribers, drawing about one thousand people.[55] Promotional film events such as these, as well as the promotion of the Korean Products Competitive Exposition (Gongjinhoe) held at the Kyeongbok Palace in Seoul in 1915, were used to spread ideas and images that were central to the Japanese Imperial agenda.

Following the close of the 1915 Gongjinhoe, the *Maeil Shinbo* helped to showcase Japan's administration of Korea by organizing nationwide documentary screenings of the event as a way of celebrating its success. Also in 1915, the *Maeil Shinbo* and the *Kyeongseong Daily*, another newspaper published by the Korean Colonial Government, jointly sponsored the distribution and exhibition of newsreels of Emperor Taishō's coronation ceremony at cinemas across fifteen different Korean cities in an effort to unite audiences behind the regime and build a sense of Japanese nationalism.[56] Subscribers of these newspapers received discounted admission tickets, and fervent audience responses to the film in each city were promptly published.[57] The birth of cinema in occupied Korea was accompanied by the advent of a propaganda machine designed to overwhelm audiences with pro-Japanese and later, after 1937, anti-Western rhetoric.

While commercial and educational screenings were growing in number and frequency in the lead-up to 1916, Christian associations began screening films for religious education purposes. In the process, film screenings replaced the magic lantern slide shows that missionaries had used for this purpose in the 1890s. On 8 May 1916 at the Jongno Youth Hall in Seoul, the YMCA (Young Men's Christian Association) held screenings of the two-hour (over 2,000-meter) Italian 'sword and sandal' genre film *Quo Vadis* (1912), one of the first feature films to run longer than one hour.[58] The film, which contained lavish sets of Rome and thousands of extras, is well known for having been screened at some of the largest and grandest theaters in Paris, London, and New York. Religious discussions facilitated by the YMCA followed screenings of this and similar films which, in their sheer scale and spectacle, represented cinema as a modern art form.

By 1916, most of Korea's largest cinemas were changing their programs every four to seven days due to the increasing need to share and to circulate prints, particularly those cinemas sharing joint ownership or management under Nikkatsu or Tenkatsu. Newsreels such as *Pathé Animated Gazette: From Zeppelin Perils: Erecting Searchlights at Hyde Park Corner against Possible Airship Raids* (1914) continued to fill the average program.[59] Cinemas in both Korean and Japanese neighborhoods showed these newsreels and documentary films, which portrayed modern lifestyles in Japan and the West as well as landscapes in other countries and fictional entertainment films. This pattern lasted until around 1937, when the Korean Colonial Government began cracking down on foreign film culture and showing an increasing number of Korean-Japanese co-produced feature-length propaganda films.

SEGREGATION AND 'MOVIE MADNESS'

As we have seen, audiences were influenced in their choice of cinema by considerations of locality, price, and genre. Seat prices varied according to the location of the seat or whether a customer stood for the duration of the film. However, price was not the only factor in the allocation of seating. Race, nationality, class, and gender played the largest roles in determining how audiences were organized or segregated within the public cinema space.

The authorities had other, more practical, issues to deal with as well. Overcrowding gave rise to ongoing safety concerns, especially given that cinemas commonly ran highly flammable nitrate prints through their projectors, by necessity utilizing a heat source. Around the world, many cinemas (probably the best known of which was portrayed in Giuseppe Tornatore's 1988 Oscar-winning film *Cinema Paradiso*) maintained these hazardous conditions in small projection rooms that often lacked adequate asbestos fireproofing on the walls. In addition, early indoor theaters were usually made of timber and were thus prone to fire. Indeed, two disastrous fires occurred at Seoul's Danseongsa and Incheon's Pyo Cinema in 1915 and 1916, respectively, leaving people injured and property severely damaged.[60]

Separating audiences according to gender was a practice rooted in traditional Confucian values. Elite cinemas in Seoul attempted to prevent men and women (over the age of 11) from physically interacting once they had entered the building.[61] Most of these cinemas probably had only one front entrance, and let men enter first.[62] Men and women, regardless of nationality, were ushered to different seating and standing areas that were separated by physical barriers. Despite attempts to segregate audiences by gender, some men apparently couldn't resist leering at the women—a practice which upset readers of the *Maeil Shinbo* who complained about this on many occasions.[63] Even with these separate seating arrangements, sometimes men and women mingled unexpectedly while waiting in cramped spaces before and after a show. Hence, from this early stage, cinemas developed a reputation as a public space associated with indecent behavior.

Cinemas such as the Godeung also separated audiences by race, showing Japanese patrons to the fancier tatami-mat viewing areas on the second floor while directing Koreans to the seating and standing areas on the first (ground) floor. Other cinemas also followed this dual-level segregation strategy.[64] In colonial Korea, in which the ideology maintained by the Japanese authorities focused on assimilation, practice deviated from the theory of the parallel development of two distinct but equal societies. Japan spoke about building equality and co-prosperity between Japanese and Koreans, but in practice this concept failed because colonial policy discriminated between Koreans and Japanese at many levels.[65] Racial segregation in Korean cinemas was but one example of the large disparity between the ideal and the reality of Japan's colonial project.

Almost from the moment motion pictures were introduced to Korea, they were a source of concern for the authorities as regards moral and social behavior, as well as for social commentators who generally disapproved of the lack of cleanliness and the arrogant staff that were said to plague the cinemas. Korean cinemas were beset by 'movie-mad' audiences (a phrase originating in the United States),[66] well before any government policy could have anticipated such a development. As with early film exhibition culture in the United States, Korean cinema-goers played a significant role in the institutionalization of the cinema, in the process challenging traditional notions of cultural identity which were already in flux due to Korea's colonial relationship with Japan. For Koreans, this 'movie madness' existed as a form of escapism—albeit a temporary escape from the reality of their colonial status and the remnants of Korea's traditional feudal system. Cinema-going was more than the act of going out and seeing a movie; it was also about public socialization. Bringing men and women together to watch filmed and live entertainment opened new liminal spaces for the expression of 'immorality' and 'obscenity,' whipping up excitement among local audiences who used these gatherings to step outside of their traditional modes of living. The results caused disorientation and anxiety among officials, police, Confucian scholars, and cultural critics alike.

One of the first outbreaks of this moral panic occurred in 1906 at the Hyeobryulsa in Seoul, where men and women were seated unusually close to one another. It was closed temporarily by palace officials after its managers were accused of creating 'spring fever' among its mixed audiences.[67] Other theaters such as the Gwangmudae and Wongaksa were the target of similar accusations of undermining Confucian social morality. Such fears about audiences 'behaving badly in the dark' reflected similar experiences reported from other countries in the early days of cinema.[68] In the United

Kingdom at this period, cinema lights were often kept on in an attempt to appease female cinema-goers—it is unclear whether this was also the case in Korea.[69] Nevertheless, from early on there existed a constant tension between critics of cinema culture and exhibitors who were eager to make a profit by whatever means.

Along with rowdy audiences, unsanitary and unsafe conditions in cinemas remained a concern for the anonymous contributors to the *Maeil Shinbo*'s regular Readers' Club column. They particularly disapproved of the 'un-Korean-like' flirtation between male and female cinema-goers. The publicly expressed views of these critics reaffirmed the general perception that the cinema space, including the contents of the film shown, was a magnet for immorality. While the Readers' Club may have lacked an overt manifesto, it certainly censured the cinema, and advocated tougher exhibition regulations. Given these increasing levels of concern in the 1910s, it is no wonder that provincial police began paying closer attention to cinemas and theaters as potentially unruly spaces where delinquency and obscenity festered.

Eventually, the Korean police shifted their concerns over 'immoral' behavior among audiences to the live, spontaneous performances of *byeonsa*.[70] Live narration had the potential to stir audience emotions in ways that threatened public order—or, at least, the authorities recognized the potential for these live narrators to stray from their scripts. From around 1916, it was common practice for cinemas to submit narration scripts to the provincial police for advance approval. Cinemas were also required to provide permanent seats at the rear of the cinema for local police to monitor live performances. Watching live performances in this way became part of an ongoing censorship process—duties which, until the Korean Colonial Government's expansion of the Library Department in 1926 (discussed in the next chapter), were carried out by local provincial police in an ad hoc manner.

Cinemas were potentially subversive places. In Korea, there was a cultural belief that evil lurked in the dark. Cinemas potentially provided dissidents with an opportunity to meet in 'private' in a public space, where they might discuss matters relating to the independence movement, or simply share their true feelings about the Japanese authorities and their colonial condition. At the same time, cinemas in the Japanese quarter of Seoul that offered Japanese films created a potentially nostalgic space for Japanese audiences to escape the reality of being away from home.

In other cases, heated exchanges among mixed—Japanese and Korean—audiences caused potentially dangerous tensions. According to an interview with Lee Gu-young, one of the better-known colonial-era screenwriters and directors, one such skirmish broke out when the Godeung screened a short film of a boxing match between a Western boxer and a Japanese judo exponent.[71] Police were called to the scene when a fight broke out between Koreans sitting on the first floor and some Japanese on the second floor. After this outburst, which had occurred despite racial segregation, police in Seoul began spending more time watching crowds watching films.

This story is a good illustration of the capricious nature of film culture in Korea's occupied cinema. It also suggests why the colonial authorities developed new and stricter censorship laws spanning the life of a film from preproduction, through postproduction and distribution to exhibition (see chapter 5).

Class barriers were also reflected in attendance at the cinema. 'Poorer' Koreans had begun frequenting the cinema, enjoying this product of modern technology and the distractions that it offered. However, letter writers to the *Maeil Shinbo* sensed that something was amiss at this new center of Korea's burgeoning entertainment culture. Fearing the worst, these anonymous writers, as well as teachers and parents, blamed the cinema for its 'bad influence' on society and particularly for enticing students away from their studies. By early 1914, it was not uncommon for around one-third of some cinema seats to be occupied by students.[72]

Despite the occasional Christian-sponsored film screenings, criticism aimed at cinema's perceived negative impact on youth intensified. A special 'Children & Motion Pictures' column published in the *Maeil Shinbo* voiced these concerns, alleging that foreign films were corrupting children's imaginations, leading them to confuse illusion and reality.[73] Late afternoon and evening screenings to which women were supposedly bringing their children were singled out as the primary problem. Cinema-going was seen as a luxury for mature adults and therefore inappropriate for children, especially those from poorer (uneducated) backgrounds who might not know any better. The basic fear was that children would mimic what they saw on the screen. (As we will see in chapter 5, the Japanese authorities probably counted on this mimicry process when they facilitated the production of military and other feature-length propaganda films between the late 1930s and mid-1940s, films primarily aimed at youth.)

In response to these supposed social problems associated with places of public entertainment, in 1915 Seoul police began enforcing a new law requiring all local cinemas to segregate men and women over the age of eleven.[74] In addition, doctors and primary-school teachers persuaded Seoul police that a large percentage of films were exposing children to confronting issues of sexuality, and were therefore dangerous to adolescents. As a result, police began enforcing local bylaws banning children under the age of eleven from cinemas and theaters. Anyone violating these edicts, including men and women caught 'unscrupulously' sitting together, was threatened by the local police with punishments including beatings and possibly jail time.[75]

The authorities' desire to clean up the city before the arrival of international guests at the 1915 Exposition (held in September–October, at the Royal Palace) was also probably a contributing factor to these social-control measures. Given that this would be the first international trade event held in Korea following its full annexation, and that the eyes of the world would be observing the Japanese administration, the colonial government would not have wanted to risk any display of dubious morality in the capital. Predictably enough, the anonymous contributors to the *Maeil Shinbo*'s Readers' Club column welcomed the stricter provincial reforms initiated by Seoul police.[76]

The advance of cinema culture in the era before national censorship reached its peak in 1916 contributed to the formation of a new consciousness that was inseparable from a peculiar Korean and colonial consciousness, particularly as Koreans were not producing any films of their own at this time. Nevertheless, the exhibition of foreign cinema as part of the larger consumption of entertainment in Korea did provide opportunities for Koreans to participate, albeit indirectly, in the construction of colonial modernity through the influence of what they were seeing on screen. As we have seen, local audiences in Korea were generally separated along racial lines, viewing different types of films and being entertained by different (Korean or Japanese) *byeonsa* or *benshi*. In this way, cinemas catering to Korean audiences managed to maintain a space that predominantly involved Korean-language as well as foreign (but not Japanese) films. Although these choices were made by Japanese cinema owners for marketing purposes, they offered audiences an opportunity to escape from the realities of colonization awaiting them in the world outside the cinema.

At the end of 1916, as Hasegawa Yoshimichi replaced Terauchi Masatake as governor-general, the colonial government began formulating new plans to restrict and mould the public expression of this so-called modern culture. One notorious achievement of Hasegawa's administration was the promulgation of film regulations which attempted to restrict not only the exhibition of foreign films in Korea, but also the production of local films—even before they were made—in anticipation of the further development of film culture in Korea. It is no coincidence, then, that 1916 is the *official* year of the birth of permanent film production, distribution, and exhibition in Korea.[77] With this fundamental change in place—and with considerable irony, given the occupying authorities' hostility to Western modernity—American films began to establish dominance in the Korean market. With France and Italy caught up in World War I, studios in the United States were presented with an opportunity to capitalize on their production foothold and share of exports across world markets. By mid-1916, American films, which had developed a reputation as exciting action stories, had become audience favorites, outstripping the more conservative Pathé and Gaumont films with which they had competed previously.[78]

The provincial regulation of cinema culture reached a watershed in 1922, when the Gyeonggi provincial governor passed the Regulations for Exhibition and Exhibition Halls, which also included new measures for script censorship and testing for all *byeonsa*.[79] Seoul, the seat of power in Gyeonggi Province, set new standards for investigating—effectively censoring—film content in addition to policing public performance spaces and screening venues. While no other specific guidelines appear to have been released following the 1907 Press Law, the Gyeonggi provincial regulations were most probably inspired by the Motion Picture Regulations passed in Japan in 1917.[80] In turn, the measures adopted in Gyeonggi Province provided the basis for the development of national film regulations in 1926.

PRECURSORS OF LOCAL FILM PRODUCTION

By 1916, film importation and distribution systems were becoming more competitive with the increasing popularity of American and European films. In 1915, J. H. Morris, an American missionary who ran an orphanage and later invested in the mining industry, established the Morris Trading Co. in the Bonjeong area of Namchon, the Japanese Quarter, which since annexation had become one of Seoul's lively business hubs. From this location, which was relatively close to Seoul's other major cinemas, including the Godeung, Morris distributed films acquired on an informal basis from Japanese agents of Universal Pictures. In 1926, Universal hired him to set up a formal branch office in Seoul and to expand the company's activities in Korea through his locally established networks and experience.[81] Universal Pictures (Japan) Ltd. provided Morris with his largest source of films until he later added films from Paramount and Fox.[82] Until his retirement, Morris supervised the entire territory of Korea on the basis of 10 percent of all Universal sales, making himself guarantor for all accounts. Universal's Korean exchange operated under Universal Pictures (Japan) Ltd. from 1926 to 1946, when a local direct distribution branch office in Seoul was incorporated during the period of the United States Army Military Government in Korea (USAMGIK).

Other new foreign distributors included the W. W. Taylor Co., which distributed First National and MGM pictures (in addition to selling Victrola gramophone systems).[83] George R. Allen entered the film scene in 1922 after extending his larger gramophone and sewing machine sales operation. Importers and agents such as Morris, Taylor, and Allen purchased American film prints directly from the Universal and Paramount exchanges and distributed them to cinemas in Korea—a different method from that used by the cinemas screening Japanese films.

Western entrepreneurs such as Allen and Morris participated actively in the establishment of Korea's early exhibition market by forming direct links with American studios such as Paramount and Universal. Japanese entrepreneurs also noted the business opportunities, and quickly expanded their influence over the exhibition market by constructing and running new cinemas and setting up distribution deals with Japanese film studios such as Nikkatsu and Shōchiku. Koreans like Park Seung-pil and Park Jeong-hyun worked to create cinema spaces catering to Korean audiences. As a result of all this activity, a rich film-literate environment developed in which local productions would eventually flourish.

The total population of Korea in 1910 was a little more than thirteen and a quarter million people, including nearly 172,000 Japanese and about 12,700 other foreigners.[84] In 1920 the total population had increased to seventeen and a quarter million people, with the population of Japanese and other foreigners doubling. As a result of these changes, cinemas increasingly catered to mixed audiences. In addition to the established system of targeted screenings, new promotional strategies emerged in response to Korea's gradually diversifying population.

Thus Koreans were increasingly exposed to (largely Western) modernity through the big screen—encountering a variety of narrative themes, filmic images, and the customs and manners of a disparate crew of fictional and (to a lesser extent) nonfictional characters. Foreign films opened new windows onto the world, in many cases localized by a live narrator. Local newspapers, under the censorship control of the Japanese colonial government, also played a key role in the spread of cinema culture, and modern ideas more generally, regardless of whether their readers ventured out to the cinema or not. Newspapers used the lure and excitement of motion pictures as a promotional device to increase subscriptions and to spread a sense of (Japanese) nationalism.

As well as promoting local and foreign film culture, the editors of the *Maeil Shinbo* continued to publish emotional reader responses to local film screenings and their potential harm to society. Newspapers generally became a mouthpiece for a conservative element that was ardently opposed to the coming of cinema (and modern ideas more generally). They also published articles about the film industry, providing background information about advanced Western filmmaking and acting techniques.[85] Responding to public interest in the industry, the newspapers informed readers how to create train crashes and airplane flight scenes, how to build life-size studio sets, miniature models and natural locations, and how to film people and animals. In February 1916 an article in the *Maeil Shinbo* offered instructions on shooting a kissing scene involving a newlywed couple.[86] News reports about American film stars also littered the *Maeil Shinbo*. Updates on Chaplin and Fairbanks (and their lucrative contracts) appeared regularly, for example. Published for thirty-six years almost without interruption, the *Maeil Shinbo* is one of the richest sources available for studying film culture during the Japanese colonial period.

This plethora of 'how-to' articles on Western filmmaking techniques can be read as a significant prelude to the production of Korea's first homegrown film, a 'kine-o-rama' called *Righteous Revenge* (1919). Through such material in the media, Korean filmmakers had several years in which to contemplate how to make films before launching their own productions.

Carried out on a province-by-province basis, film censorship remained an uneven process during this period. By early 1913, the number of entrepreneurs importing 'banned' films from the United States and Europe began rising in tandem with the increasing number of cinemas. Exhibitors were answering a local demand for global culture, which, according to contemporary newspaper reports, meant Western films containing scenes that violated traditional morality. Interestingly, these 'immoral' films were among the most widely attended.[87] This barrage of seemingly 'objectionable' films, which inspired the need for stricter regulations in some provinces, included *Three-Fingered Kate* (available in the United Kingdom since 1909); one-reel live action shorts *Mutt and Jeff* (USA 1911), based on the popular comic strip; *Lieutenant Rose* (UK); *Dr. Gar-el-hama* (Norway); *Arsene Lupin Contra Sherlock Holmes* (Germany); *The Adventures of Dick Turpin*; *Alkalie Ike*; *Desperate Desmond*; Louis Feuillade's French crime serial *Fantomas* (Gaumont); *Sherlock Holmes* (France–United Kingdom); *What Happened to Mary?*; *Who will Marry Mary?*; *Pearl White Crystal Comedies*; *Lieutenant Daring* (United Kingdom); and *Merely a Millionaire* (1912).

These ad hoc measures, passed in response to the perceived threat to public order created by these types of films and their 'movie-mad' audiences, anticipated by a decade the formation of a cohesive national film policy in Korea in 1926 (discussed in chapter 3).

Meanwhile, after Korea's first film company, Chosun Kinema Co., was established in Busan in 1924 with Japanese capital, Koreans saw their first silent-film star, Na Un-gyu, in the national hit film *Arirang* in 1926, which Na also scripted and directed. In response to the rapid development of the Korean film industry, the colonial government created a Bureau of Motion Pictures for propaganda purposes in 1920, and the systematization of film policy and censorship regulations began in 1922. While all these changes set the foundations for Korea's boom of silent cinema (1926–1934), it also foreshadowed the strengthening of the government's control of content and propaganda dissemination through the film production and exhibition industry. In chapter 3, we discuss the dynamic impact of official film policy on the distribution and consumption of foreign films and the production of a small number of locally produced pictures.

3 Profiting and Profiteering from the Systematization of Film Censorship, 1916–1936[1]

After 1916, the 'birth' of the film industry in Korea, and after Hasegawa Yoshimichi became governor-general, the amount of Korean culture expressed on screen declined markedly. At the same time, there was a noticeable increase in the number of Japanese, American, and European films entering the Korean market—distributed by Koreans as well as Japanese, Americans, and other foreign nationals. The numbers of documentaries and travelogue films produced by Japanese filmmakers and other films made cooperatively by Korean and Japanese production staff also increased. Filmmakers and distributors from the United States and Japan had their eyes firmly fixed on the Korean market. Between the late 1910s and the mid-1920s, Japanese exhibitors expanded their operations in the cities and reached out into rural areas by opening new cinemas or purchasing established cinemas. These included the Gyeongseong Cinema, the Gyeongryonggwan, and Junganggwan in Seoul, the Gukjegwan, Sangsaenggwan, and Yurakgwan in Busan, and the Chosungwan, Geumjwa, and Shinheunggwan in Daegu.

Between 1916 and 1926, well-established Japanese film companies such as Nikkatsu, Shōchiku, and Tenkatsu dominated the exhibition side of the cinema industry. Shōchiku provided films to the Daejeonggwan and the Hwanggeumgwan, while Nikkatsu and Tenkatsu supplied films to the Hirakgwan and the Danseongsa, respectively. Nikkatsu, Shōchiku, and the Teikine group also began producing films in Korea. In 1918, Nikkatsu led the way when it opened a local production office in Seoul and installed Sadashichi Kojima from Japan as manager. Shortly after, Teikine, known for its films of live plays, also opened a branch in Seoul, and in 1921 Shōchiku opened a production office in the capital, with Sotarou Takahashi as production manager.[2] These three Japanese film companies served as the backbone of the film industry in Korea over this period.

In 1918, Korea entrepreneur Park Seung-pil bought and then renovated the Danseongsa, running it with regular screening programs until he retired in 1927.[3] Given the close distribution relationship between the Danseongsa and Tenkatsu, Park benefitted from an immediate source of high-quality films when he took over in 1918, securing (and indeed advertising) advanced screening programs from Universal and Gaumont.[4] Park's contacts with the Japanese film industry proved invaluable when he produced Korea's first film *Righteous Revenge* (*Uirijeok Guto* in Korean) and the documentary *Landscape of Seoul Vicinity* in 1919. Park also established the Danseongsa Film Company, which produced *The Story of Janghwa and Hongnyeon* (1924), one of the earliest films made with an all-Korean production crew. Park Jeong-hyun, who had worked for the Umigwan Theater as a projectionist and later became the manager of the Danseongsa, joined the film as its cinematographer.

Amidst these industry developments, Admiral Saitō Makoto replaced Hasegawa as governor-general in August 1919. Saitō's legacy to Korea was the creation of a new cultural policy designed to relax Japanese administrative control over Korean cultural and artistic activities across the peninsula. However, Saitō also attempted to streamline the country's administration and police operations, encouraging the Korean Colonial Government's pursuit of 'co-option' and 'cooperation' among Koreans as a key strategy of his reforms.[5] During Saitō's term, government offices and provincial police throughout Korea intensified their encouragement of Koreans to support Japan's colonial (and nationalistic) agenda, a drive that was formalized in 1938 under Governor-General Minami Jirō as the assimilationist policy of *naisen ittai* (*naeseon ilche* in Korean), or 'Japan and Korea as One Body.'[6] In response to the March First Movement in 1919, which had inspired a number of nationalist protests against the Japanese occupation of Korea, Saitō was anxious to reshape Korea's relationship with Japan so that it could take its place within the empire.[7] Writers, actors, filmmakers, and theater entrepreneurs took advantage of this new opportunity and began creating spaces for the expression of Korean culture within the wider context of Japan's emphasis on a national culture. This was an inspiration for Korean intellectuals and artists, and cinema became a 'node of cultural construction,' a phrase used elsewhere to describe radio.[8] Thus, by moving Korea closer to Japan culturally and politically, Governor-General Saitō and his cabinet facilitated the further development of the film industry, including Korean cinema, albeit in a small way.

Allowing Koreans to gain film production training and experience—or at least not entirely preventing them from doing so—stimulated the birth of a Korean cinema. One of the earliest Korean films, *Righteous Revenge* (or *Loyal Revenge* or *Loyal Vengeance*), a multimedia 'kine-o-rama,' was made in 1919, and first shown in public on October 27 that year.[9] *Righteous Revenge* is a story about a family dispute over property. As far as we can tell from the cursory descriptions that survive, the film portrays a young man who seeks revenge on his evil stepmother, who had plotted to murder him and steal his wealth. The date of the film's release is commemorated in the Korean national film day, which since 1966 has been celebrated annually to honor the birth of the Korean 'cinema' as distinct from the birth of the film industry in Korea. Immediately following the success of *Righteous*

Revenge, Koreans began making other films with both all-Korean, and mixed Korean and Japanese production staff.[10]

In addition to the production of fiction films by private companies during this period, public-service films were also produced by the Korean Colonial Government's powerful Central Council. In 1920, its Board of Information (renamed the Investigation Section in 1922) created a motion picture corps, which was charged with filming the daily life of Koreans—capturing the 'real Chosen' on film. The completed films were then sent to Japan to educate and amuse audiences there. Conversely, the motion picture corps arranged the duplication and 'road-showing' of documentary films about daily life in Japan to audiences in urban and rural Korea.[11]

The one-reel *actualités* or nonfiction documentary films shot in Korea by the government's motion picture corps captured an eclectic picture of life in the peninsula. They included footage of cars and trams moving around Seoul, young children in school, scenes of village and urban life, local agricultural and fishery techniques, forestry and mining operations, nurses training and Red Cross meetings at hospitals, Christian missions and Buddhist temples, customs such as drying salt in the sun, local funeral ceremonies, art exhibitions, a parade of firefighters, horse racing, and musical performances in the Korean royal court. Other films celebrated the construction and completion of new municipal buildings, the emperor's birthday and his twenty-fifth wedding anniversary, the crown prince's return to Korea from Japan, and the crown prince's wedding. Longer travelogue documentaries included three-reel films of mountain walks and five- and six-reel films of travel between Korea and Japan, as well as a royal delegation sent from Korea to Manchuria.[12] It was perhaps inevitable that, after 1919, Koreans used their newfound filmmaking skills to explore and express their cultural heritage and later to contribute to feature-length propaganda productions. As discussed in chapter 5, they were strongly motivated, at least in part, by Japan's plans to modernize Korea and its efforts to exhibit this achievement throughout the Empire and beyond.

This 'hopeful' period between 1923 and 1934 generated a new skill set as well as ninety feature films. The four most popular genres, ranked in order of frequency, were melodramas, action films, literary adaptations, and historical dramas.[13] These films contributed to a remarkable upsurge—not quite a 'golden age'—but a boom in the number of 'silent' films made by or with Koreans during this time. (Actually, as we discuss in the next chapter, few of these films were silent as they were accompanied by live narration performed by *byeonsa*.)

Two of the earliest feature films made with a predominantly Korean cast and crew were *The Border* (1923), produced by Korean exhibitor Park Seung-pil, and *The Story of Chunhyang* (1923). According to reports in the popular press, *The Story of Chunhyang* drew huge audiences over an eight-day release period, generating larger-than-expected profits.[14] Other films produced around this time were *The Vow Made Under the Moon* (or

Promise under the Moon, 1923), directed by Yun Baek-nam and produced by the Korean Colonial Government to encourage saving among Koreans, and *Arirang* (1926), Korea's most celebrated nationalistic film, starring Na Un-gyu, the country's leading filmmaker and silent star (1902–1937). Na Un-gyu's achievements—he made a number of pro-Japanese films before his death in 1937—are fraught with a tension between his patriotism and his collaboration with the Japanese colonial authorities.[15] In the following two chapters, we explore this tension in the work of other filmmakers, including their collegial links and working relationships with Japanese directors, writers, cinematographers, and investors in both Korea and Japan, as well with as the Japanese film company Nikkatsu. The wealth of experience gained by Koreans in the films produced before 1926, along with the rapidly developing exhibition culture in the major cities, contributed to a filmmaking 'boom' between 1926 and 1934.

The feature films shown in Korea during World War I and the 1920s were predominantly Western films (mainly from France and the U.S.), with Charlie Chaplin comedies and action films being especially popular. Other films included *The Iron Claw* (1916), *Civilization* (1916), *Joan the Woman* (1918), Mario Caserini's *Resurrezione* (1917), *Hearts of the World* (1920), *Intolerance* (1922), *The Four Horsemen of the Apocalypse* (1923) and *The Cabinet of Dr. Caligari* (1922) (Lee 2004: 91–95). These popular foreign films imported into Korea provided local filmmakers with crucial knowledge of new filmmaking trends, and it is no surprise that, in the 1920s, Korea's film production industry began to grow steadily through exploring new aesthetics.

During this period, although films were not restricted or banned by a national censorship authority, local police in Korea's thirteen provinces retained individual authority to block the exhibition of particular films before, during, or after their screening. Their decisions may have been guided by the censorship standards that had been in place in Japan and circulated among police stations there since around 1910.[16] Under these internal regulations, applications made to the provincial police to exhibit a film had to meet a number of specific requirements. They had to show that the film in question avoided the subject of adultery and the portrayal of obscenity and lust, eschewed the glorification of crime, cruelty (seen as immorality) and hooliganism among youth, and, finally, avoided political satire and any other suggestive content that might undermine public order.

As Korean cinema developed, so did the rules governing it, again following practice in Japan. Regulatory adjustments made at provincial level in Korea during 1922–23 and again in 1924 mirrored policy changes in Japan in 1917 and 1925. Before 1917, Japan had decentralized film regulations enforced by local police, a situation that had proved problematic for exhibitors. For example, in 1911 the Ōsaka police created its own regulatory guidelines concerning performances by *benshi*, obscenity in films, and limiting attendance by children to protect them from the possible bad influence of films[17]—all similar to concerns observed in Korea. In response to escalating complaints and difficulties experienced by local police, the Tokyo Metropolitan Police announced the Tokyo Moving Picture Regulations, which took effect in August 1917. This law centralized control over film censorship in the capital and introduced other related regulatory measures such as seating separation for audiences, the *benshi* licensing system, cinema building-code standards, and limited cinema opening hours.[18] The 1917 regulations mirrored increasing concerns arising from Korea's burgeoning film culture in the 1910s. As a result, the regulations regarding exhibition announced by the Gyeonggi Province police in 1922 and 1923 replicated Japan's 1917 regulations, with the exception of a centralized censorship regime.

However, in 1924 a number of factors led to the perceived need for a centralized film censorship system in Korea: an increase in popularity of publicly viewed films; the subsequent increase in the number of film imports; and the administrative load on police resulting from the multiple and decentralized censorship processes currently in force. In April 1924, the Gyeonggi Province Police Department convened a meeting of local provincial police chiefs.[19] In June 1924, a centralized film censorship system was initiated involving the three cities of Seoul, Busan, and Shinuiju (an important linking city in the northern part of the Korean Peninsula bordering China), although Seoul was the only center with the appropriate equipment to screen films.[20] Later in Japan, in 1925, the Criminal Affairs Bureau of the Department of Home Affairs announced that the Korean Colonial Government would also follow Japan's systematized film censorship system, in the form of the Motion Picture Regulations passed in July 1926. This law established the core censorship mechanism for the national control of newspapers and other printed materials, as well as films.[21]

In 1926, as part of Governor-General Saitō's cultural policy, the Library Department was established, charged with overseeing the publication of Korean-owned printed materials. As a result, newspapers such as the *Chosun Ilbo* and *Donga Ilbo*, which began publication in 1920 and 1921, respectively, were now governed under the Publication Law and censored by the Library Department. The same regulations were also applied to film. Saitō's relatively relaxed administration of cultural affairs led to an increase in printed materials as well as the production of films, while also providing the Korean Colonial Government with a practical reason for exercising centralized censorship through the Library Department. In essence, the 1926 regulations shifted the regulatory focus of the 1910s from controlling film-viewing culture to controlling content.

In 1927, under the management of the Chief Censor Ōka Shigematsu, the Library Department employed a total of nine Japanese and Korean staff to administer film censorship. Ōka, who served in the Library Department until 1937, was an influential figure in the development of the censorship process in Korea. He was the author of numerous articles on censorship in magazines and official gazettes, and had access to extensive industry networks.[22]

This new cohesive national censorship framework coincided with the end of the relatively liberal 'Taishō Democracy' period and the beginning of Japan's Shōwa era in 1926. It formed part of the beginning of a military-driven agenda to strengthen the Japanese Empire. Increasingly throughout the remainder of the colonial period, Japan embraced totalitarianism and ultranationalism at home and throughout its colonies, a stance that fed the development of the 'Greater East Asia Co-Prosperity Sphere' and peaked with Japan's invasion of China in 1937—the beginning of the Second Sino-Japanese War.

In the context of this increased militarization, the Peace Preservation Law (1925) aimed to suppress socialism, communism, and other 'subversive' movements and activities. Here, the key instrument was the expansion of the Special Higher Police (*tokkō*) within the Criminal Affairs Bureau of the Department of Home Affairs; they were charged, along with the regular force, with administering the surveillance of Koreans and other foreigners in Japan, labor relations, and censorship. The outcome was the establishment of 'Japan's interwar thought-control system,' which was aimed at preventing any form of unrest that might threaten the security of the Empire.[23] In Korea, they were also called the 'publication police,' because of the critical role the Library Department played in supporting their activities.[24] One of their key publications was entitled the *Korean Publication Police Gazette* (the counterpart of the *Publication Police Gazette* in Japan). Even with this increased level of surveillance and systematized film censorship, Koreans, Japanese, and other foreigners living in Korea still managed to contribute to the advancement of the film industry.

A SYSTEMATIZED APPROACH TO FILM CENSORSHIP

Micromanaging the film industry in colonial Korea was a government priority because film was thought to exert a powerful influence over society and culture. Indeed, the Japanese authorities had exploited the media as a propaganda tool as far back as 1868, when the early Meiji press policy was formed. Since that time, the Japanese government, as well as private industry in Japan, had learned to appreciate the importance of the mass media as a powerful tool for communicating ideological messages to the general public.[25] It was with this knowledge, then, that the Korean Colonial Government applied these early regulatory precautions to the exhibition, distribution, and, later, production of films in the Korean market.

When Japan assumed legal force over Korea in 1905, authority over all matters concerning the production, editing, and distribution of information was delegated to a Police Advisory Board in each of Korea's thirteen provincial areas.[26] Whether they knew it or not, the experiences of local cinema audiences were dependent on the province in which they attended screenings—albeit while sharing a communal feeling of escapism. Though the regulation of the cinema was overlooked at the national level, the micro-management exercised at the local level was effective enough to control film content as well as the live narration that accompanied screenings and spectator behavior.

The colonial government's promulgation of new and explicit laws addressing public entertainment built upon several tangential laws already in place by 1907 that aimed to maintain its political and ideological control in Korea. Even before permanent cinemas were built in the 1910s, the resident-general had used his authority to regulate all theaters, exhibition halls, and temporary spaces for viewing films. Regulations for these itinerant screening spaces were modeled on those previously established in Japan under the Theater Regulations of 1900, where an early attempt had been made to censor live performances and film screenings by having entertainment venues seek police sanction for such performances.[27] Anything or anyone identified as a potential threat to public order and social morality was banned from these venues. Although similar policies were applied later in Korea than in Japan, preliminary measures were enacted in relation to the press and social security, providing a precursor of a sort to film regulations proper.[28]

By the early 1910s, the gradual expansion of entertainment culture in Korea signaled a need—for the authorities, at least—for a comprehensive and centralized form of regulation. There was a great disparity between how cinemas were run and how cinema culture was regulated from province to province, and audiences and officials could not help hearing about how things were being done elsewhere. Because there was no national film policy, police officials in the provinces surrounding Seoul, Incheon, Pyongyang, and Busan each had their own views about objectionable content and obscene behavior, and their own methods for regulating these issues. However, Busan was more proactive than other cities. In 1910, its provincial authorities developed detailed regulations for theater performances and film exhibitions through Provincial Government Law No. 2, which gave the police effective control of the exhibition and performance of events through their oversight of public security, theater hygiene, ticket pricing, and hours of operation. The police could use their authority to suspend any performance or film that was deemed to threaten public morality or security.[29]

However, on August 1, 1926, Governor-General Saitō's administration enacted Government-General Law No. 59, which became Korea's first systematized, national film censorship regulations. Law No. 59 mirrored the regulations ratified in 1925 in Japan proper. The whole empire now had a cohesive approach to film censorship, giving the minister of home affairs a greater degree of oversight over the importation and exhibition of moving images. The Japanese Government, through the Korean Colonial

Government, was thus able to control the exhibition of domestic and foreign films through stricter central censorship regulations, while continuing to delegate regulatory power to provincial police authorities to deal with censorship issues at a local level. The new law reinforced a hierarchical system that operated at international, national, and local level—but one which, in reality, was not always easy to control completely.

The new censorship regime was chiefly directed to monitoring the exhibition market, which was inherently complex. While this approach seemed justified due to the expanding size of the exhibition market in Korea at the time, it should be noted that Japanese expatriates in Korea and Japanese cinema chains dominated the exhibition market, complicating the execution of the censorship apparatus and its potential impacts. In Korea, official censors had to negotiate harder with Japanese producers, exhibitors, investors, and audiences because of the multilayered relationship between the colonial government and the different classes of citizen in the colonial state.[30]

Supplementing Law No. 59, Saitō created a national censorship board within the Korean Colonial Government's Library Department. The board methodically recorded a plethora of data—the total number of applications, reels, reel lengths, script and reel rejections, types of restrictions imposed, and total fees imposed on all domestic and international feature and nonfeature films censored. International reaction was swift in coming. According to the *Film Daily Year Book 1925* (one of the key sources in the United States for international film trade data and news), the Motion Picture Producers and Distributors Association of America (MPPDA) immediately expressed its concerns about the implications of the stricter censorship regime. The MPPDA was worried about anything that might hinder the distribution of Hollywood films throughout the Japanese Empire, especially in Korea.[31] The association's fears were well-founded. The censorship apparatus rejected very few American films outright, but they still experienced a degree of subjective censorship treatment upon entry. Nevertheless, Hollywood films were warmly accepted, along with their associated censorship application fees. In addition, Hollywood's cause was assisted by a tactical error on the part of a coalition of some of the major Japanese film companies in Korea.[32] In mid-1924, these companies met to develop and improve self-censorship standards and lobby the government for lower tax obligations. They also planned strategic actions including an organized boycott of American films. However, the boycott proved to be a failure because it lasted only about two weeks and never made it to the Korean market. In the end, this temporary embargo caused Japanese exhibitors to lose more business than American distributors. Apparently, Korean audiences preferred Hollywood movies to Japanese films, as had indeed been the case in Japan itself.

The new film censorship regime was probably enacted partly in response to the global activities of the MPPDA, which was helping both the minor and major Hollywood studios expand their distribution networks and territories throughout the world and, more specifically, in Asia. Around this time, markets in Asia, and Japan in particular, became highly valued because of the potential to earn lucrative profits from film rental contracts.[33] Hollywood distributors simply wanted to expand and maximize their profits throughout Asia, which was an increasingly important market for the United States during and after World War I due to the loss of distribution opportunities in Europe.

Despite its national reach, Law No. 59 delegated responsibility for censorship to the provincial police, who could determine whether a film was detrimental to public order and cultural customs at the local level. Socially acceptable films, by definition, avoided violating the dignity of the emperor and were 'free from impediments to the maintenance of public order, customs, or hygiene.'[34] Any film, domestic (Korean and Japanese) or foreign, which sensationalized adultery, arson, crime, murder, or attacks on the authorities was prohibited.[35]

After 1926, every exhibitor, local producer, and foreign distribution agent had to apply to the nearest provincial police station for a permit to screen a film. Once domestic and foreign films had negotiated the censorship process, including providing multiple copies of the same film for censorship, they received a formal stamp of approval. This exhibition permit process was guided by two film-rating categories: the first for films suitable for audiences younger than fifteen years of age, and a second for adults (older than fifteen). Written exhibition permits specified the period of time and number of screenings allowed. As far as audience behavior was concerned, men and women were prohibited from sitting together unless they were married.

A film that failed to receive a screening permit could be reedited and resubmitted, with additional censorship application fees, to the same provincial police station. The collection of multiple fees promoted the further growth of the censorship apparatus by providing opportunities for the local authorities to reap a steady income. In some cases, fees were remitted when the censorship board or the governor-general deemed it necessary or when it was considered a public service to do so, as in the case of educational documentaries. According to the *Film Year Book 1926*, this clause gave special preference to filmmakers whose work glorified imperial Japan, and no doubt pleased provincial police in the process.[36]

Saitō's legacy to the nascent film industry and the economic life of Korea can be seen as a mixed bag. His decision to allow Koreans to submit at least 450 domestic (Korean and Japanese) and more than 2,100 foreign films for censorship approval allowed Korean entrepreneurs and businesses to contribute to the growth of the film industry as they contributed to other manufacturing and production industries, thus encouraging an expanding consumer class to offer indirect support to local filmmakers and entertainment entrepreneurs. At the same time, Saitō's regime introduced stricter regulations and an increased police presence (police numbers increased from around 2,300 in 1919 to 18,400 in 1924).[37]

Another way of interpreting Saitō's actions is to see him as a canny cultural administrator who saw that Japan's film industry could benefit if film production and distribution activities in Korea were curtailed. Police played a central role in the enforcement of film policies. Aspiring Korean filmmakers, as well as the MPPDA, witnessed the tightening of film regulations by provincial police at the same time as Japanese film studios were showing an eagerness to exploit the Korean exhibition market—a market which included hundreds of thousands of Japanese citizens who had begun entering Korea after annexation in 1910.[38]

Despite impediments to local initiatives, film culture in Korea flourished throughout the Japanese colonial period. As we discuss below, both individuals and groups in the Korean film community—perhaps in a comparable way to the economic contribution to colonial Korea made by the Korean business elite[39]—played a noteworthy role in the growth and development of a national cinema.

THE NEXT GREAT IDEA

After 1926, nonfeature films (also called 'noncommercial' films in censorship documents) that were locally produced and made in Japan, and designed to educate Korean and Japanese audiences, were exempt from paying censorship application fees. The fees generated from an abundance of Hollywood feature films helped to subsidize screenings of these films. Soon after his appointment as governor-general in June 1931, Ugaki Kazushige requested that more propaganda films be screened in Korea. Japanese distributors eagerly supplied so-called public films, which were educational films intended for a wide audience. Public films were highly regarded by the censorship board and were exempt from application fees. This development provided an incentive for Japanese film companies to increase the production of cultural and educational propaganda films, which in turn served to promote Japan's assimilationist ideology to Koreans and gave a further boost to the Japanese film industry.

In 1933, a new censorship building was constructed in the Korean Colonial Government complex in Seoul, representing a significant technical achievement in the first decade of the Japanese Shōwa period. This 146.45 *tsubo* (approximately 44.4 square meters) building stood on the site of the current Gyeongbok Palace in central Seoul, and was equipped with state-of-the-art silent and sound film projection equipment compatible with all international film formats (16mm and 35mm dual sound-on-disc and sound-on-film sizes, sprocket dimensions, etc.).[40]

The decision to build a new facility came at an opportune time. According to detailed Japanese censorship statistics and other archival documents discussed in this chapter, the new facility, which cost ¥50,475, was built to meet the demands of a massive increase in the number of films undergoing censorship.[41] More than ¥250,000 in total fees (approximately US$58,256), generated from thousands of censorship applications for both feature and nonfeature films between 1926 and 1936, helped to pay for the new building.[42] Although the revenues generated from this exercise may have equaled only a fraction of the entire revenue generated by the Korean Colonial Government, the censorship office was of more than symbolic benefit to the state treasury. According to official records, total ordinary revenue generated in 1935, for example, was ¥240,463,427.[43] During this decade, the total number of film reels censored was 84,441, equaling more than 20,232,874 meters of film and equating to revenues of ¥262,080.[44] Censorship application fees collected by the Korean Colonial Government between April 1, 1935 and March 31, 1936 alone amounted to ¥29,568.

Generally speaking, the business of film censorship was profitable enough for the government's censorship operation to remain self-sufficient. The steady stream of fees paid for most, if not all, of the film censorship office's day-to-day operating expenses, including employee salaries, equipment, and other administration costs. As table 3.1 shows, fees paid by censorship applications from the United States and other countries amounted to 39 percent of all fees paid for the 1926–1935 period.

The sheer volume of censorship statistics compiled from the period between August 1, 1926 and March 31, 1936 is astounding. As expected, the censorship fees generated from processing this number of films were likewise impressive. The film censorship operation in particular exploited the large number of American and Japanese films imported into the colony. Regrettably, very little revenue from this windfall was reinvested in the Korean film industry. Rather, a sizable amount was redirected in 1933 to building the new administrative and screening facility discussed above.

In the mid-1930s the colonial government enforced strict regulations after Governor-General Ugaki initiated a higher exhibition quota for domestic films, while limiting the screening of American films. In general, film culture in Korea was seen as part of a very young industry and as a relatively new form of cultural expression. Its power to influence the masses and make an impact on society was reflected in the authorities' eagerness to regulate the sector, using means similar to those applied to the telecommunications, transportation, mining, and agricultural industries.

Distribution agents and importers handling Japanese and American films contributed a great deal to the viability of the censorship apparatus, both as a process and an authority. From 1926 to 1936, Japanese, Korean, American, and other foreign distribution agents based in Tokyo and Seoul lodged applications to exhibit 14,288 feature films. Among the total of 5,626 foreign films licensed during the period were 5,078 American films: 762 from Universal, 412 from Fox, and 514 from Paramount; the remainder (3,390 films) were obtained from other smaller producers and distributors. Representing other countries (not including Japan) were 548 films—an average of about one per week for the censors to appraise. The number of foreign

Table 3.1 Censorship Statistics, 1926–1935[1]

Entertainment and Non-Entertainment Feature Films[1]	Total Japanese Historical (H) Films vs. Total Japan Contemporary (C) Films[2]			Total Foreign Films			Total American Films			Total Universal, Fox, and Paramount Films[3]		
	J	K	O	J	K	O	J	K	O	J	K	O
Censorship Applications[4]	H: 3811 / C: 3538	H: 36 / C: 170	H: 87 / C: 960	3,122	1,974	530	2,822	1,749	507	470	1,027	191
Total number of films censored (total applications)	H: 26,962 / C: 6,305,579			31,505			27,610			10,136		
Total number of reels censored	H: 6,123,624 / C: 6,305,579			7,803,671			6,816,759			2,582.932		
Total number of films censored												
Total handling fees collected (in yen): ¥227,946.28[5]	H: 77,521.30 / C: 61,588.91			88,836.07			78,466.97			U: 11,360 / F: 9,685 / P: 8,995		
Number of films rejected — Reels	H: zero / C: 9			52			52			U: zero / F: zero / P: 10		
Number of films rejected — Length (meters)	H: zero / C: 1,577			14,067			14,067			U: zero / F: zero / P: 2,919		
Number of scenarios restructed	H: 289 / C: 326			568			471			U: 53 / F: 54 / P: 46		
Percentage of restrictions out of total number of films censored — Public peace (safety) — Number of parts	H: 202 / C: 270			630			520			U: 75 / F: 63 / P: 51		
Public peace (safety) — Length (meters)	H: 1,028.75 / C: 2,343.69			4,885.13			4,313.73			U: 506.9 / F: 324.34 / P: 557.74		
Public morals (manners & customs) — Number of parts	H: 138 / C: 161			3,772			3,474			U: 435 / F: 502 / P: 519		
Public morals (manners & customs) — Length (meters)	H: 957.02 / C: 810.44			6,832.5			5,917.55			U: 606.79 / F: 795.94 / P: 966.52		

Table 3.1   Continued

[1]A majority of these statistics concern entertainment films; approximately 13% of all Japanese films submitted for censorship were non-entertainment types while only 5% of all foreign films were non-entertainment types.
[2]From Shōchiku, Daitō, Nikkatsu, Shinkō, and 'other' Japanese studios.
[3]These were the 3 biggest, and therefore the only American film companies identified by name in the censorship records.
[4]Censorship applicants: Japanese (J), Korean (K), and Other (O).
[5]For comparative purposes, this is equivalent to $106,849.82 and $65,992.73 in 1926 and 1936, respectively.
Source: Censorship Statistics, 1 August 1926 to 31 March 1935. Governor-General of Korea, Police Affairs Bureau, Archives Section. Serial# CJA0002448, File# 101-7-1-2. Government-General of Korea Archives, Daejon, South Korea.

films submitted for censorship over this period rises to a total of 7,515 if we include nonfeature (and noncommercial) films classified as military documentaries, publicity (propaganda) documentaries, and advertisements.

About 90 percent of all foreign films submitted were produced in the United States. Not all American films passed by the censor reached their intended audiences. In some cases, the censorship board used the tactic of granting censorship approval to a film and then at the last minute prohibiting it from being screened. A number of different pretexts, such as fire hazard or threat to local order, were used to suppress a film after the censorship approval process had been completed. In this way, the Korean Colonial Government was able to control the number of foreign films introduced to Korea while generating sufficient revenue to sustain its censorship operation. Although it is unclear exactly how many films were actually *screened*, it is clear that the American film industry made a substantial contribution to film culture in Korea and to the stable operation of the censorship apparatus. While the rise of a film-viewing culture in Korea since the 1910s has been well documented, the contribution made by this continuous cash flow from Hollywood through the censorship regulations is less well recognized. By subsidizing the growth of the Korean Colonial Government's censorship apparatus, the American film industry unintentionally helped to legitimize the Japanese colonial authority by supporting it financially.

We turn now to another aspect of colonial film censorship policy—the ways in which its development helped the MPPDA reach its goal of expanding Hollywood's worldwide cultural hegemony while continuing to reap heavy profits from the Korean and larger Asian region.

Censorship application fees were based solely on film length. In Japan, for example, a short, 1,000-meter film cost the applicant (the film owner or rental agent) ¥16.66, or $7.78. A feature-length film of 2,400 meters cost ¥39.98 or $18.74.[45] The fees for censoring additional copies of the same film amounted to 40 percent of the cost of the first copy. Major Hollywood studios often sent multiple copies of the same film to a single market in order to arrange simultaneous screenings in different capital cities. Applying for re-censorship also incurred fees of 40 percent of whatever applicants had initially paid for the first copy of the film. Newsreels and other current-event films, often inspected by provincial authorities rather than a centralized censorship board, were charged 1 *sen* (0.4 of 1¢ in 1926) per length of 3 meters. Given the considerable cost involved in applying for censorship approval in Japan proper, only the more financially stable organizations, especially those that had survived the Great Depression, could afford to distribute and exhibit a large number of films in Japan. This probably explains why, in the mid- to late 1920s, films made by the major Hollywood studios occupied a share of the Japanese market of between 22 and 30 percent, while European films only attained about 3 percent.[46]

At the beginning of the censorship regulations in 1926, the stated censorship fee in Korea was 5 *sen* (2¢ in 1926) for 3 meters of original film and 2 *sen* per 3 meters of the second copy of the film.[47] Apart from restricting content, censorship fees provided additional financial burdens for both distributors and exhibitors. Japanese distributors in particular must have been inconvenienced by this measure since their imported (Japanese and foreign) films to Korea had already passed censorship in Japan proper and many of them had already been screened at cinemas there. This means they were charged for censorship twice. Besides, the fee was higher in Korea than in Taiwan, another Japanese colony, which was 2 *sen* (0.8 of 1¢ in 1926) for 3 meters.[48] As a result, the Motion Picture Industry Association, which consisted of exhibitors and distributors, mounted a campaign to lower censorship fees.[49] Their efforts were successful. With the revision of the censorship regulation in September 1928, fees were reduced to one *sen* per meter of footage for the first (original) print and one-half of one *sen* per meter of footage for duplicate copies—50 to 60 percent less than applicants paid in Japan.[50] These considerably lower fees were an economic incentive for Hollywood film distributors to flood the Korean market with their products well into the 1930s. Hence, audiences in Korea (Korean nationals, and Japanese and other expatriates) enjoyed a huge variety of Hollywood films that spanned many years.

According to the *Film Daily Year Book of Motion Pictures*, the share of Hollywood films in the Korean market remained higher than in Japan proper, amounting to up to 40 percent of the total length of film actually screened in Korea. The proportion of total audiences attending American films, as well as the number of film rentals in Korea, also exceeded those in Japan.[51] In August 1934, according to the American consulate-general in Seoul, American films dominated motion picture screens in Korea, with as much as 62 percent of the market. More than half of Seoul's major cinemas were screening foreign, primarily American, films, which outnumbered films from all other countries combined fivefold. Although box-office figures are not easily retrievable for the 1930s, after Hollywood films the most numerous were German, British, French, and Russian films, in that order.[52] During this time, Fox, Paramount, Warner Bros., First National, Universal, independent agent J. H. Morris, and other agents representing Columbia, MGM, RKO, and United Artists—all controlling members of the MPPDA—had direct distribution offices in Seoul. Korea was unquestionably a key territory for Hollywood distributors.[53] There was no better market in Asia for Hollywood films than colonial Korea. As chief censor Ōka complained in 1933, Korean-owned cinemas regularly turned away large numbers of Japanese films in order to exhibit foreign films, with the result that, at this period, twenty million Koreans were watching foreign films almost exclusively.[54]

HOLLYWOOD'S FIRST GOLDEN AGE IN KOREA

In 1919 Korea's first film magazine, *Nokseong,* featuring French actress Rita Jolivet on its cover, was published by Bang Jeong-hwan, a well-known publisher and children's rights activist. Inside, the magazine was filled with pictures of Hollywood actors such as Geraldine Farrar, Molly Malone, Eddie Polo, and Grace Cunard. An advertisement for the Danseongsa occupied one page, promoting its capacity for screening color films. Stories about films—including how to make action films—also entertained readers.

The rise of foreign films since 1910, in particular Hollywood films, on account of their sheer entertainment value is clearly illustrated by the contents of this magazine and the increase in newspaper and magazine articles that documented Hollywood film releases and American actors and actresses. For example, in November 1925 the newspaper *Donga Ilbo* ran a series of articles about Hollywood and related topics, reflecting the popular demand for information about Hollywood and how it worked. These topics included new film projects and their producers (including First National, Universal, and Paramount), news about actors, and the inner workings of Hollywood, including details of studio sizes, technological matters, fees for day laborers, and animal actors.

By far the most popular stars in Korea at this time were Mary Pickford and Douglas Fairbanks.[55] Fairbanks had developed a strong fan base among both Japanese and Korean audiences as a silent-film action hero.[56] Both Japanese and Korean distributors aggressively sought out his films.[57] As a result, in November 1926 his film *The Black Pirate* (1926) was simultaneously released at the Danseongsa and Hwaggeumgwan to satisfy both Korean and Japanese audiences—but only after protracted and heated negotiations between the Japanese and Korean exhibitors, Koyama (the Japanese agent for United Artists), and the police.[58] (Usually, a film was released first at a cinema in Seoul and then the print was circulated to other provinces until it finally deteriorated.)

The American films exhibited in Korea (and Japan) in 1929 included numerous movies starring Pickford and Fairbanks.[59] Most of these had already played to financial and critical success in the United States.[60] These films had been forwarded from United Artists' offices or distributors in China, Spain, Italy, and France, once other markets had tired of them.

Hence, Korea served as an important dumping ground for older prints— many of which must have been damaged and missing sections.

Of the 31,505 reels of feature films censored in Korea between 1926 and 1935, a paltry 52 reels were rejected. In addition, a mere 472 scenarios (or 9.3 percent) of all American feature films censored during this decade were restricted from being screened. Sections cut from all foreign films for reasons of public peace and order comprised only 4,885 meters out of the total of 7,803,671 meters of film censored. Similarly, an insignificant 6,832 meters of film parts were cut for their unacceptable depiction of manners and customs or for being an affront to public morals.

'Hollywood' was not a monolithic agent operating in colonial Korea. Between April 1935 and March 1936, all Universal films were handled by Japanese agents, while Koreans handled 99 percent of all Paramount films. Other foreign (most likely American) distributors/importers handled all of the Fox films during the censorship process. This was a significant change from the period between 1926 and 1935 when two-thirds of all Universal films were handled by Korean agents, and two-thirds of all Fox films were represented by Japanese distributors/importers. Nearly all Paramount films from this decade were represented by Koreans.

This diversity was also expressed in the types of film favored by each company. In 1936, Universal films averaged 3.48 reels; Fox averaged 7.89 reels, and Paramount 7.55 reels, illustrating the diversity of approach by the Hollywood studios in distribution and exhibition strategies in the Korean market. Universal aimed primarily at the exhibition of short films, while Fox and Paramount concentrated on feature-length films. In this period, the censorship board approved the contents of nearly all American films; in other words, American films were not seen as jeopardizing public order, displaying immoral manners, or undermining imperial Japan's 'good and beautiful customs.'[61]

The ease with which the Korean Colonial Government's censorship officers passed so many American feature and short films is not difficult to explain, given the widespread self-censorship practiced in the American film industry in the late 1920s. During this time, all of the major and minor studios and producers (members of the MPPDA) conscientiously attempted to avoid highly objectionable scenes in their films—or at least they were perceived as having done so. In order to enhance the 'moral value' of their films and, more importantly, to have their films passed by both American *and* foreign censors, MPPDA members (each in its own way) solicited immediate feedback from key state censors in order to customize—albeit in a nuanced way—their films on a state-by-state (and country-by-country) basis. Their general aim in making these revisions was to portray 'questionable' content—scenes depicting crime, nudity, kissing, 'dirty dancing,' vulgarity, gambling, profanity, and sacrilege—more subtly and adroitly than originally portrayed.[62] While it might have helped to smooth the way for exporting American films overseas, it was impossible to customize all film contents to suit each country's moral standards. As censor Ōka testified, between 1928 and 1931 American films needed to be cut 'here and there' due to many scenes containing 'problematic' hugs and kisses. During the same period, only one Japanese and Korean film received the same treatment.[63]

Their relative ease of acceptance by the censorship board made the distribution of American films in Korea extremely convenient for Hollywood distribution agents and exchanges (and their local Korean agents). It may be that Hollywood distributors exploited the censor's motives in order to submit every possible print for exhibition. In turn, the Korean Colonial Government profited from thousands of censorship applications and their associated fees. In any case, the bulk of Hollywood films gained censorship approval with little or no resistance, though in many cases particular scenes were cut in the process. Many of the foreign films imported into Korea at this time were action films that often dealt with national battles, class struggle, revolution, and crime. The censors were worried that these types of films might negatively influence local audiences, and cut many of them in the interests of national security. Other films depicting romantic scenes were also cut because of their treatment of sexual relationships.[64]

When scenes were cut, they raised alarm bells for the U.S. film industry. On 14 March 1927, F. L. Herron, a U.S. news correspondent in Japan, sent the following biting market report to the MPPDA:

> And speaking of censors—they are not college-bred individuals, for after one has graduated from college in this country [Japan], he is supposed to be amenable to reason. I think they are first kidnapped from the rural granite quarries when they have become sufficiently headstrong to travel 3rd-class into the cities, get measured for uniforms and thus qualify to become policemen. After a couple months training as custodians of the peace, which does not exist they are transformed into censors—henceforth and naturally they are a bone of contentions with no such attribute as peace. The more intelligent of these acquire the habit of getting a monthly salary of 150 Yen, but the lesser lights do not bother much about money—they just sit in quietude and amass a vocabulary which sounds like 'kut-kut-kut' and they become proficient in its use.[65]

In this context, the systematization of censorship after 1926 has an uneven impact on the ways that American films were distributed and exhibited in terms of their treatment by the censorship apparatus.

In any case, censorship applications were warmly accepted, regardless of the quality of the prints in question. In this mutually satisfactory relationship, both Hollywood and the censorship board could benefit. Moreover, the overabundance of American films in the Korean market during the 1920s and 1930s possibly inspired Korean filmmakers. It is interesting to note that the boom in Korea's production of silent films[66] coincided with the deluge of Hollywood films into Korea. In 1936, director Na Un-gyu

Table 3.2 Censorship Statistics, 1935–1936

Entertainment and Non-Entertainment Feature Films[1]			Total Japanese Historical (H) Films vs. Total Japan Contemporary (C) Films			Total Foreign Films			Total American Films			Total Universal, Fox, and Paramount Films		
Censorship Applications			J	K	O	J	K	O	J	K	O	J	K	O
Total number of films censored (total applications)			H: 573 C: 564	H: 14 C: 48	H: 7 C: 157	500	154	65	463	101	62	88 (all Universal except 1)	70 (all Paramount)	36 (all Fox)
Total number of reels censored			H: 4,842 C: 4,701			4,194			3,463			1,123		
Total number of films censored			H: 1,087,429 C: 1,034,339			1,012,591			829,982			277,930		
Total handling fees collected (in yen): ¥29,032.87			H: 10,315.53 C: 9,025.81			9,691.53			7,922.89			U: 752.06 F: 712.69 P: 1,281.66		
Number of films rejected	Reels		H: zero C: 1			zero			zero			zero		
Number of films rejected	Length (meters)		H: zero C: 53			zero			zero			zero		
Number of scenarios restructed			H: 38 C: 38			85			65			U: 1 F: 7 P: 9		
Percentage of restrictions out of total number of films censored	Public peace (safety)	Number of parts	H: 44 C: 34			76			59			U: zero F: 5 P: 4		
		Length (meters)	H: 192.2 C: 150.85			441.65			354.65			U: zero F: 16.1 P: 28.8		
	Public morals (manners & customs)	Number of parts	H: 26 C: 40			3772			3474			U: 435 F: 502 P: 519		
		Length (meters)	H: 188.55 C: 158.3			858.45			686.3			U: 30.3 F: 50.95 P: 100.5		

Table 3.2 Continued
Source: Censorship Statistics, 1 April 1935 to 31 March 1936. Source: Governor-General of Korea, Police Affairs Bureau, Archives Section. Serial# CJA0002471, File# 101–7-2–1. Government-General of Korea Archives, Daejon, South Korea.

recalled that his film *Arirang* (1926) had been an extremely risky venture because it adopted a Western filmmaking style. According to Na, local audiences were passionate about Western action and spectacle films such as D. W. Griffith's *Orphans of the Storm* (1921), laughing and crying in reaction to the exciting storylines and scenes materializing before them. In comparison, Korean films were perceived as boring and the number of people paying to see them was on the decline.[67] As Na explained, *Arirang* was made with a mix of Western elements represented by action (fighting) scenes and montage techniques, demonstrating the extent to which local productions were influenced by Hollywood and other foreign films.

Hollywood was by no means the only target of the Korean censor's scrutiny; Japanese films were also in the frame. According to comments made by the Bureau of Police Affairs in 1935 before the Sixty-Ninth Imperial Parliament, censorship in Korea had to be 'strict' and 'careful' because Korean customs and ways of thinking differed from those in Japan.[68] In effect, the assimilationist approach was easier said than done. Censorship laws restricted freedom of expression throughout the empire and suppressed films that criticized the existing social order or glorified revolution. Given the massive number of Japanese films submitted to the censor in colonial Korea, it is fair to say that Japanese films, too, were gouged. Between 1926 and 1936, 14,550,971 meters of Japanese feature films and 1,447,610 meters of nonfeature films passed through the censors' hands, generating ¥162,507 in application fees—a colossal sum.

One would have expected the censorship regime to target films with socialist themes, too. Nevertheless, between the late 1920s and the mid-1930s, members of the Korean Artists Proletarian Federation (KAPF) in Korea and the Nippon Artists Proletarian Federation (NAPF) in Japan were not prevented from meeting and talking about making a small number of socially conscious films.[69] Members of these two groups had maintained a collegial relationship during this time because of their shared frustrations with a censorship regime that was becoming increasingly strict (particularly in Korea). In early 1930, Korean filmmakers visited the NAPF Kyōtō studios, at which time their Japanese colleagues expressed desire to learn more about and to support the work of their fellow filmmakers in Korea, sending a clear message of solidarity.[70]

For almost seven years, the Japanese Department of Home Affairs and the Korean Colonial Government overlooked these interrelated groups of proletarian filmmakers, until films with socialist themes were stifled by the so-called cultural crackdown in 1936, when Minami Jirō took over as governor-general from Ugaki. Given the strict film laws of the time, it is remarkable that these left-wing filmmakers were able to make 'subversive' films for as long as they did. More research is needed to explain how, between the mid-1920s and the early 1930s, KAPF and NAPF succeeded in encouraging filmmakers to join the resistance against oppressive film laws and inspiring them to make films containing covert and, at times, overt social criticism.[71]

From the colonial government's point of view, feature and short films, as well as 'kine-o-ramas,' were entertainment. On the other hand, educational films, commercial and public relations advertisements from organizations such as the Meiji Confectionery Company and the Tokyo Electric Light Company, and documentary films fell into the non-entertainment category. A third set of film genres contained a mix of both education and entertainment and included cartoons, current events, industrial topics, newsreels, public information, health and hygiene, science, sport, tourism, battlefield reconstructions, and war reports. On 2 June 1927, the chief of the Bureau of Internal Affairs of the Korean Colonial Government sent a catalogue of some of these non-entertainment genres to the mayor of each municipality.[72] The three most prevalent types of film in this list were cultural films (*bunka eiga*), 'public' films, and short- and feature-length propaganda films (*puropaganda* or *senden geki eiga*). Cultural films aimed to educate Japanese and foreign audiences as to the uniqueness of Japanese culture. Examples are a two-reel film called *Kokumin kaiyei* (Let Every Japanese Learn to Swim), a one-reeler, *L'Art des Fleurs au Japon* (The Floral Art of Japan), and *Aki no sanya* (Secret of Nature in Autumn), all popular films released in 1937.[73] Public films had imperialist themes and contained actual war footage. Propaganda films often presented imperial and overtly nationalistic (*naisen ittai*) themes through narratives featuring action, adventure, and espionage.[74] In both types of film, *naisen ittai* sentiments were exploited in Korea to serve the colonialist agenda and to act as inspirational recruitment tools for the war effort. These film genres, combined with the widespread availability of both critical and fan-based film and popular culture magazines—such as *Samcheolli*, *Movie Age*, *Korean Film*, and *Popular Film*—as well as a plethora of newspaper articles about local and international cinema, contributed to the growth of a film-literate society.[75]

Three categories of non-fiction film in particular experienced censorship problems—historical or period films (*jidai eiga*); modern and contemporary films (*gendai eiga*); and documentary films made in Korea by all-Korean or part-Korean and part-Japanese production crews.[76] *Jidai eiga* films sought to give audiences a flavor of feudal life by dramatizing everyday relationships between Japanese and Korean society from the early seventeenth to the mid-to-late nineteenth centuries. *Gendai eiga* films portrayed aspects of contemporary life and the social mores of the early twentieth century. Titles that sounded overtly revolutionary were changed for fear that they might inspire protest. Scenes too critical of the Japanese Empire were cut or re-shot. One of the earliest censorship cases involving a Korean film occurred in April 1925, when the censorship board changed the name of the film *Dark Light* (*Amgwang*), produced by Chosun Kinema Production, to *Make-up of God* (*Sinui Jang*), and made substantial cuts, forcing its Japanese director Kancho Takasa (known in Korea as Wang Pir-yeol) to reduce its initial fourteen reels to ten. Though directed by a Japanese film-maker, all the actors in *Sinui Jang* were Korean. The next film to be heav-ily censored was director Lee Kyeong-son's *King of the Mountain Bandits* (*Sanchaewang*), completed in September 1926 by the Kerim Film Associa-tion (Kerim Yeonghwa hyeophoe), an all-Korean film company. Though the film eventually passed the censors, the producers had to cut *Sanchaewang* from seven to five reels. The film was finally released in October 1927, but failed to attract a large audience.[77] Although *Sanchaewang* dealt with a love triangle between two men and one woman, it seems that it was the film's portrayal of a bandit leader that raised objections from the censors because of its overt depiction of social resistance.

Arirang, one of the most influential films of the Korean cinema, and (in some interpretations) a nationalist call to arms, was made by Chosun Kinema Production in late 1926. With the exception of Katō Kyōhei, a Japanese cinematographer, it employed an all-Korean production crew. Na Un-kyu, one of Korea's most popular silent-film stars, directed and starred in the film. Although, incredibly, the film passed through the censorship process unscathed, its accompanying promotional leaflet contained an offending line and had to be reprinted. According to Lee Gu-young, pub-licity manager of the Danseongsa cinema, who designed the leaflet, the Library Department unaccountably demanded that one line from the film's theme song, 'Arirang'—"There are hundreds of stars in the sky, and there are so many stories in our lives"—should be deleted. This minor incident piqued the public's interest and people flocked to see *Arirang*.[78]

Despite its reputation as the most 'nationalist' film produced in the colo-nial period, the film is in fact a simple melodrama. Yeong-jin is a mentally unstable young man, living with his father and younger sister Yeong-hee. Yeong-jin's friend Hyeon-gu meets Yeong-hee and falls in love. Oh Gi-ho, an unscrupulous employee of the village landlord, tries to rape Yeong-hee. Hyeon-gu and Yeong-jin fight with Oh, and Yeong-jin eventually kills him. Shocked by all the blood, Yeong-jin suddenly becomes sane and is jailed on a murder charge—after being taken over the Arirang Mountain by Japa-nese police officers. Since the film is lost, and only the storyline and the *byeonsa* script remain, we have little idea of how the nationalist themes were played out on the screen, apart from the bare bones of the plot. Some critics see the insertion into the opening scene of a fight between a cat and a dog as symbolizing the relationship between Korea and Japan; also, Young-jin's madness could have been induced by Korea's colonial status, and Oh might represent the pro-Japanese element in colonial Korea.[79] However, the film's reputation as a vehicle for nationalist sentiments might also have resulted from its treatment by *byeonsa*, who anticipated what audiences wanted and then responded spontaneously by improvising scripts and clarifying ambiguities where necessary—and within limits enforced ruthlessly by local police.[80]

From what we know, *Arirang* was indeed full of ambiguity and polysemic meaning. For example, Young-jin is introduced as a young man who became mentally unhinged while studying philosophy at university. No further explanation is given. There is evidence that, in their commentary (when they were able, without interference from the police), the *byeonsa* explained this as the effects of torture received by Young-jin for his part in the March First Movement.[81] Performing as a *byeonsa* was a risky business. Korea's last living *byeonsa*, Shin Chul (1929–), disclosed to the authors in an interview that, as a teenager, he had been arrested by the Japanese police during a performance of *Arirang* in his youth, when he had yet to master the protocols followed by senior *byeonsa*:

> During one of my first Won San Cinema performances of *Arirang*, which was very popular as the increasing number of patrons showed each day, I made a mistake at the end of the film. A policeman arrested me, held me for 3 days, and beat me severely. It was Showa 18 (1943), and I was only 14 years old. My crime was to shout the following words during the scene where Young-jin kills Oh Gi-ho after Oh tries to rape Young-hee: "Young-jin asks his friends to take care of his father and sister and says, 'Sing me "Arirang," the song I used to sing so much when I was insane. When I go over the Arirang hill, I cannot come back again. I killed a man who was a traitor and a running dog of the Japanese—I could not stand him any more.' "[82]

While such political interpretations of *Arirang* have continued to hold sway, the important point is that audiences at this period saw what they wanted to see, regardless of what they were watching. Whether we call it escapism or resistance, it seems that audiences in the 1920s and 1930s played a more active role than contemporary film viewers by creating alternative storylines and infusing what they were watching with emotional content. As we have seen, cinemas in Seoul catered to the tastes of particular audiences by bringing out their favorite genre films and using either Korean or Japanese *byeonsa*. The role of audiences in actively creating a Korean film culture persisted until the mid-1930s, when the age of silent films and *byeonsa* drew to a close.

Another film with potential censorship issues was *Ben-Hur* (1925), which its Korean importer, Lee Gu-young, described as a spectacle hit film that Koreans went to great lengths to see and hear when it was exhibited in 1931.[83] The film deals with suffering of the Jews at the time of Christ at the hands of their Roman occupiers, and was thus ripe for contemporary political interpretations. Lee went to considerable trouble to get the film passed by the censors, including sweet-talking the board members and even distracting them during the censorship approval screenings. These tactics worked and the film was passed without difficulty. As Lee had hoped, when the film was released the *byeonsa* took pains to narrate the story with clarity and expression, thus helping to ensure the film's commercial success.[84]

Around the time of General Ugaki's appointment as governor-general and the escalation of the Manchurian Incident in 1931, filmmakers in Korea began to experience the tightening of film regulations. This was part of Japan's stricter control of cultural policies and the general suppression of Korean culture that took effect during this period. These more restrictive film policies began to shut Korean audiences off from foreign films as a higher exhibition quota of Japanese films came into force. All aspects of the film industry were now subservient to Japan's wartime regime, which prioritized the war effort over all other social, cultural, economic, industrial, and political concerns in ways similar to the restrictions applied to the German film industry in the lead-up to World War II.

On April 26, 1933, Governor-General Ugaki passed Law No. 40, requiring that all foreign films shown in Korea must first be imported into Japan and only then distributed to the colony. Hollywood's formerly successful direct distribution strategies were no longer possible. Korea became a dumping ground for thousands of older and third- and fourth-run prints of American films that would normally have finished their lives in Japan and elsewhere. Governor-General Ugaki was attempting to create a stricter approach to the distribution and exhibition of foreign, primarily American, films in Korea as part of a larger 'surveillance state.'[85] However, reports emanating from Japan told a different story; the correspondent for the *Motion Picture Almanac*, Tani Chikushi, writing in Tokyo in late 1935, claimed in English: "No restriction has been set by the [Japanese] government upon the exhibition of foreign pictures [in Japan]."[86] Nevertheless, bureaucratic mechanisms now threatened Hollywood's golden age and the cultural autonomy of the American film industry in the Korean market.

On 7 August 1934, the Korean Colonial Government passed the Motion Picture Control Rule (Hwaldong sajin yeonghwa chwiche gyuchik) as Government-General Law No. 87, reflecting the government's increasing need to control the exhibition and export of films. By the end of 1934, each imported film was subject to a system of double censorship. First, prints were examined by customs officials at the Japanese port of entry, and then subjected to closer scrutiny by the Japanese Censorship Bureau in Tokyo. Locating and deleting 'objectionable' scenes—such as those showing riots or containing alleged anti-authority, revolutionary, and communist propaganda—continued to be the focus of censorship activity. The censorship board allowed images of naked bodies, but kissing was prohibited. According to the *Motion Picture Almanac 1935–1936*, images or narrative content offensive to the Japanese Empire or the monarchy were strictly prohibited.[87] The Russian films *Battleship Potemkin* and Pudovkin's *Mother* were both banned from exhibition in Japan (and hence Korea) because of their social and ideological content.[88] Still, only ten out of around 2,400 imported films were banned in Japan in 1933, comprising eight American, one Russian, and one German film. Between January and September of 1934, only one American film submitted for censorship was banned outright.[89]

Among the titles submitted from Warner Bros.–First National Pictures which received censorship approval in 1934 and which were subsequently screened in Korea were: *Footlight Parade* (1933), *Gold Diggers of 1933* (1933), *Captured!* (1933), *I Am a Fugitive from a Chain Gang* (1932), *42nd Street* (1933), *Crowd Roars* (1932), *Winner Take All* (1932), *Fashions of 1934* (1934), *Son of a Sailor* (1933), *Tiger Shark* (1932), *Central Air Port* (1933), *Frisco Jenny* (1932), *The Little Giant* (1933), and *The Last Flight* (1931).[90] These were visually entertaining sound films that Korean and Japanese audiences could readily appreciate because they assumed little knowledge of the English language. Hollywood films were not dubbed at this time, although it would not have been illegal to do so. It was standard practice to add Korean or Japanese subtitles and other explanatory notes to most prints.[91] Censorship applications for all English-language films required two copies of these explanatory notes or the whole dialogue transcript translated into either Japanese or Korean. All inter-titles and subtitles had to be provided in English, as well as one of the local languages. Censorship application requirements became more demanding with the advent of sound, as descriptions and transcripts of all spoken dialogue had to be submitted.[92]

Through the Government-General Law No. 82, ratified on August 7, 1934, Governor-General Ugaki mandated that 25 percent of all pictures shown in Korea had to be of 'domestic' origin—Japanese or Korean. Ironically, this stricter policy stimulated Korean film production because Korean films were now categorized as 'domestic' (*kokusan*) products.

Another potentially positive outcome for Korean filmmakers in the late 1930s was an expanding exhibition market in Japan proper and Manchuria, which was an expanding part of the empire. According to the International Cinema Association of Japan, this situation presented 'one of the most hopeful signs for the future of the Korean cinema.'[93] Although the industry remained unstable primarily because of a lack of funding, 115 films (including twelve 'talkies') were produced in Korea between 1926 and 1937.[94] Hence, we can call this period the first golden age of cinema in Korea (rather than the first golden age of *Korean* cinema), without overstating the facts. It also coincides with Hollywood's first golden age of cinema in Korea.

During this period, an average of one film was made in Korea every five weeks, and a new film company was formed each time a new production began. Roughly 113 of these productions were staffed entirely by Korean filmmakers, while fifty-four were staffed by a combination of Korean and Japanese crews. Korean and Japanese producers and filmmakers utilized this one-off funding strategy until 1942, when the Korean Colonial

Government took complete control over film production and consolidated all film companies into a single entity called the Chosun Film Production Co.—much as Adolf Hitler did in Germany when he assigned Joseph Goebbels to take over the Universum Film AG (UFA) studios in 1933.

Throughout the late 1920s and 1930s, Korea's film culture expanded through these closer ties with Japan. Korean filmmakers gained production experience by traveling back and forth to Japan. This occurred despite the limited view expressed in the United States that 'only a small number of moving pictures are taken in Chosen, they being by amateurs for personal use and government agencies for propaganda purposes.'[95] On the contrary, film culture was thriving in Korea through these contacts with Japan. For example, Lee Pil-wu, the cinematographer for Korea's first successful and most famous talkie, *The Story of Chunhyang*, spent time in Ōsaka studying at the film library of the *Ōsaka Mainichi* newspaper, which opened its doors to both commercial and art-house filmmakers in July 1927. According to an article in the *Ōsaka Mainichi* (1933), "Education through the Movies," the library contained feature and documentary films from all over the world, including Italy, France, Austria, Canada, Mexico, Peru, Brazil, and the Philippines.

By early 1931, Korean filmmakers no longer needed to travel to Japan to gain similar experience, as local branches of the *Ōsaka Mainichi* film library and training center were opened in Seoul and Daegu. Both libraries were generously supplied with projectors and films from the main *Mainichi* library. Weekly screenings of educational and cultural films were arranged at the two Korean branches and basic production classes were offered as well. The main objective of this initiative was to increase the level of education regarding films and filmmaking through a hands-on approach.[96] The library and training program sponsored by the *Ōsaka Mainichi* was an innovative attempt to consolidate imperial attitudes through the medium of film. Armed with technical know-how, social and business contacts with Japanese filmmakers, and an intense desire to express themselves through film, Korean filmmakers continued to sharpen their production skills and turn out more films.

While Korean filmmakers were gaining production experience, distributors and importers were focused on profiting from the exhibition side of the industry. Between 1 August 1926 and 31 March 1936, Korean entertainment entrepreneurs such as Park Seung-pil, Lee Gu-young, and Jo Jeong-hwan, as well as producers and directors such as Lee Pil-wu, Kim Dong-pyeong, and Lee Chang-geun, applied for censorship approval to exhibit 2,396 American, Korean, Japanese (most likely from the smaller Japanese film companies), and other international feature films, for both entertainment and educational purposes.[97] Averaging around 217 films per year, these figures demonstrate that Korean entrepreneurs had a far more active role in this golden age of occupied cinema than previous studies have allowed. While ongoing financial support for local film production was lacking over this period, there were literally thousands of opportunities for Koreans to facilitate the exhibition of American, Japanese, other foreign, and a small number of Korean films.

Despite these gains, as Hollywood film distributors were forced to import their films to Korea via Japan, Korean film companies suffered from a lack of distribution profits and regular funding, especially for experimentation with and conversion to sound-on-disc technology in the early 1930s and sound-on-film technology in the mid-to-late 1930s. As a result, Japanese film companies with access to ample funds increased their distribution opportunities throughout the Korean market. Over the same eleven-year period, Japanese distributors/importers in Korea submitted 12,108 Japanese, American, other international, and a small number of Korean feature films (both entertainment and educational) to the censorship board.

At the same time, Japan's stricter film policy helped to regulate and reduce the influence of so-called bad culture in foreign films on Korean audiences while the Japanese were preparing for war. Despite attempts by the Japanese authorities to use a screen quota to control foreign films, and the steady stream of income generated by censorship applications, it was difficult to enforce the double censorship policy because of limited human resources. According to the *Film Daily Year Book of Motion Pictures 1936*, in 1934, of a total of 17,468 film reels submitted to the censorship bureau in Japan, only 651, or less than 4 percent, were rejected. About 48 percent of those rejected were from the United States.[98] The Department of Home Affairs in Tokyo, as well as its branch in Seoul, simply lacked sufficient censorship staff. For example, in mid-1925, Tokyo's censorship board employed forty-four staff. According to statistics for the period between 1926 and 1936, the domestic and foreign films submitted for censorship totaled approximately 20,320, amounting to 93,407 reels.[99] Censors throughout Japan and Korea would have had their hands full and eyes blurred.

At the end of 1935, Governor-General Ugaki moved to protect Japan's domestic film industry further by strengthening the laws regarding the market share allocated to domestic films in the Korean and Japanese markets. The domestic (Japanese *or* Korean) screen quota system was raised from 25 percent to one-third, increasing exhibition market barriers for American and European distributors and their silent and sound films. The loss of distribution opportunities for foreign film exchanges was only exacerbated in 1937, when newly appointed Governor-General Minami declared that at least half of all films screened in Korea had to originate domestically. This had significant implications for distributors of American films. The American distributors voiced their complaints in American film industry journals such as the *Motion Picture Almanac* and at numerous industry conferences.[100]

Eventually, as a result of the quota limits placed on the number of imported American films and the more stringent censorship regulations, the MPPDA was forced to come cap in hand to the Japanese Department of Home Affairs and the Korean Colonial Government and plead the cause of the sidelined Hollywood distributors. During this period, according to archival documents held by the Supreme Commander for the Allied Powers (SCAP), hundreds of thousands of dollars in film rental profits were at risk as American films had previously been screened extensively and were well received throughout Japan and Korea. When the Sino-Japanese War broke out in 1937, the Japanese Empire was being run according to the 'total war' regime. The Japanese government prioritized the protection of its domestic film industry and the education of its Imperial subjects. In effect, the Korean Colonial Government no longer needed to exploit Hollywood censorship applications because it had already accumulated sufficient funds to run the censorship apparatus.

In 1938, when the film import quota was reduced to 100 features per year, Hollywood distributors were unable to recover the market strength gained during the first golden age of American cinema in Asia. The Japanese authorities seemed paranoid about the potential for Hollywood films and American culture to adversely influence citizens of the Japanese Empire. According to the trade bulletin from the Department of Commerce issued on August 31, 1936, almost all *benshi* (or *byeonsa*) performances accompanying foreign films had ceased in Japanese-controlled Manchuria, as foreign films were now regularly titled with Japanese dialogue along the sides of the film frame. This meant that the Japanese authorities potentially had much improved control of film content and could block any undesirable interpretations reflecting the views of audiences.[101] Then, when the United States entered World War II in 1941, the remaining links between the American film industry and the Japanese and Korean markets were broken completely; all American films and related materials in local Hollywood distribution offices (exchanges) were impounded.[102]

THE AFTER-EFFECT

Throughout the colonial period, the production of domestic (Japanese and Korean) films, as well as the distribution and exhibition of international (American, British, Chinese, French, German, Italian, and Russian) films, were flourishing activities. The development and enforcement of colonial film policy, including censorship, were designed to manage Korea's burgeoning film culture in the interests of the empire.

Further exploration of the censorship status of the thousands of Hollywood films screened in Korea during the colonial period is needed. It would be revealing to learn more about the specific scenes that were cut or eliminated from the very large group of American films that passed through the censorship process. In addition, in accordance with censorship application requirements, this total would have included multiple copies of the same film. While it is clear that the censorship apparatus was chiefly directed at collecting a mass of application fees rather than preventing films from being screened, more research is needed to better gauge the actual number of films screened in the Korean market in this period.

The research presented in this chapter corroborates the view that Japanese censorship policies in colonial Korea were overwhelmingly directed at revolutionary themes and motifs, rather than 'Western' ones. This helps explain why the rejection rate for American films was so low—a fact that complicates our understanding of the impact of the early cinema on Korean culture. One might ask whether the watching of thousands of Hollywood films during the Japanese colonial period constituted, for Korean audiences, a form of passive resistance, or at least a temporary escape from their harsh reality. Unfortunately, it is difficult to substantiate this interpretation with empirical evidence since few relevant source materials have survived. Indeed, there is a dearth of published material documenting and analyzing the political economy, audience reception, and cultural transformation of the film industry in Korea during the colonial period. Surviving archival materials, business records, and government files are scarce—not to mention the fact that few films made in Korea before 1945 exist today in any form.

Until the mid- and late 1930s, when Governors-General Ugaki and Minami began restricting the expression of many facets of Korean culture, the Korean Colonial Government had permitted Korean filmmakers to create spaces—given moderate parameters—within which they could express a national culture and spirit. However, censorship was complicated in Korea because of the unpredictable impact a film's content might have on Korean audiences and the dynamic role potentially played by *byeonsa*. Given the perceived influence of the development of talkie (sound) technology on Korean society, the authorities—and the police in particular—treated the production, distribution, and exhibition of films seriously. The censorship board may well have believed that listening to the Korean native tongue on film was tantamount to participating in a cultural or nationalist activity. At the same time, the authorities recognized that Korean films could subvert the colonialist agenda, and they viewed them with great seriousness as a result.

4 The Coming of the Talkies to the Cinema in Colonial Korea

Between the mid-1920s and late 1930s, national film industries across the world experienced fundamental changes in the production, distribution, and exhibition of sound films. During this global transformation, enormous capital was wagered on the development and adoption of 'modern' screen technologies. Despite the risk of financial ruin during the Great Depression, hundreds of new cinemas were built, and thousands were wired for sound equipment—speakers, amplifiers, and electric motors. The silent period began inexorably to fade and, although somewhat chaotic and uneven in its introduction, sound production became a symbol of adventure and progress.[1]

A Western (American and European) cartel drove this fundamental, but not uniform, cinematic change across all countries and languages. Between 19 June and 22 July 1930, the German Tobis-Klangfilm and American Western Electric-ERPI and RCA Photophone companies assembled at the Paris Picture Sound Conference. Through the 'Paris Agreement' signed on the last day of this gathering, they divided the world into three commercial regions—an exclusive German, an exclusive American, and a 'neutral' sales territory which included Japan and its colonies.[2] In addition to this major territorial carve-up, hundreds of local sound recording and projection innovations flourished all around the world. Often characterized in film trade magazines as underdogs in some kind of 'talkie war,' these alternative systems helped to wire up thousands of cinemas in suburban locations that the big electric firms could not reach or simply had no interest in servicing.[3] Developments in Korea occurred much later than in the United States and Europe, and in ways that diverged significantly from these wider regions. In Korea, the exploration of new possibilities in sound production emerged from within a complex colonial environment.

In this chapter, we explore the ways in which Korean filmmakers embarked on a project of modernization that incorporated a mix of old and new cultural and artistic traditions and technological innovations, all while working under colonial rule and constraints on cultural expression. We argue that the advent of the talkies in colonial Korea helped Korean filmmakers and technicians create fertile conditions for the success of domestic sound films, thereby inadvertently furthering the cause of a national film and cinema culture. Far from their getting an easy ride on the back of a Japanese-dominated, modernized industry, we show how Korean pioneers of sound cinema had to reckon with a difficult political, cultural and economic climate, and a complex set of internally and externally driven motives. While the film industry was firmly controlled by the Korean Colonial Government, the history of cinema in colonial Korea is more complex than a tale of 'good' Korean films and filmmakers versus 'collaborative traitors' and the propaganda films they churned out. Sound cinema, and film production more generally, became a 'node of cultural construction,' similar to the case of radio, in which Korean filmmakers contributed to both a local and a national/imperial cinema at the same time as they actively negotiated, challenged, and reaffirmed Korean culture (and, later, Japanese or 'Imperial' culture) through film. The all-Korean films and Korean-Japanese coproductions on which they worked infused a significant productive energy into the creation of a modern, popular culture in Korea within and despite the political and cultural boundaries of colonialism.

In terms of the larger picture, industry and commerce were experiencing rapid growth at this time.[4] Governor-General Saitō was charged with softening the image of the Japanese Empire following the defeat of the abortive March First independence movement in 1919. He aimed to relax (or at least give the appearance of relaxing) Japanese administrative control over Korean cultural and artistic activities.[5] Writers, actors, filmmakers, and theater entrepreneurs took advantage of this new environment and began developing and negotiating spaces for the expression of Korean culture. Studying filmmaking, producing silent films, and experimenting with sound films formed a major part of their activities. As we saw in chapter 3, this was a time of hope for Korean intellectuals and artists. According to a search of the Korean Movie Database administered by the Korean Film Archive (KOFA), between 150 and 160 feature films were produced in Korea and forty-five Korean nationals were formally registered as directors during the colonial period. Cinema-going audiences were increasing both in the peninsula and across the Japanese Empire. In 1932 alone, the annual total of cinema-goers in Korea reached 6,500,000—about one in every three people.[6] These audiences had developed a strong appetite for Hollywood movies. According to the *Film Daily Year Book 1937*, the percentage of actual meters of foreign (primarily American films) exhibited in 1932 (amounting to 63 percent) overwhelmingly exceeded the total length of Japanese and Korean films exhibited in Korea. (The inverse was true in Japan, where about 70 percent of all films screened were domestic and 30 percent were of foreign origin.[7])

Most filmmakers would have been aware of the cinema's potential to make an impact on local (and probably foreign) audiences. The Korean Colonial Government, too, was aware of cinema's impact and, when it eventually overturned the imbalance of foreign versus 'domestic' (including Japanese) films, its actions had an enormous impact on the local film industry, precipitating a production boom. By 1937, the artistic merits of Korean films such as Na Un-gyu, Lee Gyu-hwan, and Lee Myeong-wu's *Omongnyeo* (1937); Ahn Seok-yeong, Lee Gi-se, and Lee Myeong-wu's *Shim Cheong-jeon* (*The Story of Shim Cheong*, 1937); and especially Lee Gyu-hwan's *Nageune* (*The Wanderer*, 1937, made by the Korean Sung Bong Film Co. and 'supervised' by the Japanese Shinkō Studio's Suzuki Shigeyoshi) had begun to attract the attention of audiences in Japan and Manchuria. Based on its commercial success, and the fact that it was considered by the Japanese film industry as the 'first outstanding work from Korea,' Shinkō had planned to export *Nageune* to Europe and the United States.[8]

Availing themselves of the opportunities afforded by their colonial occupation, rather than being restricted by it, Korean filmmakers were able to make a number of domestic sound and silent productions during this period. Many of these productions, which focused on the misfortunes of the poor, were known as *shinpa* films—excessively sentimental melodramas based on popular novels and romantic stories.[9] Korean scholars have seen these films as embodying a sense of Korean nationalism.[10] While these productions might have been read by some as a subversive metaphor for the struggle against Japanese colonialism, it seems they were non-threatening to the colonial state. Although few if any have survived, we assume that they lacked overt socialist and communist references—banned under the 1926 censorship regulations—as otherwise they would not have been exhibited at all.

Despite the unequal relationships existing between them, Korean filmmakers and technicians sought and received collegial assistance from Japanese filmmakers and film companies. They gained formative experience by working with all-Korean production crews and Japanese filmmakers in Korea, and training (as apprentices) with big film studios in Japan. In 1930, three out of the twelve feature films completed were 'co-productions,' employing either a Japanese film editor or cinematographer along with a Korean cast and crew. In 1931, the number of co-productions increased to five (out of fifteen feature films made), with some employing Japanese directors, actors, and screenwriters alongside Korean casts and crews.[11] While detailed economic data on film production in colonial Korea are difficult to obtain, it seems likely that these film companies survived only by courting Japanese investors who controlled a significant percentage of the overall film business. Thus Koreans gained invaluable experience working on a combination of their own and Japanese films, while outwardly conforming to the Korean Colonial Government's assimilationist ideology, summed up in the catchphrase 'ninety million fellow countrymen.'[12]

At the same time, the development of the film industry in Korea contributed to the industrialization of Japan's film industry by serving as an expanding market—especially in the face of the Western-style modernity flooding into Asia from the United States. In this era, Hollywood maintained its domination of feature films on the world's screens, not only in terms of sheer quantity and quality but also in film recording and projection/exhibition technology, raw film stock, and promotional and distribution strategies devised in America and executed across the globe. But Japan had its own strategies in mind. Film production in occupied Korea undoubtedly played a central role in the Japanese government's long-term aims of infusing Korean culture with Japanese language and cultural values while also diffusing those same values throughout its Asian empire.

THE NOVELTY AND POWER OF MODERN SOUND TECHNOLOGY

Korean-language studies provide little sustained discussion about the coming of the talkies to colonial Korea, opting instead for the by-now ritualistic repetition of the legends surrounding the making of *The Story of Chunhyang* (1935), the 'first successful' sound film, which we discuss later in this chapter.[13] Even more recent scholarship, which includes the cinemas of both North and South Korea in its purview, collectively brushes over the pursuit of sound technology and its integral links with Korea's larger cinematic history.[14] While a few Japanese film-industry trade reports from this period touch upon films and filmmakers in Korea, only a handful of the specialist English-language studies of Japanese cinema history include colonial Korea.[15] Repeatedly, these studies point to 1935 as the year when the talkies simply 'emerged' in Korea. However, archival documents and industry trade reports tell a more detailed and vibrant story about when and how the talkies came to Korea, and the myriad ways in which they influenced and enriched the development of a uniquely Korean cinema.

In the mid-1920s, the motion picture industry in Korea (and Japan) began pondering a switch to commercial sound, a changeover that had already happened in countries such as the United States, Australia, Britain, France, and Germany. Demonstrations of the American De Forest Phonofilms brand (sound-on-film), which took place in Japan in 1924 and Korea in 1925, had planted the seeds of the inevitable transition. In late February 1925, as a one-off event, four Phonofilms were screened at the Umigwan cinema in Seoul.[16] These documentaries and part-talkies were part of a huge range of approximately one thousand short sound films produced by De Forest. This screening, which was cosponsored by the major newspapers *Maeil Shinbo* and *Gyeongseong Ilbo*, included *President Coolidge, Taken on the White House Ground* (1924), a violin performance and a political demonstration in Washington Square. One can only speculate about the impact that the first film featuring an American president recorded with sound would have made on Korean film pioneers.

The next developments occurred between May and October 1927, when technical and cultural discussions about 'modern' sound technology began appearing in Korean newspapers.[17] At this time, the *Donga Ilbo* had published several articles on the subject, including the exploits of Lee de Forest and his sound-on-film talkie technology. The impact of sound films on society and the art of filmmaking were topics of particular interest.

Then, in January 1928, documented talkie screenings took place at the Umigwan Cinema, astounding audiences with footage of Charles Lindbergh's pioneering nonstop solo flight from New York to Paris in May 1927 in the *Spirit of St. Louis. Donga Ilbo* subscribers could bring a coupon to the cinema entitling them to 50 percent discount.[18]

Within eighteen months of these screenings, foreign sales engineers from both the German Tobis-Klangfilm and American Western Electric-ERPI companies began thinking of ways to occupy the market. Their initial strategy was to give equipment demonstrations in the region. However, as Koreans learned about the difficulties involved in the coming of the talkies to other countries, they too realized that few Korean exhibitors could afford to lease or buy one of these high-end Western systems.[19] Nevertheless, local newspapers continued to publish reports about the talkies.

In a typically enthusiastic piece published in October 1931, the *Chosun Ilbo* discussed how the Union of Soviet Socialist Republics (hereafter USSR) and Germany had been researching and developing sound film technology since 1926; the entire Soviet film industry was reportedly converting to sound as a result of the overwhelming popularity of talkies.[20] In further articles published under its columns under the headings 'Modern Knowledge' ('Hyeondae Jisik') and 'Film Knowledge' ('Yeonghwa Sangsik'), the newspaper offered readers historical overviews of the talkies in the United States and Japan, citing specific examples of the use of sound effects. While critic Lee Chang-yong appreciated the novelty of hearing (and seeing) a cat meow and a door slamming, he believed that the adequate expression of the spoken word was still problematic. Lee found the overt disavowal of talkies by Charles Chaplin, whose films were extremely popular in Korea, a telling sign of the questionable future of this latest development in motion pictures.[21] Such articles reminded readers of the limited ability of early sound technology to reproduce and amplify sound in ways that human ears were used to hearing.

Despite its faddish character, the quality of early motion picture sound was generally poor. Low admission prices barely seemed to compensate for this nascent technology. Hence, it took more than a few talkie demonstrations in the mid-1920s to convince the public of the viability of sound films.

By the end of 1928, fewer than 10 percent of the estimated fifteen thousand American cinemas had been converted to sound but, by mid-1930, just over 75 percent of cinemas in the United States had been wired. By this time, equipment costs had begun to come down and public opinion was changing after the quality of amplification improved. It looked as if sound was becoming an irreversible trend in the American and European film industries.

From the start, the Korean film community was both intrigued and frustrated by the adoption of sound by film industries around the world. Lee Chang-yong considered that producing sound films was completely out of the reach of Korean filmmakers, who could not even dream about using imported sound equipment because of the cost. On the one hand, Korea's colonial situation was not exclusively to blame for this limitation, as investment capitalism was still in its initial stages in the peninsula. Filmmakers in Japan, on the other hand, could afford this technology because of the more mature state of the country's film studios and production infrastructure. Despite his contradictory feelings about the changeover, Lee Chang-yong looked forward to savoring American and European talkies; as a representative voice of the Korean film industry he was excited by the novel spectacle they seemed to offer.[22]

In the early 1930s, Lee Gyu-hwan was working as Suzuki Shigeyoshi's assistant director at Shinkō's studios in Kyotō when it released the smash sound-on-disc film hit *What Made Her Do It?* (*Nani ga kanojo o sō saseta ka*).[23] At this time, Lee Gyu-hwan wrote a series of newspaper articles about sound technology in which he promoted the talkies as a potentially modernizing vehicle for filmic expression and the evolution of the industry.[24] He openly admired the way in which Hollywood directors and studios were engaging with the infant technology. His articles emphasized the novelty and popularity of talkies in Japan while pointing to their undeveloped state in other parts of the empire. Although Lee was writing from his knowledge of the Japanese industry, the level of detail about sound technology he disclosed in these articles gave him the appearance of an expert. It was a clever strategy, designed to ingratiate himself with the Korean film community in advance of his return to Korea, and may have opened opportunities for him to study filmmaking in the United States.[25]

The knowledge Lee expressed in these newspaper articles must have proven frustrating in 1932 when he made *The Boat without the Boatman*, a silent film portraying the difficulties experienced by Korean farmers, that was (and still is) considered the quintessential nationalistic film, despite being lost today.[26] Despite his advocacy of sound technology and the talkies before his return to Korea, Lee could not afford to make his debut film with sound. However, despite the gap between theory and reality in his pursuit of sound, Lee Gyu-hwan's knowledge and ideas inspired other practitioners such as Lee Pil-wu and his brother Lee Myeong-wu to gain further industry experience and training in this area. Lee Gyu-hwan maintained his position at the cutting edge of the film industry during his long career—highlighted by his landmark 1955 version of *The Story of Chunhyang*, which kickstarted the 'golden age' of Korean cinema in the 1950s and 1960s.[27]

For Lee Chang-yong, Lee Gyu-hwan, and many others at the time, sound recording and projection equipment seemed to be the last word in film technology. Even so, in the early 1930s talkies had a long way to go before reaching the heights that silent films had attained as an art form. Both men doubted that the Korean film community could successfully experiment with sound because their access to *silent* cameras and associated equipment was already severely limited. Opinion was divided among exhibitors, too, with some from the smaller centers firmly opposed to sound, while others were beginning to import talkies, instigating a kind of battle between silent and sound films. Sound may have been sweeping over the United States, but it was off to a very slow start in Korea—limited by the attitude of colonial authorities, who were more concerned with influencing the distribution and exhibition of Japanese and other foreign (primarily American) films than with developing the production infrastructure in Korea with modern equipment and financing the creation of well-equipped studios like those in Japan.

In the late 1920s talkies first appeared in the capital, Seoul, and then spread to the smaller cities. Seoul had by far the largest number of cinemas and total seating capacity as well as the most advanced American and Japanese sound equipment—not to mention the country's most modern roads, railroads, post offices, telegraph and telephone exchanges, banks, electric-power plants, hospitals, hotels, restaurants, and schools. Seoul was fast evolving into a city of the future and a city of opportunity within the Japanese Empire. Seoul was the metropolis, Korea's site of change and urban modernity, and nowhere more so than in the realm of entertainment and popular culture. Six out of eleven of Seoul's most prestigious cinemas, catering to Japanese audiences and showing Japanese features, shorts, and animated cartoons from the Nikkatsu, Shōchiku, Shinkō, and Taitō studios, were wired with the Nippon Sound System (manufactured by Japan Wireless Telegraph and Telephone Co.).[28] Seoul's other five flagship cinemas, mostly frequented by Koreans, screened mainly foreign (American, British, French, German, and Russian) and Korean films on American sound-projection equipment provided by Western Electric-ERPI.

In the provincial cities of Pusan, Pyongyang, Daegu, Weonsan, and Incheon, with one cinema apiece, primarily Korean audiences watched foreign films on American sound equipment. Admission prices differed across Korea at this time. Tickets for general cinema seating in Seoul cost from 40 to 60 sen (between approximately 11¢ and 17¢). The small discounts offered to students and the larger ones (up to 50 percent) to children were intended to entice the young not only into the realm of popular entertainment but also to explore more serious documentary films and cultural issues. The sound-film genres to which they were exposed, many sourced from Japan, are documented in the English-language *Cinema Year Book of Japan 1936–1937* and *Cinema Year Book of Japan 1938*, and included military (army and navy), tourism, education, sports, manners and customs, public health, science, the arts, politics, and popular music.[29] Engaging young Korean audiences in this way represented a further avenue for the dissemination of Japanese cultural ideals in Korea, and in particular into the minds of youth.

Between 1926 and 1936—what has been called the first golden age of American cinema in Korea—Hollywood films, both silent and talkie, were overwhelmingly dominant in the Korean market.[30] As the previous chapter demonstrated, a regular supply of American films, which were imported first into Japan, accompanied the gradual but inexorable spread of sound technology from the United States.[31] Musicals and gangster films were two of the most prolific genres that were submitted to the Korean Colonial Government for censorship. In 1930, a continuous supply of American sound films began arriving, first in Japan and then Korea, imported by the local MPPDAA offices. Culturally, this had two important consequences. On the one hand, colonial Korea was unquestionably a key territory for Hollywood (and a smaller number of European distributors) and, whether they were aware of it or not, its agents were promulgating Western modernity as a set of cultural attitudes closely linked to advanced technology. On the other hand, the popularity and availability of Hollywood films in Japan facilitated their distribution into Korea, offering new sources of inspiration to local filmmakers and helping them develop their skills. Hence, the plethora of foreign films (as well as a small number of Japanese films) flooding into the peninsula encouraged Korean filmmakers to make and exhibit sound (and silent) films of their own. The first attempt was in 1930, when a Korean production company tried its hand at making a talkie.

KOREA'S UNTOLD TALKIE STORY: THE MODERNIZATION OF TRADITION

Most film histories assert that sound cinema began in 1935 with *The Story of Chunhyang*, a film that briefly reinvigorated a depressed local film industry. While *The Story of Chunhyang*, directed by Lee Myeong-wu and with Lee Pil-wu as sound engineer, is remembered as 'Korea's first successful talkie'—corresponding to *The Neighbor's Wife and Mine* (1931) in Japan—it had in fact been anticipated five years earlier.[32] In 1930, Korean filmmakers first tested the waters of the modern cinematic era with the attempted production of *Secret Story,* to be filmed by Lee Pil-wu (born in Seoul in 1897) and directed by Na Un-gyu, who had acquired huge star appeal and popularity from his work in *Arirang* (1926).[33]

Secret Story aimed to modernize Korean tradition by emulating changing Western production and exhibition practices. The technical coup it sought to achieve was to synchronize a prerecorded phonograph disc with a silent film, a method that had already achieved successful results in films like Warner Bros.' *The Jazz Singer* (1927). In February 1930, Lee launched his talkie project by visiting Japanese entertainment entrepreneur Minagawa Yoshizō and his Minatalkie Company in Japan, negotiating a contract for the purchase of multiple sound-on-disc recordings. Although Minagawa was willing to provide Lee with a continuous supply of discs for ten won each, Lee had insufficient funds to underwrite the deal. In retrospect, ten won was probably a bargain, as the average cost of a phonograph record was between 1.35 and 2.5 won.[34] According to a newspaper interview with

Figure 4.1 Advertisements for the unreleased sound-on-disc film *Malmothal Sajeong* (1930). From top to bottom: Malmothal Sajeong (1930, unreleased). *Daejung Yeonghwa* #4 (July 1930); and Malmothal Sajeong in *Chosun Ilbo* (9 August 1930): 5 —reappearing in *Chosun Ilbo* on 10 and 11 August 1930. Author's own collection.

Lee Pil-wu's brother, Lee Myeong-wu, film songs cost about sixty to seventy won to record.[35] The outlay involved was between two and a half and three times that of a simple phonograph player, which only wealthy Koreans could afford.[36] Had the deal been successful, Minagawa would have done Lee a favor while at the same time getting rid of his unwanted discs.

Despite this setback, Lee kept the project alive by creating an ambitious media campaign to generate interest in sound technology in general and to attract the financial backing required for the film's completion. An early advertisement for the film appeared in July 1930, covering the full back page of *Daejung Yeonghwa*, a popular Korean film magazine. According to the advertisement, *Secret Story* aimed to be the 'first talkie production in Korea,' with plans for screening at the well-known Danseongsa Cinema. This Won Bang Gak production, as it was styled, had the financial backing of Park Jeong-hyun, the Korean owner and manager of the Danseongsa, one of the oldest permanent cinemas in Seoul and authorized by the Japanese police to screen foreign films. Multiple newspaper advertisements in the *Chosun Ilbo* exploited Na Un-gyu's name as director and promoted the film as a *fait accompli* talkie, scheduled for release in August 1930 (figure 4.1).

Despite the enthusiasm reflected in the publicity campaign, funding problems persisted and *Secret Story* failed to eventuate.[37] Lee Pil-wu and Na Un-gyu eventually had a falling-out. Although Na Un-gyu never made a talkie film as famous as his silent *Arirang*, he did write and direct a second sound film, *Arirang Part 3* (1936), while working for the Korean Hanyang Film Studio.[38] Both Lee Pil-wu and Na Un-gyu were convinced that the time had arrived (in terms of opportunities for training experience, expertise, and funding) for Koreans to make their own talkies, regardless of their reception by the public.[39] They must have felt that the end of the silent era was near.

Prior to the making of *The Story of Chunhyang* in 1935, the chronology of Lee Pil-wu's activities is somewhat obscure. However, in 1931 he traveled to Shanghai to observe the exhibition of sound films and to acquire as much knowledge of the new technology as he could. Commercial sound and talking films had been exhibited in Shanghai since February 1929. Lee probably wanted to learn more about the American Movietone sound-on-film recording system, which Fox news crews were operating there.[40] Shanghai was a major center for film production and distribution in China and an ideal location for Lee to learn how to resolve some of the technical obstacles he was facing.

After his return from China, Lee spent time in Japan studying further aspects of sound production. Here he made contact with the Tsuchihashi brothers, who were developing an innovative sound-film-recording system (based on RCA equipment developed in the United States) for Shōchiku.[41] The Tsuchihashi system was well known at the time through the commercial success of Shōchiku's talkie *The Neighbor's Wife and Mine* (1931). Lee Pil-wu's contacts in the Japanese film industry enabled him to negotiate a technical cooperation contract with the Tsuchihashi brothers. This most probably involved the sharing of publications (readily available in Japanese and English) containing detailed specifications of various sound systems, the acquisition of spare parts, and general advice about constructing sound recording and projection equipment.

However, the acquisition of technical know-how was only a part of the equation for success. Desperate for funding, Lee imported Fritz Lang's first talkie *M* (1931) from Japan for exhibition in Seoul. His fascination with this now-famous example of *film noir* illustrates Lee's advanced tastes in film. Although Lee took the trouble to rebuild a projector for the sound projection of *M*, the film failed due to its lack of commercial appeal; and as it was in German, audiences could not understand the dialogue.[42] There is no record of Lee using a live film narrator to make the film more accessible to audiences in Seoul. Apparently, Lee's modified projector was also ineffective.

Throughout the early 1930s, Lee Pil-wu worked with the cream of the Japanese film industry, people working at the cusp of the technological conversion to sound. He brought back to Korea new skills and ideas, as well as his unquenchable thirst for knowledge of the unparalleled changes transforming the cinema during this period. It is unclear whether Lee returned to Korea for patriotic reasons, because he had reached a plateau in his training in Japan, or because he was able to secure new funding opportunities in Korea. Whatever the reason, his overseas experiences fed his passion to contribute to the global motion picture revolution. Lee became obsessed with sound and used every chance to ingratiate himself with like-minded people. His time in Japan had enabled him to gain valuable experience in Ōsaka, where he had worked for two major production companies, Nikkatsu and Shōchiku, and befriended film production technicians and amateur radio enthusiasts.

These experiences and connections would prove invaluable to Lee when he returned to Korea and began making *The Story of Chunhyang* with sound. Lee Pil-wu's life story, as told through interviews, suggests he was modern in a culturally hybrid sense, following new, Western trends in dress and music, yet at the same time working to put a distinctively Korean face to a new style of cinema insofar as the constraints of colonial status would allow. Lee's personal lifestyle thus reflected the modern technological age he was so eager to engage.

Between 1931 and 1935, while sound may have been the Next Big Thing, the Korean film community continued to contribute to the growth of a local cinema by making silent films. While no further Korean sound films are known to have been made during this period, the American distribution exchanges continued promoting and distributing both sound-on-disc and sound-on-film films. The growth of sound during this brief period was meteoric. In 1933, 21 percent of the films exhibited were talkies. In 1934, the number of talkies nearly doubled to 40 percent of the total number of films screened and, in 1935, this total more than doubled again to 85 percent of the market.[43] The talkies exhibited included Warner Bros.–First

National's (Vitaphone) *On with the Show* (1929) and *Top Speed* (1931); Universal's *Outside the Law* (1930) and *Dracula* (1931); United Artists' all-talking documentary *Around the World in 80 Minutes with Douglas Fairbanks* (1931); Fox's (Movietone) Oscar-winning *Bad Girl* (1931) and *Young as You Feel* (1931); as well as Chinese talkies produced in Shanghai. It is important to record these titles not only because they have been hitherto overlooked but also because they reveal the diversity of spectacle films to which Koreans were exposed in the early 1930s.

One notable Korean sound pioneer was Lee Gi-se. Owner of the Gaeseong-jwa cinema in Gyeonggi province built in 1912, he established the Gishin Yanghaeng distribution company and represented MGM and Paramount films after inheriting George R. Allen's Paramount distributorship in 1927. Lee expanded his business through contracts with Russia's Sovkino and British International Film in 1928.[44] In the mid-to-late 1930s, Gishin Yanghaeng made a noteworthy contribution to the diffusion of talkies in Korea by securing an exclusive exhibition contract with the Chosun Geukjang Cinema for *The Story of Shim Cheong* (1937). Yang Geun-mo, president of the Dongyang Film Company, was another Korean who helped build up the local distribution market.[45] As a result of the domination of the market by foreign operatives, he imported films from the relatively small Hollywood producer-distributor FBO, which was known for dealing in low-budget silent romantic melodramas, as well as action and comedy films. Albeit on a small scale, Lee Pil-wu, Korea's pioneering cinematographer and sound-recording engineer, also attempted to break into the distribution business by acquiring prints of *Way Down West* (1920) and Fritz Lang's *M* and exhibiting them in Seoul to subsidize the production of talkies.

The reception of sound films was complicated in Korea by the use in many cinemas of live narrators or *byeonsa*. William R. Langdon, the American Consul-General in Seoul, followed developments in the film industry closely. He was pessimistic about the future of talkies in Korea, even though the exhibition market was steadily experiencing the transition to sound.[46] As far as we can tell from the available evidence, most imported films were old and damaged from overuse, projectors were substandard compared with those used in the United States, and speaker volumes (while muffled in the best circumstances) were lowered to create a more favorable environment for performances by *byeonsa* during film screenings. And because this practice elided the need for subtitles, it made it possible for distributors of Hollywood films to diffuse their products widely throughout Korea over a long period. In fact, so important was the role of the *byeonsa* that Korea could be described as a major dumping ground for second-run Hollywood films.

As we saw in chapter 1, Korean *byeonsa* (*benshi* in Japanese) shared some of their traditions with the *pansori* dance and theater performances. Resembling the live narrators of nineteenth-century magic lantern presentations and *pansori* performances, male and female *byeonsa* stood off to the side of the screen and engaged film audiences by giving a running commentary on the narrative and providing emotional explanations of dialogue. They changed voices for each character, and offered sentimental interpretations of the imagery unfolding on the screen. Like *pansori, byeonsa* performance appealed to the common person because of its basic emotive style, transforming missionary slide presentations as well as silent and sound films into a simplified format and often offering an alternative narrative to the original, thus 'neutralizing' the confronting content of many of the Hollywood films exhibited between 1926 and 1936.

Thanks to the *byeonsa*, exhibitors and showmen were able to offer audiences an increasing flow of foreign films because live narrators elided the need for language-specific explanations, particularly when performing alongside American, European, and Japanese films, whether silent or sound. While the popularity of live film narration in Korea owed an important debt to the magic lantern technology and culture introduced by Christian missionaries, it was also partly modeled on the Japanese *benshi* tradition, which had begun in 1896 when silent film was first introduced to Japan.[47] Top *byeonsa* performers attracted fan clubs and regular followers and held their own against the foreign talkies being screened in Korea's larger cities.

Nevertheless, the popularity of Hollywood films in Korea owed a great debt to the *byeonsa* tradition. Spoken language was easier to follow than subtitles in Korean or Japanese. After the talkies arrived, *byeonsa* demanded that the sound volume be turned down in order to better project their voices. As in other countries, talkies also competed with musical accompaniment, which in Korea formed a backdrop for the *byeonsa* performances. Because *byeonsa* vied with the talkies for audience attention, sound films were not initially as popular in Korea (or Japan) as they were in English-speaking countries. In short, Koreans (and Japanese) retained a cultural proclivity for live narrators who projected their own sense of heightened realism onto a film and made the talkies seem less impressive, and possibly less necessary, especially since recorded, mechanically produced dialogue was inferior, in both auditory and entertainment terms, to live voice.

According to filmmaker and critic Lee Gyu-hwan, screening imported foreign talkies, shown in their original languages and accompanied by a *byeonsa*, was the cinematic equivalent of preparing a tasteless bowl of *bibimbap* (rice and mixed vegetables). Lee recognized that Korean filmmakers still lacked the technological expertise to engage with sound, unlike their counterparts in the United States and other Western countries. Perhaps ironically, the belated adoption and diffusion of sound technology and the delayed proliferation of American sound films in Korea proved to be major incentives for the development of Korean talkies. Screen quota regulations, propagated as early as August 1918 and strengthened significantly on 1 January 1937 by the Korean Colonial Government, had begun to call attention to, and to address the dominance of, Hollywood films in the region, thus encouraging the production of more 'domestic' (Korean and Japanese) films.[48] In the mid-1930s, after Governor-General Ugaki approved a higher exhibition quota for Korean and Japanese films, blocking the flow of foreign (primarily American) films, exhibitors with wired cinemas were anticipating the arrival of more 'local' (Korean *and* Japanese) sound productions.[49] The time was ripe for the local contribution to sound.

THE POLITICS OF INTERPRETATION:
THE STORY OF CHUNHYANG

Although the attempt to make *Secret Story* in 1930 was a significant failure, involving a premature attempt to use sound-on-disc technology, the production and exhibition of the 'first' Korean talkie, *The Story of Chunhyang*, in 1935, proved that Koreans could construct their own spaces for cultural expression within the constraints of colonial rule. The film opened up a new industry pathway, bringing together Korean production crews and Japanese financial backers in the making of local sound films, a process that had begun with the silent version of *The Story of Chunhyang* in 1923.

The Story of Chunhyang talkie was produced by the Gyeongseong Film Studio, an all-Korean-staffed organization, with funding from a Japanese entertainment entrepreneur. While it is impossible to know if the Japanese investor was fully aware of the nationalistic implications of the project, his status as a Japanese national would no doubt have eased the film's review before the censorship board. Given the increasing presence of Japanese film distributors in Korea at this time, involving a Japanese investor was probably part of director Lee Myeong-wu's plan from the outset. At the same time, it may have also lent an aura of 'innocence' to the movie. This anonymous entrepreneur was not the only Japanese to invest in Korean productions, which, after all, were desperate for funding. In 1934, still eager to bring sound to the Korean cinema, Lee Pil-wu contacted a Japanese colleague with whom he had worked at the Shōchiku studio and asked him to bring a sound-recording machine to Korea. Lee purchased the machine for 1,200 won, modified it, renamed it the P.K.R. system, and used it to make *The Story of Chunhyang*.

The Chunhyang story was a well-known traditional folk tale and hence was a smart choice to adapt into a talkie. Based on a popular old novel from the Chosun Dynasty, it reflected the intimacies and uniqueness of Korean culture and society. The film tells the love story of a noble scholar and Chunhyang, the daughter of a *gisaeng* (*geisha* in Japanese), traditionally regarded as part of the lowest social class, to whom he is secretly married. The story unfolds against a narrative involving a corrupt official and a covert envoy sent by the king to inspect the regional bureaucracy. Seduced and threatened by the corrupt official, the heroine nevertheless maintains her fidelity to her husband. The scholar reveals his true identity, saves Chunhyang and punishes the offending official for his maladministration. A silent version of *The Story of Chunhyang*, directed by a Japanese filmmaker in 1923, had already proven itself a box-office hit.[50] Every frame of the 1935 sound version embodied a sense of Korean-ness—which nevertheless evaded the Korean Colonial Government's censorship apparatus. This and other locally-made films produced around this time provided spectators with glimpses of Korean landscapes and traditional ways of life, as well as some of the changes brought about by state-sponsored industrialization.

Although the folk tale on which *The Story of Chunhyang* is based was several hundred years old, audiences may well have seen it as a metaphor for the Korean struggle against the colonial and military authority—the corrupt official on the one hand, and the secret envoy as the savior of Chunhyang and the local villagers on the other representing the occupying power and the hope of Korean independence, respectively. Given this powerful if subliminal nationalist message, and its success in representing Korean culture on the big screen, it is hardly surprising that *The Story of Chunhyang* was the first successful talkie in Korea.

As a prominent advertisement in the *Chosun Ilbo* announced, *The Story of Chunhyang* was released at the Danseongsa Cinema on 4 October 1935. The text listed the cast and crew and made some extravagant claims: "A great story . . . the world has been waiting for this . . . the premiere of the first Korean talkie." When *The Story of Chunhyang* was released, audiences originally rushed to see it for its novelty value, breaking box-office records. The film's success with local audiences was a good omen, suggesting a promising future for local sound productions and proving that a sound film could be made within an industry that lacked modern facilities and large numbers of trained engineers and production assistants.

However, while the film received considerable popular acclaim, many leading Korean filmmakers were not confident that its success could be repeated.

Figure 4.2 Advertisement for Korea's first successful talkie, *The Story of Chunhyang* (1935). *Chosun Ilbo* (4 October 1935):2. Courtesy of Yonsei University Library Newspaper Collection, Seoul.

Ahn Seok-yeong, a Korean film director and prominent film critic writing for the *Chosun Ilbo*, was 'shocked' by the success of the technological aspects of the production as no-one had known whether or not it could be done. He questioned whether the success of *The Story of Chunhyang* would lead to a rise in production and distribution of Korean films as he was unsure whether there were sufficient sound recording engineers, actors with speaking experience, and editing specialists to build an ongoing sound industry. All the same, he hoped for a day when more young people would enter the film business, making all Koreans proud of their accomplishments.[51]

Initially, the film's director, Lee Myeong-wu, and his brother, cinematographer Pil-wu (no doubt chastened by his experience on *Secret Story*), had seen the project as little more than an ambitious plan due to the lack of facilities and the underdeveloped technology at their disposal.[52] Nevertheless, the pair was keen to accomplish as much as they could.

Although, by this time, advances in sound technology in Europe and the United States were offering audiences and exhibitors (those who could afford it) a better sound experience, exhibitors in Korea had yet to invest in and employ the new technology on a broad basis. After all, Korean filmmakers were still working to perfect their silent filmmaking skills. For Korean-born Park Gi-chae (1935), another *Chosun Ilbo* writer, the significance of making an all-Korean talkie under colonial rule went far beyond the overcoming of technical limitations; it had injected a new stimulus into the Korean film community and society at large—an influence that no doubt extended by word of mouth to citizens beyond its immediate audience.

While *The Story of Chunhyang* made a profit at the box office partly because of its novelty—*The Jazz Singer* (1927) in the United States and *The Neighbor's Wife and Mine* in Japan had enjoyed similar success—the acting performances and the technical side of the film left a lot to be desired. While the production efforts were in many ways commendable, the presentation of backdrops, costumes, and characters remained underdeveloped. The talkie's subject matter was not as fully expressed as in the silent version of the same story. Moreover, the enunciation of the Korean dialogue was not clear. Although the film may have failed to live up to the high expectations created for it as 'Korea's first talkie,' Korean audiences were quick to forgive its lack of quality. It was a cultural triumph to hear the national language spoken by Korean actors on the silver screen, a spectacle which seemed to legitimize, at least in part, a national identity under threat from colonial rule and the influence of Western media. The awkward and clumsy-sounding dialogue was understandable given that talkies in Korea were in the exploratory stages.

Despite its technical imperfections, *The Story of Chunhyang* received high praise from many newspaper critics. After watching the film, Indol (aka Seo Hang-seok), a cultural critic for the *Donga Ilbo*, said that he felt like someone who is finally offered *kimchi* after a steady diet of lamb. According to Indol, Korean audiences had fallen in love with *The Story of Chunhyang* despite its deficiencies. The film's nationalistic appeal was unquestionably reflected in this overwhelmingly positive critical reception.[53]

Still, some Korean critics were pessimistic about the future of local talkies, choosing instead to reject the modernization of the arts. According to the well-known novelist Shim Hun, Koreans were not ready in the mid-1930s for the new spectator practices required to enjoy talkies. Nor did he feel that there was a need to hear Korean language spoken on screen purely for the sake of novelty. Shim accepted the fact that talkies were increasingly popular in Korea, but saw this modern filmmaking tool as part of a technological bubble that was expanding too rapidly to control. His comments are reminiscent of Charles Chaplin, who believed that sound tainted the beauty and aesthetic qualities of silent film. In any case, Shim Hun was clearly a traditionalist on questions relating to cultural practices. He believed that sound film in Korea was in danger of skipping some key stages in the development of this technology—chiefly, the production, distribution, and exhibition of sound-on-disc films, as had been the case in most other countries developing talkies. Moreover, like others, he argued that the film industry in Korea had only just begun to perfect the art of silent filmmaking.[54]

Other filmmakers and critics such as Song Yeong asserted that Korean talkies were yet to reach their full potential and, by portraying largely Western themes (free romance and capitalism, for example), literally dressed up to look Korean, they represented Korean culture only superficially. At the same time, Song (1936) expressed the wish that his fellow filmmakers would make talkies featuring iconographic Korean images, such as women's silhouettes in doorways, and commonly heard sounds such as the pounding of ironing (laundry) rods, as well as sad sighs and laughs for dramatic effect.

Although *The Story of Chunhyang* no longer survives, there remains a rich legacy of newspaper and magazine articles and editorials, advertisements, still photographs, and interviews with members of the production crew—material that retains a sense of the excitement surrounding its production and exhibition. The popular success of *The Story of Chunhyang* led to further talkie productions as other filmmakers followed in Lee Myeong-wu's footsteps. The all-Korean Gyeongseong Film Studio also made *Honggildong-jeon Part II* (*The Story of Honggildong*) in mid-1936. A part-talkie with a Japanese producer, it was directed and written by Lee Myeong-wu, and Lee Pil-wu recorded the sound. It was released on 10 June 1936 at the Danseongsa Cinema in Seoul.[55] According to Kim Gwan, a critic for the *Chosun Ilbo*, *Honggildong-jeon Part II* also suffered from poor audio quality.[56] However, the film demonstrated the Lee brothers' commitment to perfecting Lee Pil-wu's P.K.R. sound-on-film system and to making more sound films.

As none of his films survives, Lee Pil-wu has not left posterity any cinematic legacy apart from his testimonial interviews. According to the KOFA Korean Movie Database, the oldest prints of Korean sound films still in existence include the 1936 melodrama *Mimong (Sweet Dream)*, also produced by the Gyeongseong Film Studio and directed by Yang Ju-nam and written by Choe Dok-bung; and Ahn Seok-yeong's 1937 feature *Shim Cheong-jeon (The Story of Shim Cheong)*. The Lee brothers had a hand in both these productions. Surviving stills from Lee's 1936 film *Honggild-ong-jeon Part II* include some showing the production crew. Lee Pil-wu is shown sitting with synchronized sound-recording equipment and wearing a pair of headphones (figure 4.3). A boom microphone and two audio assistants are also in the shot. This photograph more than likely shows Lee Pil-wu's P.K.R. system, which was made by remodeling existing equipment—a common practice in many countries throughout the transition to sound, especially as older equipment was passed down to those who could not afford the latest models. Unfortunately, as far as we know, Lee's unique P.K.R. system no longer exists, and only one reel (a total of about thirteen minutes) of *Shim Cheong-jeon* survives.

As a result of Japanese modernization efforts and the widespread distribution of American (and European) silent and sound films, Korean filmmakers and technicians working in the difficult cultural and financial climate of the colonial period had gained a firm grasp of the thinking behind industrialization and modernity. Individual and, at times, shared experiments

Figure 4.3 Lee Pil-Wu and the film crew on the set of *Honggildong-jeon Part II*, circa 1936. Courtesy of the Korean Film Archive.

with sound enabled a diverse group of Koreans to do more than dream about contributing to a modern, popular culture: they did whatever they could to gain production experience and training and to make films by exploiting opportunities provided to them through the enforced modernization of the country under Japanese control and the influx of foreign films, while outwardly conforming to the demands of the colonial regime. The tacit permission granted to Koreans to gain commercial film production training and experience under the cultural policy reforms launched by Governor-General Saitō Makoto after 1919 stimulated a boom in Korea's silent cinema.[57]

In addition to feature film projects, non-commercial work became available after 1920, when the Korean Colonial Government established a Motion Picture Corps under its Central Council Investigation Section as part of the administration's larger aims of promoting the colonial Korean project in Japan and beyond.[58] This relatively prosperous and hopeful time for Korean filmmakers faded after 1937 with the wide-scale suppression of Korean language and culture following the outbreak of the Sino-Japanese War. One can only guess at the direction local developments in sound technology might have taken without the gradual imposition of Japan's wartime preparation system. Within this atmosphere of repression, discussed more fully in the next chapter, the Korean film industry had little choice but to place its ambitions on hold and to follow Japan's assimilationist agenda. As the war progressed, filmmakers found they could only gain experience making pro-Japanese propaganda feature films, newsreels, and cultural films for distribution throughout the empire; several of these were made with the assistance of Korean technicians such as Lee Pil-wu and Lee Myeong-wu.

The case of *Secret Story* and *The Story of Chunhyang,* on the one hand, and the experience of Lee Pil-wu, Lee Myeong-wu, Lee Chang-geun, Lee Gyu-hwan, and Ahn Seok-yeong, on the other, represent the different pathways taken and contributions made to a complex and evolving national cinema. These individuals were part of an active and diverse group of cinematographers, writers, producers, directors, actors, and exhibitors who were seeking to modernize the cinema in Korea, whether they were working for (or alongside) Japanese filmmakers and entrepreneurs or with all-Korean production crews. Modern sound technology was used as a tool with which to impose cultural modernity on Korean audiences, but films in the Korean language could also evoke powerful nationalist sentiments; many Korean film historians see these efforts as attempts to articulate national feelings against oppression by the colonial authority.[59] And, on a more pragmatic level, they may also have simply sought to compete with some of the American talkies already screening for a number of years with American sound projectors.

During the challenging years of Japanese colonial occupation which heralded the coming of sound to Korean cinemas, Korean filmmakers and technicians embraced every opportunity to pursue their various objectives within the industry. Some were keen to develop new skills for personal gain or fame, or for greater opportunities to work and train at home or in other parts of the Japanese Empire; some even aspired to Hollywood. Others combined financial motives with a desire to be part of the great push for modernization, with the comfortable and cosmopolitan lifestyle that went along with it. Some were motivated by creativity and the desire to make films as an art form. For others again, the creation of entertaining commercial films was a leading motive.

In addition, there were others—the cinematic and politically inspired innovators—whose motives embraced broadly nationalist goals: to seek enhanced funding opportunities for more Korean films through 'collaboration' on Japanese co-productions; to express Korean language, culture, and nationalism (either overtly or subversively); or to escape their colonial environment in either a literal or figurative sense.

The making of *The Story of Chunhyang* signified a momentous achievement in terms of available technology and limited production facilities. One might even guess that the film's success surprised the Korean Colonial Government, especially as there is no evidence to suggest the administration helped fund it or other Korean productions, other than a very few. The earlier attempts in 1930 to make the sound-on-disc talkie *Secret Story* are even more surprising. Although endeavors to generate funds for *Secret Story* came to nothing in the end, the production can be interpreted an overt attempt to forge a contemporary consciousness—to help bring modernity to Korea, and to be part of global trends. Although Na Un-gyu and Lee Pil-wu failed to complete *Secret Story*, it nevertheless demonstrated that pioneers in the Korean cinema were attempting to catch up with the global transition to sound.

Ultimately, a national film industry developed through the efforts of those who had been able to spread modern sound technology, a development which originated from the combination of a desire to tell Korean stories and, later, cooperation on a small number of propaganda feature films. While Korean film pioneers may not have privately acquiesced in the state agenda of modernizing the empire, they found ways to exploit the opportunities that were offered to them and bend them to their own objectives.

In the next chapter we explore how Korean filmmakers negotiated their connections with the occupied film industry, which experienced major changes initiated by government measures: the promulgation of the Film Law in Japan in 1939; the enactment of the Korean Film Law in 1940; the Korean Colonial Government's complete consolidation of the distribution and production arms of the film industry in 1942; and the harnessing of the industry to make feature-length propaganda films that glorified loyalty to the Japanese Empire and recruited Korean volunteers for the war. At each of these stages, which placed a different set of demands on the whole film industry, Korean filmmakers did whatever they could to practice their craft and continue their training with their Japanese colleagues.

5 Collaborative Film Production Under Japan's War-Preparation System, 1937–1945

By mid-1936 the film industry in Korea began experiencing fundamental changes. The balance of control over American films in the Korean market began to shift into Japanese hands. The number of American films distributed by Korean agents dropped to almost zero by the end of March 1936, while those represented by Japanese agents sharply increased. Korean businessmen responded by increasing the distribution of films acquired from other countries.

In 1937, as Japan escalated its war-preparation efforts, it unleashed a program of 'unbridled nationalistic consciousness' throughout its empire.[1] As part of this effort, the Korean Colonial Government's censorship apparatus began blocking the entry of films with 'Western' themes by banning nearly all films imported from the United States and the Allied countries. While Japanese films had previously enjoyed a moderate market share, Korea now became a key exhibition market for Japanese films. Although the resulting exhibition vacuum was eventually filled by a host of films imported from not only Japan, but also from Nazi Germany and fascist Italy, it was difficult to replace the sheer volume of American and European films that had flooded the market over the previous two decades.

As the ideology behind the procurement of entertainment films changed, so too did official thinking about what was produced for 'educational' purposes at home and in Japan's colonies. Given wartime priorities, almost all print and visual media production was expected to serve Japan's war-preparation system, following the principle 'education is the guiding force behind national culture.'[2] Under the banner of 'education,' Korea's film industry was radically transformed into a propaganda tool to support Japan's war machine. After the consolidation of distribution companies under one banner in April 1942, and with the support of a domestic film industry keen to do its part for the war effort, the Japanese Department of Home Affairs churned out newsreels and dramatic feature films and strongly encouraged audiences to see these films, often for free.[3]

Of the fifty-nine known films made in Korea between 1936 and 1945, almost all were produced to imbue Koreans with the ideology of *naeseon ilche* (*naisen ittai*): Japan and Korea as one body.[4] In simple terms,

Governor-General Minami Jirō aimed to use these films to help 'mould our national character, to form our national morals, to cultivate a firm and fiery national faith . . . '[5] Implementing these goals came at the expense of support for independent productions, which as a result became financially unviable, and eventually prohibited under Minami's heavy-handed rule (1936–1942).

As suggested elsewhere, during this 'dark age,' Korean filmmakers had little choice but to appear to collaborate with Japanese filmmakers on state-driven propaganda films.[6] To further the ideals of the Greater East Asia Co-Prosperity Sphere, they showed Koreans and Japanese working together to protect the Japanese Empire in the event of a 'Western invasion,' bound by an amorphous concept of Asian unity. Nevertheless, some post-1937 colonial-era co-productions managed to resist the *naeseon ilche* ideology, resulting, in the words of Kim Ryeo-shil, in a kind of 'chimera,' a hybrid animal with the incompatible characteristics of a lion, a snake, and a lamb.[7] Examples of these types of films are discussed in detail in this chapter. The authorities in Korea struggled to implement the rhetoric of *naeseon ilche* as thoroughly as they wished, because linguistic, class, and ethnic distinctions prevailed despite the imposition of a foreign national language. These 'hybrid' films were perhaps the natural outcome of clashing ideals, in which the filmmakers' desire for artistic and commercial success was at odds with the colonial administration's desire for increased ideological control.[8]

In this chapter we investigate the collaborative pathways pursued by Korean filmmakers both before and after the industry was fully consolidated and dominated by the state authorities. Major industry changes such as the promulgation of the Korean Film Law (Chosun Yeonghwa-ryeong) in August 1940 and the establishment of the Chosun Film Production Corporation (Chosun Yeonghwa Jusik Hoesa) in September 1942 challenged filmmakers to rethink their role as well as asking how to ensure their economic survival. The critical question, then, is not why, but *how* filmmakers, audiences, critics, and other intellectuals associated with the industry engaged with *naeseon ilche* in the context of an atmosphere of patriotic fervor and rising war hysteria. We first investigate how those within the industry responded to these events, and then explore how the challenges they faced impacted on the types of films produced by analyzing representative films of the period. Although the Greater East Asia Co-Prosperity Sphere initiative ended abruptly with Japan's surrender in 1945, the Korean Colonial Government's attempt to use film to unify its social, cultural, industrial, political, and economic ideals and ideology forms a pivotal chapter in the history of cinema in Korea.

BEFORE THE KOREAN FILM LAW: GEARING UP FOR THE NEW INDUSTRIAL SYSTEM

Although significant relationships between the two countries had been established as early as 1912—through cinema chains and Japanese producers and investors based in Korea—in the late 1930s the political environment demanded even closer collaboration involving direct exchanges of manpower as well as equipment and facilities. Seeing this as a chance to reach out to a larger market, young filmmakers such as Lee Chang-yong, president of the Goryeo Film Association, embraced the situation, which had created what he believed was an opportunity to develop a co-production model between Korea and Japan.[9]

Several films made before the Japanese and Korean film laws took effect, in 1939 and 1940 respectively, illustrate the dynamic ways in which filmmakers in Korea were exploring and interpreting the concept of *naeseon ilche*. The success of the talkie version of *The Story of Chunhyang* (1935) had increased awareness of the Korean contribution to the local cinema among Japanese filmmakers. Another film that earned mutual respect and recognition of Korean aesthetic and technical achievements was Lee Gyuhwan's *The Wanderer* (1937), one of the few Korean films to be exported to Japan and Manchuria.[10]

While Japanese filmmakers sought increased collaboration between Korean film companies and Japanese studios, which would act as a springboard for them to expand Japan's colonial cinema, at the same time many of Japan's top filmmakers and critics acknowledged the dynamic role that film played in colonial politics and identity building, and encouraged readers of film and entertainment magazines such as *Kinema Junpō*, *Eiga Hyōron*, *Nihon Eiga*, *Eiga Junpō*, *Eiga no tomo*, *Shin Eiga*, and *Nagai New Film* to take a closer look at Korean films. While opinions differed over how much 'Korean-ness' should appear in Korean films, the consensus among Japanese critics was that Korea's film market was a new exhibition and production frontier with great potential for collaborative projects. At the same time, as co-productions were aimed mainly at colonial states such as Korea and Manchuria, they were supported by the Japanese government's desire to amplify its propaganda efforts and imperial ambitions.

Inherent in these efforts at increased collaboration between Korean and Japanese filmmakers in Korea was the desire to create new crossover content for the Japanese-owned cinemas in Korea. Korean audiences were seen as critical for expanding the market for Japanese films, given the exhibition vacuum created after the colonial government's suppression of American and other foreign films after 1937. Increasing the number of productions, particularly co-productions, could also potentially increase exhibition opportunities in Manchuria and the larger Chinese market.[11] This change of direction coincided with the promulgation of the Japan Film Law in August 1939.

Two early films that resulted from Japanese and Korean collaboration were *Tuition* (aka *Tuition Fee*, 1940) and *Miles Away from Happiness* (1941), both the work of Lee Chang-yong. As 'a businessman with a Pan-Asian perspective,'[12] Lee was well-connected in the Japanese film industry and experienced in both Japanese production techniques and Western distribution methods. He began his career as an assistant cinematographer and actor for the Chosun Kinema Company, and went on to study advanced cinematography in Japan at the Shinkō Kinema.[13] On his return to Korea, Lee became the distributor for the Korean Gishin Trading Co. in Seoul, the exclusive direct distribution agency for Paramount Pictures in Korea. While at Gishin, he negotiated nationwide distribution deals, including print rental and exhibition contracts for the Korean talkie, *The Story of Chunhyang* (1935). Anticipating the changes that were coming, Lee formed the Goryeo Film Association in 1936, with plans to export Korean films to markets such as Japan and Manchuria. Its first film was a mediocre melodrama, *Fooled by Love, Hurt by Money* (1939), with an all-Korean cast and crew, but other films followed, most notably *Miles Away from Happiness*.[14] Subsequent projects were all planned as co-productions, either by employing a mixed cast and crew of Koreans and Japanese or working with the Manchurian Motion Picture Association. This approach suggests that Lee was aiming to tap into larger markets outside Korea, especially those countries bound together through the political and economic ideal of East-Asian Co-Prosperity.[15]

Miles Away from Happiness was an ambitious project that aimed to appeal specifically to Koreans and Japanese living in Manchuria. It was a story about Korean immigrants living harmoniously in the region. Complex shooting schedules in multiple locations created delays until Lee connected with the Manchurian Motion Picture Association in 1939.[16] The film was finally completed in 1941, the same year that Choi In-gyu directed the smaller-scale *Tuition* and *Angels on the Streets* (released in both Korea and Japan). All three films were released in Japan in 1941.

These films and others, such as *Military Train* (1938) and *Garden of Victory* (1940), which were made before the film law was promulgated, have been described by some Korean film historians as 'yellow' films, meaning they deliberately chose to eulogize Japan's colonial policies before such a stance became mandatory.[17] Significantly, these films were made before the formation of the state-controlled production system, and thus before the state forced Korean filmmakers to comply with the new restrictive regulations. It seems that Korean filmmakers made these and a small number of other 'yellow' films as a result of willing co-option rather than coercion.[18]

Nevertheless, shortly after the Japan Film Law, which controlled every part of filmmaking including script censorship, came into effect in Japan in April 1939, the Asian film industry experienced a major watershed with the formation of the Chosun Film Artists Association (CFAA). While there was an expectation that the same regulatory measures would soon also take effect in Korea, as had always happened previously, the Korean Colonial Government began corralling local filmmakers into the CFAA as the first step towards consolidating all production companies under a single state-run organization.[19]

In addition, all industry members were required to register for an 'artist card' and to pass a skills test administered by the Library Section of the Bureau of Police Affairs in Seoul before they could work with their Japanese colleagues.[20] These measures effectively created a comprehensive database of those involved in Korea's film industry and ensured that the colonial authorities (as well as Japanese filmmakers) had knowledge of and access to a tightly controlled body of certified talent in Korea.

The CFAA's endorsement of this registration exercise was instrumental in facilitating major changes within the industry. The overall purpose of the group was to help the industry adhere to the measures prescribed by the Japan Film Law. In turn, Korean film people believed that they would benefit by gaining access to equipment and other scarce film supplies and by increasing their opportunities for working with Japanese filmmakers. Ahn Jong-hwa, president of the CFAA, commented that the role of the organization was not only to provide networking opportunities for its members, but also to mobilize them to respond to the needs of the nation.[21] He suggested that the CFAA industry members understood what was expected of them and accepted their responsibility to help transform members of the industry into productive citizens of the empire (Hwangguk Sinminhwa). Ahn even compared the CFAA to a samurai who followed the commands of the emperor.[22] Screenwriters such as Kim Jeong-hyeok, who participated in the planning of *Angels on the Streets*, welcomed this authoritarian body, regarding it as an opportunity for established filmmakers to combine an awareness of Korean identity with the spirit of *naeseon ilche*, a combination which he saw as the *raison d'être* for Korean cinema.[23]

Korean filmmakers had two major reasons to embrace both industry registration and the new co-production initiatives with optimism: first, as a survival tactic that would enable them to overcome technical and financial challenges they could not manage on their own; and second, as an opportunity to work with filmmakers from Japan's major studios, including Shōchiku, Toho, and Shinkō Kinema. Under pressure from the imperial government to embrace the new production system supporting the war, these three companies had their eyes on Korea as a lucrative production venue and believed it would suit them to provide Korean filmmakers with opportunities to gain advanced technical expertise. For the Koreans, collaborative pathways such as these were critical for avoiding censorship in Korea, which became much more restrictive after 1938. It also improved the chances of gaining approval to exhibit a Korean film in Japan, although this was an even harder task than passing the local censor.

Thus, the film industry in Korea was rapidly being transformed from a cinema scene dominated by commercial entertainment films to one shaped by the imperative to churn out propaganda films. The promulgation of the Korean Film Law in 1940 only hastened the process.

THE PRODUCTION SYSTEM UNDER
THE NEW KOREAN FILM LAW

After 1 August 1940, the production, distribution, and exhibition of all films in Korea came under the control of the Korean Film Law, which was an almost exact replica of the 1939 Japan Film Law. The measure set the legal foundations for the new production system.[24] Under the regulations, every member of the industry was required to follow a specific protocol in order to maintain his or her active status. Registration of Korean film artists was mandatory. By the end of 1940, fifty-eight Koreans had registered for their artist identification card, which they were required to carry at all times. By the end of 1941, the figure had increased by 150 percent to eighty-six and included fourteen male producers and ten cinematographers, and forty-four male and eighteen female actors.[25] In order to 'fit in' to the new environment created by the legislation, Korean film workers had begun using the national (Japanese) language and adopting Japanese names and—at least on the surface—expressing the nationalistic ideals expected by the colonial administration.

Koreans had little choice but to remain compliant over Japan's tightening grip on all aspects of cinema culture. The new law removed what little autonomy Koreans had enjoyed in an industry already dominated by Japanese studios and Japanese funding. While a consultative film council (included under the Japan Film Law) gave Japanese filmmakers some say in the development of their local entertainment culture, a similar provision was omitted from the Korean law.[26]

Japanese filmmakers were intimately familiar with the strict regulations promulgated by the Korean Colonial Government because they so closely mirrored their own law of 1939. Korean and Japanese filmmakers sought the best ways to accommodate the new co-production system. The contributions made by Koreans to locally produced films were a key ingredient in reproducing the ideology of 'one nation' with a nuanced, Korean flavor.[27]

In addition, Korea was seen as a needy partner requiring vigorous technical and financial support from Japan. Some Korean filmmakers, such as screenwriter Kim Jeong-hyeok, shared this view. Kim believed that films made by Koreans possessed the potential to bridge authentic Korean culture and the *naeseon ilche* ideology.[28] However, this ideal proved more difficult to achieve than expected. On paper, Korea and Koreans were meant to be treated as equal to Japan and the Japanese. However, in reality, as Caprio (2009) argues, Japan's colonization policy, which aimed for 'the unity of Japan and Korea' and 'the equality of Japan and Korea,' failed to achieve its goal because it was biased towards conditioning Koreans to become more 'Japanese' and to assist Japan's mobilization for war.

Under the new law, all films made in Korea, regardless of who produced them, were subject to censorship for both domestic and foreign audiences. One clause specifically banned any film content with the potential to create disorder in Korea. Films were also banned, both at home and abroad, if they insulted the imperial family or tarnished Japan's political, diplomatic, military, or economic reputation. Film scripts could be banned, and therefore never reach production, if they 'misrepresented' Japanese national culture or detracted from the advance of 'Japan's ideological project' and the smooth governing of Korea. Promoting or glorifying behavior that challenged authority, then, particularly the authority of the Korean Colonial Government, was strictly forbidden, as was the depiction of acts that might corrupt public morals. Finally, all films were expected to embrace the Japanese 'national' language (*kokugo*).[29] (In practice, this had its problems, as language had hitherto been an effective means of distinguishing the physically similar Koreans and Japanese.)

Nevertheless, filmmakers went to considerable lengths to hit this mark. In combination, the films made under the new law can be seen as 'soft power' tools of *naeseon ilche*, used to inspire Koreans of all ages (but primarily students) to offer their hearts, minds, and bodies to the service of the empire. And there were plenty of people to target, given that, in 1940, local film audiences reached more than 20 million viewings a year.[30]

The uncertainty, confusion, and frustration that marked 1941 produced several films that sought to fulfill this ambitious aim, each in its own way. Depicting the ideology of *naeseon ilche* was a common goal, but nothing was clear about how the country, or the film industry, would perform in reality. Ahn Seok-yeong's *Volunteer*,[31] Choi In-gyu's *Angels on the Streets*, Hinatsu Eitarō's (Heo Yeong) *You and I* (aka *You and Me*), and Lee Byeong-il's *Spring in the Korean Peninsula* all showcase some of the shared goals of the time, but with different voices. They exemplify the level of uncertainty and the subsequent aggravation individual filmmakers might have experienced. While some, like Ahn and Choi, cast an optimistic spin on their films, suggesting that all would be well so long as Koreans followed Imperial directives—chiefly volunteering for the war—some, like Hinatsu, went beyond their ideological brief, envisaging a new world where, as a result of obeying the emperor's will, there would be no distinction between Japanese and Korean. Others, like the more pessimistic Lee, tried to convince themselves of a future that would at least be acceptable for Koreans.

Volunteer is an overt propaganda piece, produced to promote the military conscription policy that the Korean Colonial Government enacted in October 1941. With this film, produced by the Korean Donga Film Company, director Ahn Seok-yeong cemented the industry leadership role that he had taken up in 1939 as president of the CFAA. *Volunteer* begins with a dedication by Korean filmmakers to Governor-General Minami. The film focuses on the son of a peasant who finds personal fulfillment after learning that Koreans are eligible to join the Imperial Army. After enlisting, he leaves his family and fiancée behind to join the troops at the front lines. Given its potential role in boosting enlistments, the Korean Colonial Government arranged the distribution of the film across Korea about four months before conscription began.

You and I also promoted the *naeseon ilche* theme. This ten-reel film (around 100 to 120 minutes long) was produced by the Korean Forces Command under the sponsorship of the Korean Government-General and the Reporting Bureau of the Japanese Forces Command. The original screenplay survives and a twenty-five-minute segment was recently discovered in Japan (May 2009), providing a further opportunity to appraise this film text. Like *Volunteer*, *You and I* follows the life of a Korean volunteer soldier who has left home to join his fellow countrymen on the front lines. The film was based on the death at the front lines in China in mid-1939 of Lee In-seok, known as the first Korean volunteer soldier. After his death, Lee In-seok was celebrated as a 'courageous flower' and posthumously promoted to corporal. His family received a gold medal on his behalf. Hinatsu and Iijima Tadashi's script used Lee's life story to promote the military volunteer system. Some critics interpret the film as a recasting of Lee's story as an ultranationalist tale about a loyal volunteer soldier of the Japanese Empire who falls in love with a Japanese woman.[32] The film combines romance and military genres while reaffirming notions of *naeseon ilche*. As a result, *You and I* is considered the exemplar patriotic film from the colonial period.

You and I was directed by Hinatsu (Heo Yeong) under the guidance of the well-known Japanese director Tasaka Tomotaka.[33] Hinatsu was an ethnic Korean filmmaker who 'passed' as Japanese in Japan by disguising his identity under the Japanese name Eitarō Hinatsu.[34] During his late teens and twenties, he studied film and performing arts at Waseda University and worked in the Japanese film industry and also for a short time at the Universum Film AG studio (UFA) in Germany. While in Japan, Hinatsu gained valuable experience working for the Makino Film, Shōchiku, and Shinkō Kinema studios in Kyōtō, as well as assisting the film pioneer Kinugasa Teinosuke.[35] Hinatsu returned to Korea with the idea of making a film about a volunteer and, after sharing the script with friends in the Education Division of the Korean Colonial Government, he was invited to direct *You and I*. His experience and social networks positioned him as an important player in the film scene in Korea.[36] Hinatsu's involvement in the film reveals important details about the complexity of undertaking cooperative filmmaking ventures between Japan and Korea.

Along with his technical contribution to the film, Hinatsu offered both Japanese and Korean audiences a 'thoroughly "colonized" psychology.'[37] *You and I* exposes the suppressed desire of a Korean man under Japanese rule to be recognized by the colonial system and therefore to 'succeed.' 'Success' is primarily defined in terms of volunteering and, indeed, dying for the empire.[38] The film includes a parallel story for Korean women, who are supposed to study hard to become more like Japanese women— that is, to serve as courageous wives of imperial soldiers. The Korean protagonists in the film thus try their best to 'become Japanese' in belief and practice.

Unlike most propaganda films, both the Japanese military and the Korean Colonial Army Information Section assisted with the production of *You and I* by supplying crucial funding and infrastructure. They also arranged special appearances in the film by Governor-General Minami Jirō and Army Commander Itagaki Seishirō, who had been chief of the intelligence section of the Kwantung Army in the early 1930s. The film showcased leading stars from Japan, Manchuria, and Korea, including Korean actresses Moon Yae-bong, Kim Shin-jae, and Hwang Jeong-soon.[39] Actress Shirley Yamaguchi (who had been born to Japanese parents in Manchuria and was also known as Li Xianglan in China and Ri Koran in Japan) also appeared in the film. The Japanese stars included Kosugi Isamu, Miyake Kuniko, Kawazu Kiyosaburō, Maruyama Sadao, Ohinata Den, and Asagiri Kyōko. With its large cast of big-name stars, generous budget, large technical crew, and backed by a sustained publicity campaign, *You and I* was undoubtedly the biggest film made with Korean involvement to date—a 'blockbuster' in today's terms.

Shot on location in Korea, *You and I* involved more than 1,000 actors and extras.[40] A mock volunteer training camp was built for the set, and the main actors were invited to live in the camp in order to give them a realistic sense of what military training involved. To accommodate the unprecedented scale of the production, and to meet its transportation needs, the governor-general provided a special commuting train, and state-of-the-art lighting gear was installed at various shooting locations for night filming. At the time, *You and I* was the largest 'inter-colonial' film project ever undertaken, bringing together Japanese and Korean technicians and years of expertise from the Japanese Shōchiku, Toho, and Shinkō Kinema film companies. Shōchiku handled the screening and promotion of the film in Japan.

Maximum publicity for the film was arranged by Governor-General Minami Jirō, who financed radio and newspaper promotions and subsidized its distribution costs. This enabled cinemas to hold free (but compulsory) screenings for primary, middle, and high-school students as well as members of the public.[41] These free screenings also included *A Pebble by the Wayside* (*Robo no ishi*, or *Roadside Stone*, 1938), a Japanese *Oliver Twist*–like story produced by Nikkatsu and directed by Tasaka Tomotaka.[42] As it happens, *A Pebble by the Wayside* was one of the first films to be highly recommended by the Japanese Ministry of Education and subsequently by the Korean Colonial Government. It also received critical acclaim from the *Cinema Yearbook of Japan, 1939* as the best film of 1938.[43]

The critical reception surrounding *You and I* is as interesting as its production background. Contemporary Korean scholars consider it to be the quintessential 'pro-Japanese' film produced between 1937 and 1945, foregrounding the *naeseon ilche* ideology in a way no other film had done previously.[44] Decades after the war, Hinatsu was seen as fake because of the lengths to which he went to appear Japanese.[45] From a Korean nationalist point of view, the famous Korean director Yu Hyun-mok, who had been taught his trade by colonial filmmakers trained by Japanese, found the film's portrayal of Koreans and Japanese working harmoniously together for the empire absurd, particularly given the coercive nature of 'volunteering' for war service.

Similarly, some Japanese film scholars have described *You and I* as a mockery because of its saturation with propaganda.[46] The film is watchable only because of its plethora of stars and the musical numbers interlaced throughout the story. Nonetheless, when it was originally released in 1941, it received the media spotlight and was swamped by favorable reviews. Director Ahn Seok-yeong affirmed that the power of *You and I* lay in the fact that it was a model film about Japan and Korea as one nation, and contained 'nothing but truth.'[47] At the time, *You and I* was valued as a tangible outcome of the cooperation between Koreans and Japanese, thus reaffirming Japan's supremacy over Korea within a 'harmonious' relationship.[48]

While few local critics dared to comment on the film's aesthetic qualities or its links (or lack thereof) to the Korean film industry, in Japan the response was a little more critical. Critic Hazumi Tsuneo praised the film's propaganda value, but also acknowledged its lack of artistic quality and limited narrative content.[49] Film magazines such as *Shin Eiga* (January 1942: 89) recognized its low commercial potential, warning theater owners 'to expect a rather scanty house after the first day or so'—thus making it an appropriate film for nonpaying audiences.[50]

Despite the film's questionable commercial and ideological success, it helped advance Hinatsu's career. Within a year of the public screenings of *You and I*, the Korean Colonial Government sent Hinatsu to work with the Japanese-backed Java Motion Picture Company in Indonesia, where he continued to make newsreels and cultural films as well as dramatic propaganda films employing local actors. His best-known Indonesian film was *Calling Australia* (1943), a wartime film made with technical support from a Japanese production crew that promoted the 'humane' treatment received by Australian prisoners of war in Japanese army prison camps. Hinatsu became an Indonesian citizen after World War Two, adopted the name Dr. Huyung, and eventually taught film in Yogyakarta. He left behind a significant legacy in Indonesia by training a new generation of local filmmakers through his company Kino Drama Atelier, ironically earning him a place among the founding fathers of Indonesia's postwar cinema.[51]

Angels on the Streets (aka *Homeless Angel*, 1941)

Angels on the Streets (see figure 5.1) was made with an all-Korean cast, including colonial film stars Kim Shin-jae, Lee Wuk-ha, Kim Il-hae, and Mun Ye-bong. A Korean-language drama about homeless children living in an orphanage in Seoul, it was produced by the Goryeo Film Association and directed by Choi In-gyu (also known as Che In-gyu or Sinkei Jaku in Japanese), who had previously directed *Tuition*. At the time of its release, and despite being mainly in Korean (with Japanese subtitles), *Angels on the Streets* was one of the most popular Korean films to be exhibited in Japan,

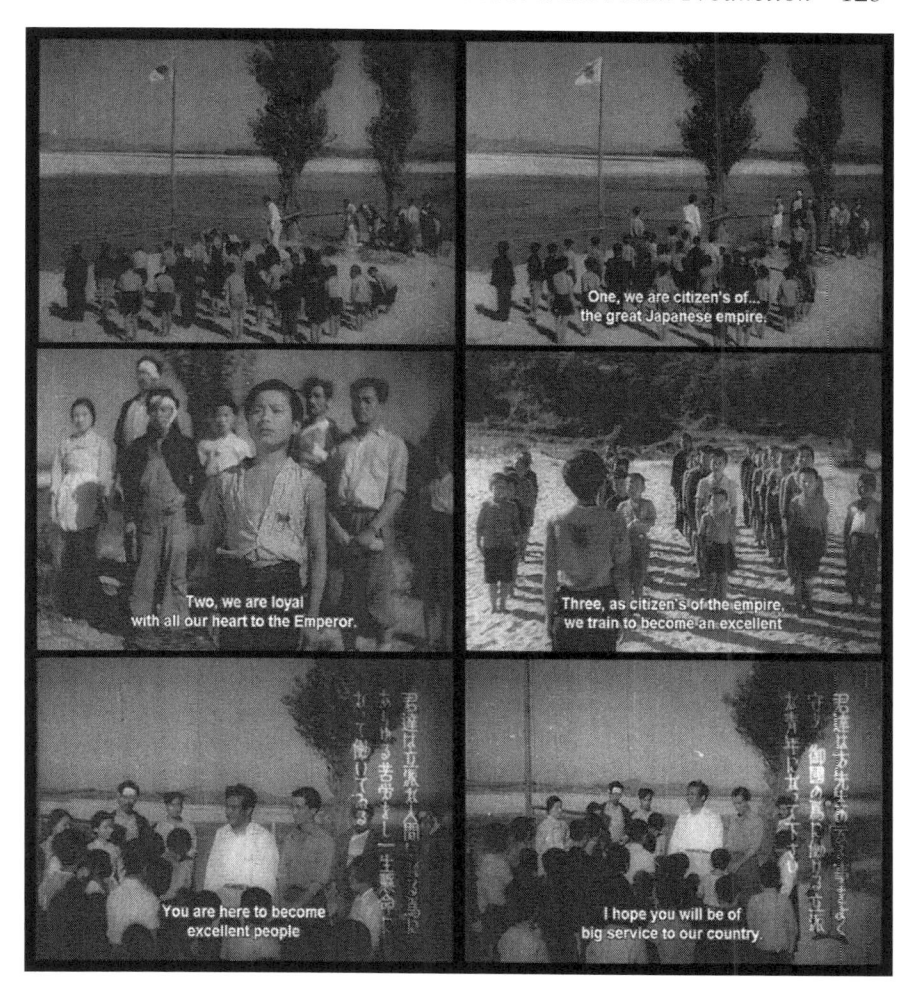

Figure 5.1   Film stills from the Korean Film Archive DVD of *Angels on the Streets* (aka *Homeless Angel*, 1941). Orphans and adults (teacher, doctor-benefactor, and parents) at the beach house near the end of the film pledging their loyalty to the Empire. Note the characters are speaking Korean and that Japanese titles appear along the right side of the frame. Images courtesy of KOFA.

receiving praise as a 'Ministry of Education recommended film.' It was approved by the censorship board in Korea in mid-July 1941, and received a special screening in Japan in September 1941.

However, at odds with this positive reception was the view expressed by the Japanese Home Ministry that the film had been tarnished by scenes portraying Koreans in traditional dress and speaking in their native tongue.[52]

Simply put, *Angels on the Streets* had violated the spirit of the Greater East Asia Co-Prosperity Sphere, primarily by not using the national language. The film reportedly embarrassed the minister of education because the ministry had supported a Korean-language film at a time when speaking Korean was frowned upon by the colonial authorities.[53] Yet the strategy of using the Korean native tongue recommended the film to many Koreans, especially those who had failed to keep up with educational requirements for proficiency in Japanese. Its reception effectively illustrated class as well as racial differences.

However, the Japanese Home Ministry's views on *Angels on the Streets* prevailed and the film was 'reedited' by its censorship office and the Ministry of Education withdrew its formal recommendation.[54] These measures undoubtedly undermined the film's distinctive flair and celebration of national culture. In the revised film, some of the Korean-language scenes were dubbed into Japanese while others were deleted. Coupled with poor dubbing techniques, these changes resulted in a loss of speech synchronization and made the Korean actors sound absurd. Audiences had to endure a seemingly random mix of Korean and Japanese dialogue. For example, the orphans and their priest/teacher mostly spoke in Korean, except when he spoke of important matters. At the end, when the conflicts between the characters have all been resolved, the priest raises the Japanese flag while a boy asks everyone to bow (see figure 5.1). The boy then leads the group as they offer the citizen's pledge of loyalty to the empire in Japanese—a language the orphans never use elsewhere in the film.

The discovery in 2005 of a print of *Angels on the Streets* has shed new light on the film and its possible reception. Watching this film more than half a century after its initial release is instructive, partly because the overt propaganda message at the end demonstrates how thoroughly the Korean filmmakers had embraced the ideology of *naeseon ilche*. There is evidence that this scene, in which the children pledge their loyalty to Japan (close to the end of the film), had been planned from the early scripting stage and was unlikely to have been demanded by the censorship authorities.[55] At the same time, producer Lee Chang-yong was no doubt aware that this ending would meet with the approval of the colonial authorities and censorship offices in both Korea and Japan.

Despite the limitations placed on the industry at this time, *Angels on the Streets* deserves some praise for its aesthetic achievements. Some Korean scholars have noted that the depiction of poverty-stricken, homeless children, played by amateur actors on real locations, predates the major works of the Italian neorealist movement.[56] The strong sense of realism in *Angels on the Streets* undoubtedly reflected the harsh social conditions under which Koreans were living at the time, although this was not intended as a critique of Japanese rule.[57] After completing *Angels on the Streets,* Choi fine-tuned his loyalty to the empire by producing stronger propaganda texts endorsing militarism, thereby elevating the concept of 'collaboration' with the Japanese to the status of a systematic program.

Spring in the Korean Peninsula (1941)

Lee Byeong-il's first film, *Spring in the Korean Peninsula* (see figure 5.2), is a self-referencing piece that provides insights into events both within and outside the film industry in the early 1940s.[58] It demonstrates once again how filmmakers embraced the concept of *naeseon ilche* using feature films as propaganda—a form of 'soft power.' This film is a melodrama, portraying a complex love triangle against the backdrop of colonial Korea's

Figure 5.2   Film stills from the Korean Film Archive DVD of *Spring in the Korean Peninsula* (1941). Top left and top right: on the studio set of the *Chunhyang* film-within-the-film; middle left: outdoor location shoot of *Chunhyang*; middle right: cinema display window featuring a promotional tie-in campaign for *Chunhyang*; bottom left and bottom right: crowds queuing to see *Chunhyang* in Seoul. Images courtesy of KOFA.

film and recording industries, which were struggling as the result of poor production conditions and a lack of funding. Its most intriguing feature is its re-creation of the making of *The Story of Chunhyang* (hereafter *Chunhyang*). This film-within-a-film story has its origins in a traditional folk tale from the Chosun Dynasty that captures the essence of Korean culture and society but also provides a vehicle for overt commentary on the dire condition of the film industry. (More description of the traditional Chunhyang story appears in the previous chapter.)

In the story, the producer of *Chunhyang* attempts to cast his friend's sister in the film, eventually securing a role for her when the lead actress is fired. Predictably, the producer and sister fall in love. The production carries on until the owner of the record company where the woman used to work tries to seduce her. When this scheme fails, he withdraws his investment funding and halts production of the film. Acting out of desperation, the producer steals money from the record company, but is caught and sent to jail. However, the police show compassion on him and free him as he has no criminal record and shows promise in the film industry. In the meantime, a new film company (Bando Film) is created.

The local film industry portrayed in the film serves as a metaphor for productions in the Korean film industry of the time. At a dinner ceremony, the company president announces that Bando will make cultural enlightenment films presenting Japan and Korea as one nation, and their first project will be the completion of *Chunhyang*. However, not everyone at the ceremony is overjoyed about the company's formation and its takeover of *Chunhyang*. The director has no money to rent a production office, and the company's filmmaking methods lag far behind those of Japan proper. His melancholy is in stark contrast to the happy scenes around him.

After all the intersecting love interests have been untangled, the producer (accompanied by his friend's sister) is sent to Japan on a special mission. As the chosen representative of the Korean film industry, he is charged with visiting all of Tokyo's film studios to learn the best methods of mutual cooperation, all in the name of *naeseon ilche*. It seems that the only real opportunities for Korean filmmakers lie in or with Japan. Collaborating with Japanese filmmakers and serving the demands of the Greater East Asia Co-Prosperity Sphere is held up as the one ray of hope for the local industry's future. Yet, a concluding shot zooming into a close-up of the director's solemn face leaves us with a radically different feeling. While the producer (and his fiancée) may be heading for prosperity in Japan, his friends are visibly downbeat about his departure. All they have to look forward to is a continuation of the bleak industrial, social, political, and cultural conditions that they are presently enduring.

During a key shooting scene, the director in the story emphasizes that a good film requires more than artistry and passion; it needs ample funding and a professional production strategy. In other words, the Korean landscapes and glimpses of everyday life captured by *Chunhyang* could have been portrayed with higher standards and production values if the film-makers had had access to better equipment and funding.

Mirroring the tensions surrounding the idea of nationalism in the original tale of Chunhyang, *Spring in the Korean Peninsula* offers complex layers of contradiction above and beyond its melodramatic themes. On the one hand, its narrative embraces Korean cultural traditions through its focus on and retelling of the Chunhyang story. On the other hand, and at another level, the portrayal of a successfully completed film under the new, pro-Japanese film company reflects some key developments in the industry—the advent of the consolidated state-run Chosun Film Production Corporation and the Korean Colonial Government's ideologically driven push for a unified front among Japanese and Korean filmmakers.

Spring in the Korean Peninsula was a box-office success, reflected in the seemingly endless queue seen in the documentary footage of the cinema hosting its opening. Interestingly, this footage was taken on the day that Shirley Yamaguchi made a guest visit to the Myeongchijwa to celebrate the release of her film *Beautiful Sacrifice* (1939), the name of which appears on a multistory outdoor billboard.[59] Other films evident in this clip that were showing at the cinema at the same time also carried messages of loyalty to the empire and praise for the expansion of the Greater East Asia Co-Prosperity Sphere and Japanese migration to its frontiers. For example, Mizoguchi Kenji's *Geido Ichidai Otoko* (or *The Life of an Artist*, 1941), a Meiji-period film scripted by Yoshikata Yoda, explored issues of loyalty among artists and aimed 'to stimulate a recognition of Japanese "spirit" through its [Japan's] most prestigious literary and artistic tradition.'[60] Also showing was *Toda-ke no Kyodai* (aka *Toda Brother and His Sisters*, or *Brothers and Sisters of the Toda Clan*, 1941), one of the first films that Ozu Yasujirō directed after his release from the Japanese military. This film, which became a box-office hit in Japan (and also probably in Korea), centers on 'various Japanese attitudes toward motherhood as an institution' within the setting of successful emigration to Manchuria.[61]

Signs of other foreign films, which also explored themes of testing the boundaries of loyalty and were actually showing in Korea at this time, can be found in the sets and shooting locations in *Spring in the Korean Peninsula*. For instance, a giant poster of Jean Benoît-Lévy's *Hélène* (1936) appears in the cinema dressing room in the film. Other large posters of Julien Duvivier's murder thriller *La tête d'un homme* (1933), Robert Siodmak's melodrama horror film *Mister Flow* (1936), and Willy Forst's *Burgtheater* (1936) appear on the walls of the small production company's office. Posters for Fyodor Otsep's *Amok* (1934) and Karl Hartl's *So endete eine Liebe* (*End of an Affair* 1934) hang in a stairwell of the cinema showing *Chunhyang*. Arnold Fanck's *Ein Robinson* (1940)—a German version of Daniel Defoe's Robinson Crusoe novel—also appears on the 'now showing' outdoor billboard advertisement mentioned above.[62] Several of these films were also exhibited in the United States Army occupation period, which is discussed in the next chapter.

With these resonances in mind, it is highly significant that *Chunhyang* was used as the story for the film-within-a-film because of the nationalistic response it could have inspired among Koreans (compare the responses to the talkie version of 1935 discussed in chapter 4). In addition, the film may have been in part an autobiographical vehicle to depict the professional jealousy that Lee's Korean colleagues may have felt as a result of his time spent in Japan with Nikkatsu between 1934 and 1940. In any event, the characters' aims and indeed the messages carried by this film mirror the challenges Lee faced working under Japanese filmmakers and with Japanese production methods. Presumably, *Spring in the Korean Peninsula* reflects his pessimism over future opportunities for filmmaking in Korea and the empire as a whole. In 1942, the Goryeo Film Association was taken over by the Chosun Film Production Corporation, forcing Lee to abandon his vision of setting up his own inter-Asian film production and distribution company.

In the heady year of 1941, individual filmmakers still enjoyed some freedom to seek ways of achieving their dreams—but with the consolidation of the film industry in 1942, even this narrow avenue was closed to them. In 1943, Hinatsu was in Indonesia, making yet another Japanese propaganda film, unaware that he would end up stranded in southern Asia. Director Lee Byeong-il was inactive for the rest of the colonial period, but made a striking comeback in 1956 in South Korea with an award-winning comedy, *A Wedding Day*. Director Choi In-gyu actively participated in the new production system by directing explicit propaganda films such as *Children of the Sun* (1944), *Vow of Love* (1945), and *Sons of the Sky* (1945), failing to follow up on his striking use of realism in *Angels on the Streets*. Only director Ahn Seok-yeong continued along his established path, directing another propaganda film, *Rural Life*, in 1942 to encourage ginseng growing.

AFTER CONSOLIDATION

The increasing number of Japanese films being distributed in Korea after 1937 signaled a need for the Korean Colonial Government to consolidate distribution before production. Following the distribution merger and the subsequent formation of the consolidated Chosun Film Distribution Corporation (hereafter CFDC) in April 1942 and the Chosun Film Production Corporation (hereafter CFPC) in September 1942, attending 'educational' films became compulsory for Koreans. This carried on a practice that had begun with the film *Japanese Capability*, made by the Seoul Talkie Film Co. (Kyeongseong Balseong Yeonghwa Jejakso) in September 1941.[63] This large-scale reorganization of the industry enabled the occupying power to increase its draconian control over the industry and to harness filmmaking as a key tool for spreading Japanese 'national' culture.

Around the time that all the distribution companies were fully merged, one of the first Japanese films to receive an official recommendation as an educational film from the Korean Colonial Government was Toho's *Horse* (*Uma*, 1941), directed by Yamamoto Kajirō.[64] This drama, set in Northern Japan, tells the story of the daughter of a poor farming family who raises a colt. The girl loves the horse dearly but, when it is grown, the government decides to auction it to the army in the annual autumn horse market. The young girl protests and in doing so demonstrates her selfless loyalty to her family and their farm, which is in debt. Other films to receive such a recommendation included *The First Submarine*; *Family of Love*; *Air Base*, Uchida Tomu's *Earth* (Nikkatsu, 1939), about the difficult lives of poor farmers; and Koishi Eiichi's 'war-in-the-air' film *Soaring Passion* (1941), about a farm boy's dream of becoming a pilot.[65]

As a result of Japan's wartime economy and regulations under the Japan Film Law, the Japanese government had begun reducing the number of films produced and film prints developed in order to conserve raw film supplies. As a consequence of this change, only three major Japanese film companies survived: Shōchiku, Toho, and Daiei. In 1942, the film law further restricted these three companies to a combined total of sixty feature-length dramatic films (20 each) to be made in Japan per year.[66] Similar cuts were also to affect Korea's film industry, but not until later, enabling the industry to prepare for the changes to come. Production and distribution companies on both sides of the East Sea were thus swallowed up by a handful of consolidated state-run companies under the pretext of ration-managing raw film supplies and producing essential patriotic films. Their combined function was to serve as a propaganda factory which existed only to create and market films promoting the empire's one-nation policy.

According to Hirokawa Sōyō of the Chosun Film Culture Research Institution, the CFPC had two purposes in producing films: firstly, to educate Korea's 'illiterate' population; and, secondly, to promote Japan's development of Korea to Japanese audiences and other peoples throughout the empire, including Koreans living and working in Japan.[67] Tanaka Saburo, the deputy chairman of the Seoul Chamber of Commerce and Industry, was appointed president of both state-run organizations, the CFDC and the CFPC, in order to streamline industry control. Given the centrality and significance of his twin roles at the zenith of the film industry, Tanaka became a very powerful man.[68] Following consolidation, the CFPC consisted of twenty-five directors, twenty-five cinematographers, forty-nine engineers, and sixty-five actors.[69] The Library Section oversaw the consolidation process and drafted the company articles. It seems that the CFPC was managed primarily by Japanese staff, who received funding from the Korean Colonial Government and technical and manpower support from Japan proper.

Prior to consolidation, ten major film companies had been the driving force of the industry; all were members of the Korea Film Association (KFA,

Chosun Yeonghwa Hyeophoe) and the Korean Film Producers' Association (Chosun Yeonghwa Jejakja Hyeophoe).[70] Before they were consolidated under the CFPC banner, more than half of these production companies had been owned by Japanese businessmen. At the beginning of 1943, due to escalating shortages of raw film stock, the Korean Colonial Government restricted the CFPC to producing only four dramatic features and four cultural films for the year, reducing its previous level of activity by one-third. However, the previous limit of twelve newsreels per year was retained. The company was under pressure to put aside profit motives. In the eyes of the Korean Colonial Government, the CFPC's ability to reach the largest possible audience was the critical measure of 'success.' The CFPC was now unable to compete with the scale and funding levels of Japanese productions, which now dominated the Korean market. The profits returned by three Japanese film companies active in the Korean market for the spring financial quarter in 1942 were: Toho, ¥172,000; Shōchiku, ¥163,000; and Daiei, ¥127,000—figures which Korean production houses could not hope to match.[71] In fact, their options were limited as a result of the vacuum created by the Korean Colonial Government with its near ban on the exhibition of Hollywood films.[72]

Although its production facilities were limited, the CFPC still possessed ample equipment to produce the *Korea Review* (Chōsen Jihō), a monthly newsreel first screened in December 1942. This series included footage of horse-riding tournaments, prayer ceremonies, New Year's celebrations in farming villages, prisoners of war, speeches by the governor-general, ice skating and other winter sports, and assembly-line workers at munitions factories. The CFPC's low-budget 'cultural' films included *Commissioner Tanaka's Speech*, commissioned by the Intelligence Section of the Korean Colonial Government; *Governor-General Koiso's Inspection Trip to the Unzan Mine*, commissioned by the Japan Mining Company; and *We Will Advance Now*, a short film that promoted Shintō practices and aimed to inspire Koreans to become 'good' imperial citizens, which were the central aims of the Korean League for the People's Collective Energy (*Kokumin Sōryoku Chōsen Renmei*, aka Korean Branch of the National General Strengthening Federation). Other short cultural films included *Angels in White Go Overseas* (*Tatakau hakui no tenshi, umi o wataru*), about army nurses, and *One Hundred Patriotic Poems* (*Aikoku hyakunin isshu*). Along with newsreel segments and feature-length films, these offerings were designed to build national pride in Japan's war effort.

The CFPC began producing feature-length dramatic films in April 1943, shortly before the seventh *Korean Review* newsreel was completed and screened. Its first two feature films were *Portrait of Youth* and *The Straits of Chosun*. When the local film industry merged into the CFPC and thus came directly under the control of the Korean Colonial Government, a number of critical questions arose: What will 'Chosun' films be like? How will 'Chosun' films differ from those produced before the CFPC?

According to Kuramochi Shūzō, a manager of the Chosun Army News Service, Chosun films were the equal of Japanese films and yet in need of something distinctively Korean, that is, 'the taste of kimchi.'[73] Films produced in Korea following the advent of the war-preparation system in 1937 had been co-productions or hybrid films, containing a mix of actors and crew from Korea, Japan, and China/Manchuria, with a mixture of Korean and Japanese languages spoken on screen. Worsening wartime conditions required the compliance of Koreans across all sectors of society, and the 'national language' (Japanese) had yet to achieve the universal adoption desired by the colonial authorities. In order to reach the masses effectively, the Korean Colonial Government still needed to employ some Korean-language material in the cultural content it produced. Nonetheless, according to the scholar Karashima Takeshi, the gradual elimination of 'Korean-ness' in locally produced films was one of the CFPC's primary aims. This situation illustrates the wide gap between the ideal and the practice of *naeseon ilche*.[74]

Karashima's assessment chimed in with the views of Japanese critics like Kuroda Shōzō, for whom the purpose of a Chosun national film was to inspire people of all types to live joyfully for the emperor.[75] Clearly, with Japan's growing involvement in the Pacific war, the nation needed to recruit more soldiers to fight at the front lines. Koreans were among the obvious candidates to be trained as loyal soldiers. Language policy was modified to this end. Even though Japanese was designated as the primary language in Korean films, government censor Ikeda Kunio believed in allowing some Korean in certain scenes involving, for example, military conscription, in order to expedite an educational effect.[76] The following discussion of three films illustrates how this effect worked on screen. The first three films produced by the CFPC, *Suicide Troops of the Watchtower* (1943), *Straits of Chosun* (1943), and *Portrait of Youth* (1943), provided a model for imperial filmmakers to follow, demonstrating how co-production ventures involving the CFPC and the Japanese film companies could be completed without any difficulty. They all contained the same message: Koreans as imperial citizens.[77] Distinct from co-productions led by an individual director or producer, these three co-produced state films were entirely planned, funded, and completed by the CFPC with the explicit support of the colonial government.

Suicide Troops of the Watchtower (1943)

A Japanese-Korean propaganda 'co-production' made between Toho and the CFPC, *Suicide Troops of the Watchtower* emulated the American action films popular with local audiences while utilizing the conventions of Japanese wartime documentaries.[78] As with *You and I*, the Korean Colonial Government supported *Suicide Troops of the Watchtower* with financial and in-kind infrastructural support over its three-year production period. It was directed by Imai Tadashi, who later became a prolific and controversial film director who infused strong left-wing ideology into his films; the assistant director was Choi In-gyu, of *Tuition* and *Angels on the Streets* fame. The film starred popular Japanese actors Takada Minoru, and Hara Setsuko, known for her many roles in Japanese war films, and the well-known Korean actors Kim Shin-jae and Jeon Ok.

Resembling American action stories of the period such as *I Am a Fugitive from a Chain Gang* (1932), *Mutiny on the Bounty* (1935), and *Captain Blood* (1935)—which also screened in Korea in the 1930s—and drawing on Japanese wartime documentary aesthetics, the film's action is set around a large border security watchtower in North Pyeongan in the north of Korea. The story portrays the selfless devotion of border policemen in Korea and Manchuria in 1935, before the outbreak of the Second Sino-Japanese War. In the village surrounding the watchtower, Japanese, Chinese, and Koreans live together in harmony. Attacks from vicious Chinese bandits (resistance groups opposed to Japanese occupation and thus enemies of the state) threaten their peaceful life. In one scene, a Korean policeman and a Chinese restaurant owner are killed while confronting these bandits. When the battle begins, villagers hide in the local police station and contemplate suicide rather than face surrender to the bandits. At the last minute they are saved by the Japanese authorities who defeat the insurgents.[79]

Most of the dialogue in *Suicide Troops of the Watchtower* is in Japanese, even when the Chinese restaurant owner converses with his son. Korean is only heard momentarily, when Koreans in the film are asked to use their native tongue. A small party scene in the yard of the police station shows the peaceful atmosphere of the border village in which Koreans and Japanese live in harmony together. Once the alcohol is flowing, the group begins singing in Japanese. Then, a Japanese policeman asks one of the Korean policemen to sing a traditional Korean folk song, at which point another Korean launches into a Korean-style dance. Despite this touching moment, various details reinforce the reality that languages other than Japanese are frowned upon—for example, signs beside a phone and in a classroom that read, 'Use only the national language.' A further example of *naeseon ilche* is seen at the end of the film when the Korean characters assert that they would rather die with their Japanese neighbors than be caught by the resistance. Even a young mother with a baby would rather shoot herself and her baby under the direction of Takazu, the police chief. This Japanese-style group suicide, a practice rarely found in Korea, is accepted unconditionally by each character as a sign of their undying loyalty to the empire. (In reality, when Japan withdrew its troops from Manchuria in 1945, many villages loyal to the empire were totally unprepared for independence and feared retaliation by Chinese insurgents, resulting in mass suicides.[80]) Whatever its shortcomings, *Suicide Troops of the Watchtower* entertained sizable audiences in Korea, earning a reported total of ¥97,148 in Seoul, Pyongyang, and Pusan.[81]

Straits of Chosun (1943)

Straits of Chosun (see figure 5.3) was produced by Tanaka Saburo and directed by Park Gi-chae, who had previously directed *Spring Wind* (1935), *Heartlessness* (1939), and the pro-Japanese film *I Will Go* (1942). Lee Myeong-wu was the cinematographer.[82] The film was shot almost entirely

Figure 5.3   Film stills from the Korean Film Archive DVD of *Straits of Chosun* (1943). Top left: Korean conscripts training to fight in the Second Sino-Japanese War; top right and middle left: Korean conscripts at the front lines; middle right: wife working in the factory in Korea – the sounds of the sewing machine overlapping with the machinegun fire; bottom left: Seong-gi and his wife's shared flashback of their romantic time together before his conscription; bottom right: ending shot with Seong-gi and his nurse staring across the Straits of Chosun, longing for Korea and his family. Images courtesy of KOFA.

on outdoor locations, featuring stars Kim Shin-jae, Moon Yae-bong, Nam Seung-min, and Dok Eun-gi and an almost all-Korean-born production staff. The film focuses on the patriotism of a volunteer soldier's family and promotes the virtues of volunteering for military service. It also showcases the need for noble Korean families (*yangban* in terms of Korea's old class system) to overcome their fear of sending their sons to war and potentially losing their descendants. Korea's long-standing tradition of protecting family lines through the eldest son became a significant obstacle to the recruitment drive overseen by the Korean Colonial Government. To overcome this objection, the government suggested an alternative way for families to continue their bloodline through their second son. It is against this background that the film encourages all male Koreans of military age to become soldiers of the empire, no matter what their background or place in their family lineage, thus glorifying Korea's participation in the war and the sacrifice of its young men as a matter of family honor. The film also encouraged Korea's daughters to play their part in the war—in ways similar to those used in U.S. government media campaigns promoting 'Rosie the Riveter' and women factory workers during World War II.

Straits of Chosun, which was spoken entirely in Japanese, deals with the unbridled dedication of a conscript and his wife, who works at a factory to support the war at home. This Korean ideal couple is willing to do almost anything to protect the unity and integrity of their family. The conscript, Seong-gi (Seki in Japanese), desires to become a proud husband and father, while his wife, Geum-suk (Kinshuku in Japanese), would like nothing more than to be a proud wife and mother. Seong-gi's elder brother, a volunteer soldier, dies in the conflict and brings honor to the family while the lazy Seong-gi brings shame to his father. Seong-gi eventually volunteers for the war to make his father happy, but leaves behind his wife, who, unknown to him, is pregnant. She gives birth to a son, and tries to make ends meet by working in a sewing factory. He is injured in battle and, simultaneously, she is shown collapsing due to fatigue. The film cuts between their hospital beds, located on opposite sides of the Straits of Chosun, and the characters are united through a phone call, with Seong-gi's parents standing at Geum-suk's bedside.

Not only does *Straits of Chosun* portray volunteer soldiers as loyal heroes of the empire, but it also praises women for doing their part in the war-preparation effort. It also makes the point that mobilizing each citizen of Korea, and thus the empire, is needed for Japan to win the war and realize the aims of the Greater East Asia Co-Prosperity Sphere. However, *Straits of Chosun* was not well-received, generally being seen as an unsuccessful attempt to introduce militaristic propaganda into the family melodrama genre that was popular at the time.[83] The injection of political ideology into drama sat uneasily with the popular Hollywood films shown in Korea between 1926 and 1936. Nevertheless, *Straits of Chosun* attracted nearly 140,000 viewers in Seoul, Pyongyang, and Pusan, generating ¥881,341 in box-office proceeds.[84]

Portrait of Youth (1943)

Portrait of Youth was another film produced explicitly to mobilize Korean volunteers for the military conscription program that was scheduled to begin in 1944. Both films were made shortly after the Korean Colonial Government announced the program in May 1942, and around the time of the formation of the CFPC. Like *You and I*, *Portrait of Youth* was produced with the crucial support of Japanese production companies Shōchiku, Toho, and Daiei, a factor which no doubt contributed to its positive critical response. Written by Hatta Hisayuki, who had been a writer for Shōchiku, it was directed by Toyoda Shirō, with cinematography by Miura Mitsuo from Toho. Unlike the films discussed above, *Portrait of Youth* was shot on location on Shirouma Mountain in Japan, and at the Daiei Studios. There were also scenes shot on location in Korea. Top Korean stars Bok Hye-suk, Lee Geum-ryong, Seo Wol-yeong, and Nam Hong-il featured in the film, along with Japanese actors Maruyama Sadao, Kiyokawa Sōji, Mitani Yukiko, and Sayama Akira from the Toho, Daiei, and Shōchiku studios.

The propaganda message in *Portrait of Youth* is eloquently summarized by Nakayama, a middle-school student who confides in his teacher his dream of becoming a soldier. Initially, he is diffident about the subject because his father wants him to become a doctor. Nakayama has nurtured this ambition since 1942, the day he learned that Koreans could join the military. In this little boy's eyes, joining the imperial forces is the way to become 'Japanese.' However, in reality, the film's message was contradictory—joining the army *to become Japanese* and thus embody the concept of *naeseon ilche* only served to remind both Koreans and Japanese that they were different from the outset. In addition, the prospect of full citizenship in the long term after the war was never more than a vague hope.

Yet, the film's message is carried beyond one boy's dream of soldiering for the empire. In one scene, the army rescues a group of skiing students who have become stranded in a snowstorm. In a thinly disguised appeal to local audiences, the Japanese commander (Tsukigata Ryūnosuke) emphatically declares that all the students are the emperor's children and therefore must be rescued at all costs. The snowstorm scenes filmed on Shirouma Mountain must have thrilled audiences at the time. The film received a formal recommendation by the Japanese Ministry of Education, and was screened in Japan in early December 1943.[85]

A number of other films produced between 1943 and 1945 recycled similar military themes to those addressed in *Portrait of Youth*. Directed by Kim Yeong-hwa, *Look Up at the Blue Sky* (1943; not to be confused with Lee Gyu-hwan's *Blue Sky* made in 1941) used model airplanes to encourage students to imagine themselves as future air force pilots. Next came *Story of Big Whales* (1944), a recruitment and educational film about apprenticing in the whaling industry and the importance of developing the industry as a source of sustainable resources, which had become scarce during the war. *Dear Soldier* (Mr. *Soldier*, 1944) extended the military conscription theme by focusing on a courageous young man who is diligently preparing to become an imperial solider. In a direct attempt to appeal to the audience and to assuage their potential fears about the enemy, the film emphasizes the deep sense of pride that the young man's parents feel as they send their son off to war. Thus, the film reassured the families of conscripted sons that they were all good servants of the empire. As a kind of sequel to Ahn Seok-yeong's *Volunteer*, *Dear Soldier* attempted to generate positive images of military training camps in order to ensure a positive future for the military conscription program. *Children of the Sun* (1944) is about a female primary-school teacher, played by Kim Shin-jae, who educates students about volunteering for the military. Other 'message films' designed to recruit young Koreans and educate them about military service included Choi In-gyu's *Vow of Love* (1945) and *Sons of the Sky* (1945). The former focuses on a newly arrived Japanese teacher at a Korean elementary school who teaches his students about Japanese customs and persuades them to embrace loyalty to the Japanese Empire. In doing so, he glorifies *kamikaze* suicide flying missions, a real-life practice that began in late 1944 and aimed to destroy Allied shipping.

Locally co-produced military recruitment films were not the only films on offer to cinema audiences in colonial Korea. Also exhibited were numerous Japanese films such as Makino Masahiro's *Opium War* (*Ahen Senso*, 1943), starring Hara Setsuko, Mizoguchi Kenji's *The 47 Ronin* (*Genroku Chūshingura*, 1941), and *The War at Sea from Hawaii to Malaya* (*Hawai Marē oki kaisen*, 1942), to name only a few.[86] These were all films that had passed censorship in Japan, but had been recensored for exhibition in Korea. After undergoing this required double censorship process, most films were given the status of a 'government-recommended film' in Korea, the equivalent of the Ministry of Education recommendation for a film in Japan. The double censorship process was an important revenue-raising mechanism that allowed the censorship apparatus to subsidize its own operations, and few films were barred as a result of this process.

Shortly after the CFDC was formed in April 1942, it began distributing the *Nippon News*, which was added to the compulsory list of film screenings. The Korean Colonial Government had strongly encouraged students to watch these newsreels (along with the ultranationalistic docudrama war films mentioned above) under the supervision of their teachers and school principals. In addition to producing newsreels, the CFPC also made short cultural and educational films such as *Revive Earth* (*Yomigaeru tsuchi*), an agricultural film about protecting crops during the winter; *The Prisoners of War Who Came to Korea* (*Chosen ni kita furyo*), a film about British prisoners in Korean prison camps; and Morinaga Kenjirō's *1944* (*Showa 19-nen*), a film about the enforcement of the Korean conscription system in 1944.[87] Other films included *Girls on the Peninsula* (Hanto no otometachi), a musical about schoolgirls and single women working in factories and on farms;

Glorious Day (Eikō no hi), a film about the naval volunteer system that was screened on Naval Day (27 May) in 1943; *Shining Victory* (*Kagayaku shōri*), a promotional film about the public donation of copper and brass for the war effort; and various documentaries about power generation.

While feature filmmaking focused on promoting militarism and volunteer recruitment, these cultural films produced during the same period dealt with a greater variety of subjects that aimed to 'educate' and 'enlighten' Koreans. Farmers and, later, schoolchildren were the primary targets of these cultural films. In the early 1940s, cinemas were located primarily in the larger cities, where cinema-going ratios per capita were high. Data recorded in April 1943 shows one cinema for every 117,607 people in Kyeonggi Province (equating to twenty cinemas), and one for every 332,068 in South Jeolla Province (seven cinemas).[88]

Between 1942 and Japan's surrender in 1945, the CFDC used its collection of cultural films, combined with the officially 'recommended' feature-length military dramas, to reach out to those Koreans who had limited opportunities to see these films at a cinema. To achieve this, the CFDC created a highly organized national traveling film network known as the Chosun Film Enlightenment Association (Chōsen Eiga Keihatsu kyōkai, CFEA). It provided workers on farms and in fishing villages, mines, and other factories with 'wholesome' entertainment while 'enlightening' them about colonial government policy and Japanese initiatives for developing Korea.[89] In effect, the CFEA was created by consolidating the mobile exhibition units that had previously been run on an ad hoc basis by the internal affairs section of each prefecture. These initiatives were ostensibly modeled on the mobile film screening units operated since around 1918 by the Russian Army out of AGIT (agitation-propaganda) trains.[90] Their main purpose, as in the case of the cultural films produced in Korea, was to maintain national morale by disseminating informative films, books, newspapers, and posters about the Bolshevik revolution to soldiers at the front and farmers and peasants in the countryside. Likewise, in the 1940s, Nazi Germany operated mobile film units in trucks with portable projectors and generators to screen current affairs newsreels to front-line troops to keep their spirits high. Given the program's reputation, few obstacles prevented the CFEA from reaching audiences, even in relatively remote farming villages. Throughout 1942, the CFEA conducted 3,665 screenings to more than 5 million people.[91] After 1943, however, the organization realized that it could have a more effective impact on Korean society by targeting public school students, the next generation of loyal imperial subjects.

The arrival of the CFEA's traveling film shows drew people from everywhere. According to a report by the Censorship Section of the Korean Colonial Government Bureau of Police Affairs, rural women carrying their babies eagerly walked up to sixteen miles round-trip in harsh weather to see a mobile film screening.[92] In this way, the CFEA was responsible for creating new exhibition opportunities for the film industry, given that the construction of new permanent cinemas was a low priority during this period. The traveling films that the CFEA exhibited played a crucial role in the Korean Colonial Government's film education strategy.

In addition to making and exhibiting films, the CFPC also began meticulously recording all film-related events and activities, thereby contributing directly to the policing of the industry.

UNFORESEEN FUTURE OF CINEMA IN KOREA

During the early 1940s, articles by scholars and government officials in Japanese film magazines were preoccupied with discussions of the future of filmmaking in Korea. 'Education' and 'enlightenment' in the context of the Greater East Asia Co-Prosperity Sphere were the concepts most frequently rehearsed. According to Karashima, a professor at Keijo University, Koreans were both uneducated and unintelligent, and thus one of the primary roles of the consolidated Chosun Film Corporation was to develop a new history and a new culture for Korea.[93] According to articles published in a range of popular Japanese film magazines during this period that are discussed in this chapter, the industrial and political changes taking place in Korea's film landscape signaled a new beginning for the local film history— one which was the ultimate culmination of thirty years of Japanese rule over Korea and its film industry. In contrast, contemporary Korean scholars view this period not as fashioning a guiding light for the future, but as the beginning of the end of any creative freedom for the industry.[94]

As we have seen, during this period of Korea's occupied cinema the nation's rulers aimed to prepare the colony and its people to transform themselves into citizens of the most advanced civilization in Asia—in other words, to be assimilated into Japan. On the surface, this idea of a 'new beginning' was shared by the Korean film industry, as its members attempted to embrace *naeseon ilche* in various ways in order to remain active in the industry. As the film examples discussed above illustrate, in the late 1930s and early 1940s Korean filmmakers were able to extend their careers and employ advanced production technology under more stable funding conditions than they had ever known. According to director, scriptwriter, critic, and film historian Hazumi Tsuneo, the level of passion shown by Korean filmmakers in the late 1930s enabled them to overcome their lack of access to modern technology.[95] In reality, however, Korean filmmakers were able to make substantial contributions to only a small number of films during this tumultuous period.

6 Disarming Japan's Cannons with Hollywood's Cameras
Cinema in Korea Under U.S. Occupation, 1945–1948[1]

In July 1950, within days of the start of the Korean War, hundreds of 16mm prints of Hollywood feature and short films and more than fifty film projectors were rushed from Japan to U.S. Army and United Nations troops in the field. With many thousands of movies and over one thousand new projectors eventually sent from the United States, the Motion Picture Division of the Army's General Headquarters, Far Eastern Command, went to great lengths to entertain the troops with some of the latest commercial releases—such as *Sunset Boulevard* (1950), *The Next Voice You Hear* (1950), *The Black Rose* (1950), and *Father of the Bride* (1950)—as well as Disney animations and current newsreels of the war.[2]

On-screen entertainment was available to soldiers in the field almost every night throughout the three-year conflict. Troops swapped foxhole assignments and huddled inside abandoned railroad tunnels, burned-out houses and half-bombed buildings, and endured rain and freezing weather to catch a glimpse of films that were often simply projected onto walls or hanging bedsheets. In the words of one anonymous soldier, "When you go to the movies over here, you get out of Korea for a couple of hours."[3] These daily Hollywood film screenings were a critical catalyst for raising the morale and national spirit of the troops on the front lines in Korea—an intriguing military strategy for bolstering the fight for democracy.

Nonetheless, this was not the first time that Hollywood films played a vital role in military affairs in Korea. Within seven months of Korea's liberation from Japanese colonial rule (1910–1945), and after the United States and Russia had carved the country in half, U.S. film distributors rushed their most popular films to the southern half of the Korean Peninsula. They were simply following the adage 'trade follows the flag,'[4] even as Lt. General John R. Hodge and his U.S. Occupation forces were disarming the Japanese military.[5] Amid chaotic social, political, and cultural change, local cinemas were inundated with a range of genre films from Hollywood. These were productions that the U.S. Army Military Government in Korea (hereafter USAMGIK, 1945–1948)—under the definitive command of General Douglas MacArthur, the Supreme Commander for the Allied Powers (hereafter SCAP), and the advice from the Central Motion Picture

Exchange (hereafter CMPE), the U.S. film industry's East Asian outpost—believed would assist them to reverse four decades of Japanese influence. In particular, these films, which are discussed in this chapter, were believed to inculcate a sense of 'liberty' among Koreans.

Despite the monumental size of this undertaking, most histories of the USAMGIK period lack a sustained discussion of this significant cultural aspect of the USAMGIK's occupation strategy and its impact on local culture.[6] These previous studies mostly focus on politics and the economy—not culture, and especially not film policy.

Until now, little has been published in either Korean or English about the hundreds of American films—made with 'Hollywood's cameras,' in contradiction to Japan's now silenced 'cannons' (see figure 6.1)—that were targeted explicitly at Korean audiences through advertisements in Korean-language newspapers.[7] Indeed, this plethora of films was consumed by thousands upon thousands of local cinema-goers, including, of course, U.S. Army personnel. Most standard Korean film histories pay much more attention to the hardships and conflicts of Korean filmmakers in the era, and see Hollywood's domination of Korean screens as a threat to local culture.[8] These studies are rightly critical of the stranglehold that Hollywood achieved after World War II. Soon after liberation, local filmmakers and entertainment entrepreneurs became frustrated at the 'undemocratic' ways in which U.S. occupation policy was restricting their activities. A wave of young and experienced filmmakers, many of whom had grown up on a heavy diet of Hollywood films between 1926 and 1936 and who had gained valuable training making propaganda films for the Korean Colonial Government, were ready to explore realist aesthetics, film as art, and narratives that resisted Japanese power. Yet, USAMGIK film policy, which was a close copy of laws promulgated by the former colonial government, kept Korean filmmakers (and their practical needs) subservient, albeit temporarily, to an authoritative agenda that aimed at restoring democratic order to the region.

After 1945, members of the Korean film industry, in common with other cultural critics, expressed their concern that Korea was simply being opened up to American goods and services, and Korean entrepreneurs were being sidelined. In fact, as this chapter shows, U.S. film distributors (like the mining industry, for instance) were simply seeking to restore the level of business that they had enjoyed in Korea before the colonial government began suppressing American film culture and commerce with America more generally.

As we have already suggested, the United States' involvement in developing a new age of cinema culture in liberated Korea was more complex than previous studies have indicated. Whereas American films received a warm reception in Japan into the early 1960s,[10] in Korea they experienced tougher market restrictions after President Rhee took office in 1948. Although the general public was enthusiastic about Hollywood 'spectacle films,' that is, films containing larger-than-life sets, remarkable natural

Figure 6.1   Images from the *Movies at War, Vol. 1* pamphlet published by the War Activities Committee, Motion Picture Industry, New York City, 1942. The phrase 'Cannon and Camera!' appears above the bottom right image (p. 3). The phrase 'Films Fight for Freedom' appears below the top right image (p. 6). Images courtesy of Special Collections, University of Iowa Library. [9]

locations, huge casts, and expensive special effects, intellectuals and the Korean government saw American films (and USAMGIK film policy) as a threat to Korean culture and tradition, and a hindrance to developing a local industry. Despite their entertainment value (and their happy endings), American spectacle films that promoted themes of violent and antisocial behavior, and frequently portrayed Western notions of 'gender equality,' had unintended consequences in Korea.[11]

By analyzing the impact of the USAMGIK's film policy, and the major themes of a cross section of Hollywood films exhibited in Korea, we explain the circumstances in which the project both failed and succeeded. Many of the spectacle films discussed here were used to evoke a sense of personal and political liberty, while distracting local audiences from the political turmoil of the period. With these themes in mind, this exploratory study provides new and important information about South Korea's postliberation film industry, which was desperate to break free from the legacy of thirty-five years of Japanese colonial rule.

After the Japanese attack on Pearl Harbor in December 1941, strict censorship guidelines prevented Korea's 120 cinemas from screening films from the United States and other Allied countries. Naturally, Hollywood distributors looked forward to the time when they could regain the market dominance in Korea that they had enjoyed during the middle years of the Japanese colonial period. The U.S. Occupation of Korea was the solution—particularly with the reopening of Hollywood distribution offices throughout the country from 1945.

HOLLYWOOD REJUVENATION

Following the end of the Pacific war, Korea was separated at the 38th parallel: the southern and northern parts of Korea were to be temporarily governed by the United States and the USSR, respectively, in order to facilitate the establishment of orderly government. The U.S. interim government had planned to transform the southern part of the Korean Peninsula into a 'self-governing,' 'independent,' and 'democratic' nation while safeguarding the well-being and rebuilding the economic livelihood of the Koreans.[12]

During this time, four pivotal players contributed to the reinvigoration of cinema culture in Korea: the Office of War Information (hereafter OWI), the Motion Picture Export Association of America (hereafter MPEA), the CMPE and the USAMGIK's Motion Picture Section in the Department of Public Information (hereafter DPI).

The OWI had been developed in the United States in mid-1942 to coordinate the mass diffusion of information at home and abroad through multiple government departments and diverse media forms. To remain as close to the American film industry as possible, the OWI operated a branch office in Hollywood. It published the *Government Information Manual* that advised representatives from across the film industry about how best to utilize educational and entertainment films as propaganda in both wartime and postwar conditions. The OWI sought to demonstrate how 'the motion picture should be the best medium for bringing to life the democratic idea'—that is, American notions of 'freedom.'[13]

The MPEA was formed in June 1945 under the Webb-Pomerene Act in order to consolidate film exports. To support the U.S. economy and to promote world peace, the organization developed influential trade strategies that successfully overcame foreign market barriers and increased distribution profits for its member companies. In early 1946 the OWI and MPEA formally coalesced under the name of the Central Motion Picture Exchange. Among other roles, the CMPE was charged with controlling the distribution rights for MPEA members' films throughout Asia.

Before the end of the war, and before the OWI was incorporated into the U.S. Department of State (hereafter U.S.-DOS) in September 1945, the OWI's Bureau of Motion Pictures had devised plans to continue 'fighting with information' in the postwar period.[14] It established key CMPE outposts in Japan and the southern part of Korea, through which the U.S.

government attempted to facilitate democracy and stability in the region. In addition to generating profits by distributing American feature entertainment films, the CMPE also distributed cultural and educational documentaries and newsreels, while the USAMGIK's DPI promulgated film policy and initially oversaw film censorship during the U.S. Occupation.[15] In U.S.-controlled Korea, the Motion Picture Section was established in 1945 under the Public Information Bureau of the DPI. The chief role of the DPI was to monitor and improve public opinion towards the United States and to democracy in general in Korea. It had the clear objective of 'disseminating information concerning American aims and policies, the nature and extent of American aid to Korea, and concerning American history, institutions, culture, and way of life.'[16]

Hollywood films became a key vehicle for indoctrinating Koreans along these lines. In Germany, the United States launched a similar project of transforming its former enemy into a democratic country through motion pictures. As suggested elsewhere, Hollywood films were seen as quintessential vehicles for disseminating 'American' ideology as 'democratic products.'[17]

During the immediate postwar period, the USAMGIK's propaganda operation in Korea was anchored by the dissemination of a flood of glamorous Hollywood 'spectacle' films across a range of genres, filling a noticeable void hitherto left by American, Korean, Japanese, and other European films. As local film critics noted at the time, the sheer spectacle and extreme 'foreignness' of the Hollywood films on show enabled audiences to forget about the political turmoil going on around them.[18] The portrayal and promotion of modern Western city life in the films discussed in this chapter was an important facet of this process.

While the criteria used to select the American films distributed and exhibited in southern Korea appear somewhat random, many were Academy Award–winning (or nominated) films such as *In Old Chicago* (1937), *Boys Town* (1938), *You Can't Take It with You* (1938), *Suspicion* (1941), *The Sea Wolf* (1941), *Random Harvest* (1942), *Casablanca* (1942), and *Rhapsody in Blue* (1945). In addition to having achieved popularity in the United States, these films represented well-dressed people scurrying along the skyscraper-lined, car-filled streets of Manhattan, Paris, and other modern cities. Heterosexual coupling was depicted as a moral norm: lovers embraced openly on larger-than-life studio sets and natural locations alike. While many films contained strong moral codas affirming the final victory of justice and the importance of hope, others affirmed women's (equal) rights, Christianity (religion), and patriotism. However, these themes were often expressed using less lofty motifs such as violence, vigilantism, public disorder, deception, desperation, suicide, theft, murder, killings, adultery, and corruption.

Through the importation of Hollywood films from the mid-1940s, Korean audiences were exposed to a large-scale, continuous series of visual and thematic representations that were totally foreign to their own cultural traditions. And, if the advertisements published in Korean language in local newspapers are any indication, Korean audiences were the primary targets of these films. Generally speaking, Koreans had had long-standing Confucian traditions that required physical separation between noblemen and commoners on the one hand, and men and women on the other hand. Confucianism provided the foundational social, moral, and legal guidelines and customs between people of all ages. Not only did cinema-going in this era enable all walks of life to mingle together in ways that were different from traditional Korean moral values, but the images, themes, and motifs presented in the onslaught of spectacle Hollywood films, which was not a new phenomenon, did continually present 'American' situations that shook the roots of traditions and caused worries among traditionalists.

Films such as Frank Capra's *You Can't Take It with You*, exhibited in April 1947, offered Korean audiences the opportunity to consider new ideas and social relationships. In fact, Americans at home were told that the newly liberated countries of East Asia were 'seeing, with awe and envy, the homes and clothes and motor cars of the world's most prosperous and least-suffering people.'[19] In *You Can't Take It with You*, an interclass couple is presented as free to pursue an intimate relationship, resulting in a 'happy ending' that portrays wealthy people sacrificing their personal gains and championing community and family values. This was one Hollywood film among many that embraced themes of social mobility and change through marriage in the face of seemingly incompatible class relationships, pitting ambition and wealth against happiness and social acceptance. The theme of heterosexual coupling and marrying without parental or family consent was linked to the desire for social mobility through acquiring material wealth in a modern society.

Tutoring Koreans in 'modern life,' as portrayed in and through American films, fitted within the USAMGIK's larger aims for the development of the country during what was anticipated to be a speedy transition to economic stability and political autonomy. Part of the process of 'reorienting' the population of the southern half of the Korean Peninsula away from antidemocratic, anti-American, and militaristic ideology espoused by their former Japanese colonial masters involved transforming the hearts and minds of local cinema audiences. Instead of thinking and acting similarly to Japanese, Koreans were now expected to think about what 'America' and democracy had to offer them.

However, seeing is a culturally constructed process, and Korean audiences saw more than they were perhaps intending to. In about half of all the American feature films exhibited at this time (and foreign films generally), what was seen on the screen was often at odds with the wholesome values ostensibly being promoted—these movies offered Koreans a mixed view of Western culture where open expressions of immoral behavior sat alongside so-called democratic ideals. Property theft, fraudulent activities, malicious intent, crimes against individuals and authority figures, and sexual contact of a kind eschewed in Confucian tradition filled local screens.

Fox's *In Old Chicago*, produced by studio mogul Darryl F. Zanuck for almost $2 million and released in Korea in April 1946, exemplified the mixed messages received by Korean audiences from Hollywood. This film showcased major stars Tyrone Power, Alice Faye, and Don Ameche, who deliver a dramatic message about overcoming poverty and fighting corruption. The film was inspired by the Great Chicago Fire of 1871, and showed how the city was rebuilt through determination and perseverance. *In Old Chicago* portrays an Irish family in the second half of the nineteenth century struggling to survive in a 'modern' society at a time when rough frontier towns were full of opportunity and where wealthy people kept African-American house servants. In the first five minutes of the film, as the family is traveling from the country to Chicago in their horse-drawn covered wagon, the father is killed while chasing a passing steam train—a sleek symbol of modernity. In the next scene, the following text appears on-screen: 'Chicago—1854. A City of easy money, easy ways, ugly, dirty, open night and day to newcomers from all parts of the world . . . a fighting, laughing, aggressive American city.'

The film is jam-packed with a wide range of positive and negative behaviors, including chivalrous men helping well-dressed women across muddy streets, unmarried couples kissing and hugging, fist fights and police raids in saloons, dancing girls in revealing clothes, and breaking and entering into private homes. Yet, as an overriding coda, *In Old Chicago* ends with the optimistic sentiment: 'Out of the fire will be coming steel'—underlining the film's projection of themes of righteousness, corruption, and manifest destiny in the context of industrialization and the expansion of America. While the physical setting of the story perhaps shares some of the gritty feel of postliberation Korean society, Asian audiences must have had difficultly in finding the democratic message in a story where 'moral turpitude' is so openly and abundantly on display.

Ironically, although it was a hit on Korean screens, *In Old Chicago* was suppressed by the U.S. Occupation authority's Civil Censorship Detachment in Japan—not because of flagrant immorality, but because of its overt portrayal of political corruption.[20] Hence, not all films bound for Korea via U.S. distribution offices in Japan enjoyed public screenings, demonstrating the differences in U.S. strategy in Korea and Japan. The difference in approach is understandable given the divergent objectives of the interim U.S. governments in Korea and Japan. In Japan, the U.S. government had spent seven years creating and maintaining political stability in its former enemy. The process of 'democratizing' Korea was seen by the U.S. government as a simpler task, achievable in just three short years and requiring a lesser degree of political vigilance.

Another potentially controversial offering was *Casablanca*, released in Korea in May 1947, which on the positive side of the ledger highlights themes of nationalism and patriotism. Yet, it too canvasses antidemocratic ideals and themes of cynicism, fighting for one's beliefs, contested loyalties, and sexual license. *Casablanca* portrays the saloon as a place of public entertainment, gambling, drinking, and close dancing and kissing between men and women. It is also a place where corruption takes root among the police and the authorities, and drunken women make public spectacles of themselves. In addition, Alfred Hitchcock's romantic psychological thriller *Suspicion* (released in October 1948) contains men forcing themselves on women and manhandling them, as well as women enjoying being kissed on the lips.

In fact, USAMGIK was well aware of the criticism directed at the undesirable nature of many of these films. According to one report from mid-1947 submitted to the U.S.-DOS, a committee of American educators that had conducted a formal survey of local attitudes in Korea was disappointed at the CMPE's failure to offer appropriate films to Korean audiences:

> To date virtually no use has been made of motion pictures for the presentation to the Korean people of American aims and policies and of American life and culture. . . . The only American films generally available to Koreans are old feature films distributed by the Korean branch of the Motion Picture Export Association. These are of inferior quality and are completely inappropriate vehicles for presenting American culture in Korea. As in other oriental countries, motion pictures are enthusiastically received by the Korean public.[21]

As previous studies have noted, in occupied Japan Hollywood films were carefully selected by General Douglas MacArthur's SCAP Office to foster democracy and gender equality while opposing any lingering feudalism and militarism.[22] This was part of SCAP's larger attempts to remold Japanese society and culture by means of a systematic and tightly controlled media censorship regime and film exhibition program.[23] While Hollywood films were shown in Korea for a variety of reasons, many—but not all—of the films distributed through official channels had appeared on a list of films first identified in the United States and then precensored and preapproved for the Japanese market.

As a result of this connection, U.S. administrators in both countries followed the OWI's larger propaganda aims—with complicity from the CMPE, whose offices in Japan and Korea shared the aim of getting American films screened in order to promote the motion picture industry in each country—while benefiting from the consolidation of supplies and manpower wherever possible. However, due to the shorter tenure of the U.S. Occupation force in Korea, and thus the lesser degree of support and protection it could offer the local film industry, the CMPE branch in Seoul was more aggressive in promoting its agenda.

HOLLYWOOD ROLLOUT

In February 1946, MPEA representatives, along with a local liaison officer who had previously worked for Paramount, one of the most active American distributors in colonial Korea, opened the CMPE's Korean branch in Seoul. For the first three months, CMPE-Korea operated out of the offices of the USAMGIK's Motion Picture Section of the DPI. However, the immediate expansion of its activities forced the CMPE to move to a high-security building with modern facilities, including a film storage vault and a state-of-the-art projection room. From the outset, the CMPE collected film rental fees from all exhibitors and documented daily box-office receipts and monthly attendance figures; it also monitored audience reactions to U.S. films as well as those supplied from other countries.[24] Exhibitors were required to pay the CMPE at least 50 percent of all box-office revenues as part of the distribution deal, an arrangement which generated severe criticism from Korean exhibitors. According to the former manager of the Chosun Film Corporation, profit-sharing arrangements had been better for Korean exhibitors under Japanese rule, when they had been only 35–40 percent. For older film industry operatives in Korea, the CMPE's higher fees were an unwelcome challenge.[25]

Government and industry representatives from the United States kept a careful eye on southern Korea. On a regular basis market intelligence was supplied to the chief film officer of the DPI, which forwarded it to the OWI Motion Picture Bureau in New York for discussion among film industry executives. The CMPE's data-collection processes helped them to cultivate the Korean and Japanese markets for future MPEA domination in what the OWI considered to be 'more normal times' to come. Referring to the dissemination of American films abroad at this time, M-G-M president Arthur Loew asserted: "What makes this world-wide distribution so significant is the fact that films are the nearest thing yet perfected to a universal language, with undeniable cultural, political, and social force."[26] While hopeful that American films might contribute to world peace, these Hollywood executives also believed that their films indirectly sold more white goods, radios, and cars than any other type of promotional vehicle.[27]

Despite this sophisticated market analysis, the USAMGIK did not immediately gain the upper hand in Korean cinemas. After liberation, and before cinemas could be renamed from Japanese to Korean names, a 'black market' emerged for the unofficial distribution and exhibition of Hollywood and Soviet films and those of other countries. Entrepreneurs and others interested in intellectual social debate, including communism, began exhibiting *soi-disant* illegal films. To assert their independence, and to make a quick profit during the exhibition vacuum left behind by the colonial regime, these entrepreneurs screened films such as Buster Keaton's *Steamboat Bill, Jr.* (1928), *The New Adventures of Tarzan* (1935), and B-grade science-fiction, gangster, and action-adventure films such as *Undersea Kingdom* (1936), *What Price Crime?* (1935), *Sea Devils* (1937), and *The Ware Case* (1938). Political films such as Leni Riefenstahl's *Olympia* (1936) and the Italian fascist propaganda film *Lo Squadrone Bianco* (1936, aka *The White Squadron*, see figure 6.2), and the romantic drama *Eravamo Sette Sorelle* (1939) were also screened for the general public. Movies from France, such as Julien Duvivier's monster film *Le Golem* (1936) and his gangster film *Pépé le Moko* (1937, see figure 6.2), and films from Argentina and China were also exhibited.

It is important to list these titles here because their screenings demonstrate a sense of initiative among Koreans that the USAMGIK eventually blocked. Their exhibition in the southern half of the Korean Peninsula also reveals a greater diversity in the national cinema scene in the earliest stages of the U.S. Occupation than was the case with Japan.[28]

Leftist entrepreneurs also stepped in to fill the gap in control of the film scene. Before the USAMGIK's role in assisting U.S. film industry representatives to spread 'American' views of so-called democracy and modernity via the exhibition of Hollywood films had begun in earnest, other organizations such as the left-wing Chosun Film Federation (hereafter CFU) began holding screenings of Soviet feature films. In the early postwar period, the

Figure 6.2 Korean newspaper advertisements for *The White Squadron* (1936) (*Shin Chosun Bo* 21 December 1945); *Puerta Cerrada* (1939) (*Hwangseong Shinmun* 14 December 1946); and *Pépé le Moko* (1937) (*Hwangseong Shinmun* 27 October 1946).

CFU had stimulated debate in southern Korea about Korea's political and social future by screening films such as Sergei Eisenstein's *Ivan the Terrible* (1944) as well as Soviet newsreels.[29] They too were interested in developing new cultural ideas and attitudes that could help Korea move away from the militaristic ideology of the former Japanese colonial government. Yet, their activities were strongly opposed by the USAMGIK authorities— particularly given the proximity of the Soviet forces in the northern part of Korea.

Before it was silenced, and before restrictive film regulations were enacted, the CFU ran articles in the daily press criticizing the CMPE for its close ties to the USAMGIK and its monopoly of the local exhibition market. Other groups attempted to screen colonial-era films such as the recently discovered and restored *Crossroads of Youth* (1934) and the propaganda film *Military Train* (1938). However, USAMGIK forces quickly confiscated these and all other films not approved by the DPI in advance of their public exhibition.

The USAMGIK eventually purged the marketplace of these 'unwanted' films under Ordinance No. 68, 'Regulation of the Motion Pictures,' promulgated in mid-April 1946. In October 1946, the U.S. Occupation forces also enacted Ordinance No. 115, which regulated the licensing of all commercial as well as educational and cultural films.[30] On paper, these ordinances abolished most of the colonial film laws, such as the Peace Preservation Law of 1925, which has been referred to as Japan's 'domination over the soul.'[31] The Peace Preservation Law was a social policy instrument that rigorously detailed the cultural values and submissive behaviors that imperial subjects were expected to show. Yet, in actuality, the two USAMGIK ordinances maintained the spirit of Japanese colonial censorship edicts, thus restricting Korean autonomy in the film industry. After April 1946, the requirement for censorship approval from the USAMGIK became an effective way of ensuring the unhindered dissemination of an 'official' American popular culture, a practice that served the interests of the CMPE and its Hollywood representatives.

The USAMGIK's new powers soon became apparent. Its censorship process required three copies of every screenplay in English to be delivered to it, regardless of the language spoken in the film in question. All films, including those already in Korea, were subject to censorship approval, a rule which attracted immediate complaints from Korean filmmakers and other industry businesspeople that found translation costs prohibitive.[32] Filmmakers argued that these extra costs would double their production budgets for a given film while paving the way for greater numbers of movies imported by the wealthier American film companies.[33]

In April 1946, the month the first USAMGIK ordinance came into force, the first batch of authorized Hollywood films arrived in Seoul. Ironically, and seemingly haphazardly, they arrived with Japanese subtitles via CMPE-Japan.[34] A rueful prologue produced by the DPI's Motion Picture

Section appeared at the start of each of film, explaining the presence of these subtitles.[35] In order to connect with local audiences, well-known Korean *byeonsa* (live narrators) were recruited to introduce each film and to explain how all subsequent *officially* distributed films would contain either Korean subtitles or part-Korean dialogue.

Shipping this first batch of prints to Korea was no doubt seen as efficient and economical, suggesting that the U.S. authorities had sent whatever prints were available—probably stock abandoned by U.S. distributors during the war. This suggests a limited effort with limited resources to control the film market in Korea—at least initially—in contrast to the situation in Japan discussed elsewhere.[36]

Almost immediately, these first Hollywood films made a splash in the marketplace as local audiences lapped them up with enthusiasm, whether or not they understood them or appreciated the cultural values they contained.[37] According to SCAP reports on USAMGIK activities in Korea, between 15 April and 31 May 1946, nearly 400,000 tickets to U.S. feature films were sold, generating a turnover of ¥4,000,000 (the equivalent of about $266,666).[38] Subsequently, DPI's Motion Picture Section stimulated a burst of censorship activity by approving 328 applications to screen American and other countries' films, including a few from Korea.[39] By June 1946 about one hundred feature, short, documentary, and newsreel films had been shown in southern Korean cinemas under the new regulations, leveling off thereafter to a monthly total of about fifty films, a flow that enabled the CMPE to harmonize its activities with the politics of the occupation. Postwar Seoul was a thriving center of entrepreneurial energy and entertainment, providing an atmosphere in which the USAMGIK was able to pave the way for Hollywood's economic and cultural preponderance in Korea and beyond.

Prints that had not been approved by the DPI were treated as black-market goods, and confiscated by the USAMGIK's Department of Police. Hence, not only procolonial and communist-oriented films, which violated the ideological spirit of the U.S. Occupation, were confiscated, but also any other films that had failed to gain approval from the CMPE. Simply put, this type of underground film trade interfered with the USAMGIK's 'reorientation' program and the monopoly that the CMPE was attempting to build in the southern Korean market on behalf of the American film industry. Thus the decision to confiscate such films was based on both economic and cultural factors.

At least a dozen unapproved films from Korea, Germany, France, and Italy were confiscated by the police in May 1946, and nine cinemas across Seoul were shut down pending the arrival of approved films to exhibit.[40] The confiscation of unauthorized films removed competition and restored the kind of market dominance that Hollywood distributors had enjoyed in the colonial period between 1926 and 1936.[41] It also solidified the MPEA's growing footprint in postwar Asia.

DAWN OF REORIENTATION

The documentaries and newsreels distributed by the CMPE arrived in Korea along with a large number of U.S. feature films which, like the former, were intended to serve the USAMGIK's reorientation program. The larger list of films screened in April 1946 included *Queen Christina* (1933), *Barbary Coast* (1935), *The Devil Doll* (1936), *Mr. Deeds Goes to Town* (1936), *Romeo and Juliet* (1936), *San Francisco* (1936), *The Great Ziegfeld* (1936), *The Buccaneer* (1938), *The Rains Came* (1939), *Golden Boy* (1939), *Honolulu* (1939), *The Under Pup* (1939), and *Abe Lincoln in Illinois* (1940). These films were 'prestige pictures' in the sense that they were 'injected with plenty of star power, glamorous and elegant trappings, and elaborate special effects'[42]—attractive packaging for presenting some of the core democratic reform values that the U.S. government wanted for Korea.

Hundreds of other films were used to lure people into the cinemas, including Cecil B. DeMille's *The Buccaneer* (1938; see figure 6.3), a quasi-fictional adventure-drama about eighteenth-century pirate Jean Lafitte and the many women he loved. The film portrays 'wild man' Lafitte and his pirate crew in the War of 1812 fighting side by side with General Andrew Jackson—whose successful battles against the British made him a national hero and contributed to his being elected U.S. president. The love triangle at the heart of the film delivers a strong message of free love, an element that was likely to have been at odds with pro-American and democratic values.

Whether or not big-budget spectacle films such as *The Buccaneer* successfully embodied or transmitted democratic ideology and other 'American' ideals to Koreans, they were regularly screened over the course of the USAMGIK period—each about once every six months (for several days at a time).

Based on the advertisements in Korean that appeared regularly in major local newspapers, a majority of the films screened at this period were talkies produced between the mid-1930s and early 1940s. Action-adventure and historical biopics were the most prevalent genres, followed by melodramas, screwball comedies, musicals, Westerns, crime/detective thrillers, science fiction, and animated cartoons. These and other films distributed by the CMPE had little competition in the entertainment field, apart from frequent live theatrical and musical performances and a few screenings of older Korean films such as Ahn Seok-yeong's 1937 talkie feature *The Story of Shim Cheong*, Na Un-gyu's silent classic *Arirang* (1926), and Choi In-gyu's colonial propaganda film *Angels on the Streets* (1941).[43] The evidence suggests that the exhibition of a small number of Korean films was allowed by the USAMGIK to placate domestic criticism of the CMPE's 'antidemocratic' practices.

Newspaper advertisements for Hollywood films distributed by the CMPE attempted to attract audiences with arousing drawings and silhouettes of film stars, action scenes, and exotic locations, promoting all the

Figure 6.3 Korean newspaper advertisements for *Honolulu* (1939) (*Hwangseong Shinmun* 14 July 1946) and *The Buccaneer* (1938) (*Jayu Shinmun* 13 May 1946). Courtesy of Yonsei University Library Newspaper Collection, Seoul.

glamour of American culture. They depicted dashing portraits of leading Hollywood stars including Robert Montgomery, Judy Garland, Bing Crosby, George Raft, Eleanor Powell, Richard Dix, Clark Gable (about to kiss Claudette Colbert in figure 6.4), and Jean Arthur as a feisty cowgirl in *Arizona* (1940).

Often, the images in these advertisements revealed little about the themes treated in the film concerned. In contrast to the happy romantic image featured in the advertisement for MGM's *Boom Town* reproduced in figure 6.4, the film portrays themes of frontier exploration and desire for material wealth, as well as jealousy and rivalry over women, and social mobility. These are all themes that would have appeared in striking contrast to the colonial ideology of the Japanese occupation, let alone the traditional values to which Korean audiences were accustomed. At the same time, the graphic imagery of the advertisements attracted non-Korean-speaking U.S. troops as well—a welcome secondary audience.

As these advertisements show, many of these films carried the 'heavy scent of "Americanism"',[44] portraying the United States as an exoticized and 'glamorous elsewhere'. Advertisements for Westerns such as *Union Pacific* (1939; see figure 6.5) displayed men in ten-gallon hats either embracing a pretty woman or pointing a gun at the reader. Those for dramas and musicals, such as *Romeo and Juliet* (1936, exhibited in July, September, and December 1946 and in October 1947), *Honolulu* (see figure 6.3), *I Wanted Wings* (1941; see figure 6.4), *The Flame of New Orleans* (1941; see figure 6.5), and *The Great Victor Herbert* (1939; see Figure 6.5), showed women in scanty clothing and couples in passionate embraces. These and other films portraying 'modern life' showcased 'film stars, dance crazes,

Figure 6.4 Korean newspaper advertisements for *I Wanted Wings* (1941) (*Jayu Shinmun* 4 May 1948); *Laura* (1944) (*Daidong Shinmun* 8 June 1948); and *Boom Town* (1940) (*Jayu Shinmun* 27 August 1948). Courtesy of Yonsei University Library Newspaper Collection, Seoul.

Figure 6.5   Korean newspaper advertisements for *Union Pacific* (1939) (*Jayu Shinmun* 5 July 1948); *The Flame of New Orleans*, (1941) (*Jayu Shinmun* 5 July 1948); and *The Great Victor Herbert* (1939) (*Jayu Shinmun* 14 July 1948). Courtesy of Yonsei University Library Newspaper Collection, Seoul.

general oddities and glamorous strangeness'[45] and the newspaper advertisements faithfully reflected this. Although exhibitors promoted programs
that mixed features with shorts and live musical and/or theatrical performances, a surfeit of Hollywood films left little room for the exhibition of
films from Korea and elsewhere: movies which might have offered alternative views of 'America'—and modernity, for that matter.

On closer inspection, musicals such as *Babes on Broadway* (1941, exhibited during the whole month of July 1947), *The Men in Her Life* (1941),
Abbott and Costello's comedy-mystery *Hold that Ghost* (1941, exhibited
in September 1948), Alfred Hitchcock's *film noir Suspicion* (exhibited in
October 1948), and other dramas such as *The Devil and Daniel Webster*
(1941) and *Men of Boys Town* (1941) presented a skewed picture of America and American culture, demonstrating once again that the selection
criteria for films shown in Korea was ultimately driven by (the CMPE's)
commercial priorities rather than any benevolent cultural agenda initiated
by the USAMGIK. Hence, the line between entertainment and 'message'
films often remained blurred.

THE USAMGIK LEGACY

The question remains how successfully the American films distributed and
exhibited in the southern half of the Korean Peninsula meshed with the
USAMGIK's occupation strategy. The films selected originated from a variety of sources, including distributors in Shanghai and U.S. film distributors' film vaults in colonial Korea that were impounded by the Japanese
authorities after Pearl Harbor. Yet, regardless of the origins of these prints,
the U.S. film industry was able to profit from the exhibition of older and
recycled films while at the same time exploiting them for their cultural
contents. In fact, before appearing in Korea, most if not all these feature
films would have undergone the self-censorship process implicit in Hollywood's Motion Picture Production Code. This industry initiative attempted
to ensure that stories and scenes contained appropriate content for domestic viewers. The USAMGIK would no doubt have been confident that these
star-driven films—often in the running for Oscars—upheld the kind of
moral values and accurate portrayals of (American) society that would not
offend Korean audiences.

However, as we have seen, while many CMPE films approximated this
model, an equal number offered a different view of America: one that depicted
opulence, feisty and independent female characters, unrestrained lovemak-
ing, violent themes, and an exotic cultural milieu that was both thrilling and
dangerous—as newspaper advertisements containing guns attest (see figures
6.4 and 6.5). This suggests that the CMPE was keen to select sensational
films that would send both locals and occupation troops to the cinemas in
droves, without carefully distinguishing between these two audiences.

The portrayal of gender themes especially was potentially problematic. Otto Preminger's *film noir* mystery-romance *Laura* (see figure 6.4) portrays the female protagonist as a successful and savvy advertising executive. Her traits and abilities are continually questioned in the context of the 'proper' conduct of women and class boundaries. And on the subject of portrayals of alternative female sexuality, one may ask how a pre-code film with a lesbian subtext such as *Queen Christina* could be seen as exemplifying American moral and cultural values.

We have no way of knowing whether the popularity of the films discussed in this article equated with their success in implanting American ideologies of democracy and gender equality in Korean audiences. DPI officials may have been preoccupied with larger issues or lacked sufficient motivation to gain a deeper understanding of Korean culture and the aspects of American movies that would appeal to Korean audiences. On the face of it, it should not have been too difficult for the U.S. authorities to select for general release films with a predominantly positive message while winnowing out their less edifying counterparts. Films such as *Mr. Smith Goes to Washington* (1939), *The Life of Emile Zola* (1937), *Mr. Deeds Goes to Town*, *Penny Serenade* (1941), *The Rains Came*, and *Random Harvest* were better vehicles for showcasing democratic and other 'wholesome' ideals and values that represented the best of what 'America' had to offer. However, there was an equal number of films that evidently catered to U.S. troops rather than Koreans.

Eventually, a steady diet of Hollywood productions—regardless of whether their narrative styles fell outside the Motion Picture Production Code guidelines—proved too much for Korean audiences, including the president-in-waiting Syngman Rhee. According to an anonymous article in 1948 in the right-wing newspaper *Chung Ang Shinmun*,[46] American pictures seduced Koreans with the 'thrill of murder and gangsterism, with fickle and promiscuous love, with frenzied jazz, and with the pleasures of life in foreign countries,' thus seriously affronting Korean cultural norms.[47] Other critics were concerned that Koreans were mindlessly consuming the eroticism, glamour, and fantasy depicted in American films without considering the massive gulf between everyday life and culture in the United States and in Korea.[48] The open expressions of sexuality and other boisterous behavior portrayed in these films were seen by American education specialists on a formal fact-finding visit to Korea as culturally insensitive and potentially injurious to Korea's Confucian traditions and national pride.[49]

The proponents of such views were more interested in seeing *and* producing films with more appropriate and edifying themes to counter those embedded in films produced during the last few years of the Japanese colonial period and the perceived vulgarity and objectionable content of Hollywood films. As such, they used editorials in newspapers to question the motivation behind the USAMGIK and CMPE operation in Korea. One article in 1948 in the *Seoul Newspaper* noted the fading of the euphoria that the Korean film industry had initially felt after Hollywood films re-entered the local market in late 1945, after years of suppression by the Japanese colonial authorities.[50] Workers in the Korean film industry were genuinely looking forward to the stimulation of the domestic industry (and improved leisure activities) that the USAMGIK potentially offered after liberation. However, the reality of the CMPE's market dominance quickly tarnished these hopes. As one newspaper editor summed up the issue: "The CMPE's coming to Korea was not to fertilize Korean cinema, but to plant a strong tree of the American cinema over the top of the sprouting Korean cinema."[51]

Clearly, however, there was a limit to what the USAMGIK and CMPE could achieve in the short time at their disposal. Nor were the CMPE and the U.S. film industry the only parties at fault. Other foreign films such as the French gangster film *Pépé le Moko* (1937) and the musical comedy *Avec le Sourire* (1936), *Monte Carlo Madness* (1932), *Burgtheater* (1936), and the sex and horror film *Alraune* (1928) from Germany, as well as *Puerta Cerrada* (1939; see figure 6.2) from Argentina, titillated audiences with provocative images both on-screen and in newspaper advertisements. The DPI failed to censor any objectionable or obscene content from these foreign films because it was more concerned with blocking films with communist sympathies and any Hollywood films obtained through unofficial—that is, non-CMPE/MPEA—channels. As a result, audiences were freely exposed to films like *Pépé le Moko*, set in Algiers' seedy casbah underworld where gunfights are common, and a melting pot of gypsies, Slavs, blacks, Arabs, homeless people, Sicilians, Spaniards, prostitutes, and corrupt officials stands in stark contrast to the (apparently civilized) French colonial authorities. The film's negative ending depicts the protagonist's suicide after losing the chance to develop love and trust with his girlfriend (who betrays him), and thus, to redeem himself.

CONCLUSION

Overseeing the film industry and facilitating the distribution and exhibition of American 'message' films was perhaps a more Byzantine task for the USAMGIK than it expected, given the level of antisocial behavior contained in the films that actually appeared on Korean cinema screens. Political turmoil on the ground posed difficult challenges for the U.S. Occupation forces and for the USAMGIK's attempts to execute a highly organized cultural reorientation campaign. As a result, the U.S. Occupation authorities most likely misunderstood local concerns and underestimated the impact that thirty-five years of Japanese colonialism had had on Korea. Nevertheless, the USAMGIK's aim of reorienting Koreans away from the legacies of the former Japanese colonial regime was achieved with surprising ease by allowing hundreds of Hollywood spectacle films back into the region. Their contents could not have differed more from the propaganda and cultural films that the Korean Colonial Government had required audiences to watch (and Korean filmmakers to make) between 1937 and 1945. In pursuing this course, the USAMGIK had indeed disarmed Japan's 'cannons' with Hollywood's cameras.

This result was achieved in the face of considerable practical difficulties. To their credit, it was no small feat for the USAMGIK and CMPE to have distributed hundreds of commercial (and documentary) films on a regular basis to over a hundred cinemas, often with obsolete or damaged equipment and facilities. They did this while trying to eradicate a black market for films and other consumables. At the same time, factors such as political and economic hardship, lack of alternative leisure and entertainment options, and low admission prices contributed to the popularity of Hollywood films among Korean audiences.

However, both these domestic audiences and the U.S. Occupation forces were too distracted by the political situation for a comprehensive Hollywood reorientation project—combined with other U.S.-controlled media such as radio and print propaganda—to succeed in generating new cultural ideas and ideals. Ultimately, the procession of glamorous images and stirring stories in films and other media kept the post-liberation euphoria flowing until the USAMGIK could stabilize the southern half of the Korean Peninsula. While the CMPE's films may not have had the immediate and solid effect on Koreans for which the USAMGIK had hoped, the entertainment and exoticism associated with 'America' certainly lingered in the minds of Korean audiences.

Despite having recruited 'expert' Korean advisors—many of whom were later accused of being Japanese collaborators—the USAMGIK was out of touch with domestic expectations for economic, political, and cultural independence and stability, as most studies of the period have pointed out. Although the USAMGIK saw all its activities as contributing to the growth of democracy, it hardly needed to work as diligently as it did to generate 'American' attitudes among Koreans because Hollywood films (and, therefore, American culture) had been suppressed for only seven or eight years before 1945. In addition, traditional Korean culture had never been completely suppressed, despite the colonial authority's efforts to implement Japanese language into everyday learning and communication.

By March 1949, only six months after the end of the USAMGIK period and the establishment of the Republic of Korea, Hollywood's economic stronghold in the southern part of Korea was already slipping. President Syngman Rhee was developing regulations to limit the number of imported American films—partly to assist the rebirth of a domestic film industry and partly to limit the public's exposure to what was seen as objectionable content.[52] U.S. film-industry representatives were anticipating a maximum of only seventeen films allowed into Korea per year. The domestic industry revived as local filmmakers consolidated their production skills and re-used equipment formerly owned by the consolidated Chosun Film Production and Distribution Co. that the Korean Colonial Government created between 1941 and 1942. It was also happy to answer the USAMGIK's call for the production of *Liberation News* shorts and a small number of 'Liberation' feature films. As a result of these and other factors, the foundations of a national film industry were laid.

Although progress was disrupted by the civil war, the Korean film industry blossomed both in terms of its size and of the quality and number of films made in the mid-1950s, starting with the release of Lee Gyu-hwan's *The Story of Chunhyang* (1955) and Kim Ki-young's *Yang san Province* (1955). Invitations to international film festivals increased proportionately. The 111 films made in 1959 constituted a dramatic increase over the mere fifteen films made in 1955.[53]

Although the full impact of the USAMGIK's reorientation film program on Korea is likely to remain unknown, a deeper understanding of its policy underpinnings, execution, and pitfalls provides new insights into how this cultural project contributed, at least in theory, to the 'Americanizing' of the region. Ironically, South Korea's love affair with Hollywood feature films revived during the 1950s and 1960s, a process well documented in McHugh and Abelmann (2005). The continuing popularity of Hollywood genre conventions, iconography, and the star system, conspicuous in many golden age classics from *Madame Freedom* (1956) to *Seashore Village* (1965), suggests that the Hollywood films distributed during the USAMGIK period may have had a longer-term cultural impact than can be gleaned from distribution and exhibition statistics alone.

Conclusion

The 'modern' concepts and technology brought to Korea by foreigners before the Japanese colonial period, and the illustration of these ideas through devices such as magic lantern equipment and, later, motion pictures, had a profound impact on traditional Korean culture and ways of living. By retracing the history of cinema in Korea back to its antecedents, this book has restored some vital missing parts to a wider historical narrative burdened by long-held but limited views of the impact of foreign cinema culture on Korea and its society.

As early as 1893, a small group of Koreans—including a select student audience and accidental onlookers—was exposed to screenings of religious and landscape imagery from around the world at outdoor talks sponsored by Christian missionaries from the United States and Britain. At the same time, missionaries began capturing 'exotic' photographic images of Korea and circulating them among local audiences in an attempt to draw them closer to their religious teachings. They also circulated these images in their home countries to educate others about their missionary work in Korea and to serve as a potential fund-raiser for this work. To Koreans, the missionaries behind the magic lanterns would have seemed worldly and intelligent, dazzling audiences with their knowledge of the novel and exotic. Certainly, as chapter 1 shows, Burton Holmes and his small film crew caused a stir wherever they went during their visit to Seoul in 1901. Professional photographers, traveloguers, sightseers, salespeople, and naval officers, whether passing through or working in the region, also recorded images of the peninsula and shared them with others in their home country. Thus there was a continual flow of pre-cinematic images in and out of Korea during this pre-colonial period—images that captivated the imaginations of both Koreans and foreigners, and that in many ways anticipated the shape of things to come. The foreign contribution to cinematic culture in Korea was soon combined with the country's rapid modernization and colonization, complicating the process of understanding and internalizing these modern images and the concepts that went with them.

So much is generally agreed to by historians. Where this study diverges from previous scholarship is in its exploration of the tensions and complexities involving not only individuals, but also economics, policy issues, ideology, and propaganda—a complex mix revealing the multifaceted relationships between the occupied and the occupier. Both groups engaged with inter-mingled elements of power and agency involving multiple (local, 'national,' international) industry and government (Korean, Japanese, American) players; at the same time, local and foreign audiences in about 160 cinemas (operating at the peak of the Japanese colonial period) gained access to films from Korea, Japan, America, Britain, China, and many other countries.

Chapter 1 highlights the powerful novelty that the 'modern' image and spectacle of magic lantern slides and, later, motion pictures held for Koreans, and how this power was maintained by those who controlled, owned, and operated the technology that displayed these visual contents. From the begin-ning, then, exhibited images were used by Western missionaries (and later foreign businessmen, foreign and Japanese film companies, Japanese authori-ties, the Korean Colonial Government, the U.S. Army, and also Korean and Japanese entrepreneurs and film producers) to direct local audiences toward a particular viewpoint. Similarly, businessmen such as James A. Thomas used film as a promotional tool to sell tobacco and other consumer goods.

Chapter 2 shows how Korean nationals would have lacked an opportu-nity in 1919 to contribute to a local cinema culture had foreigners (includ-ing major Japanese film companies) and a smaller number of Korean film exhibitors not begun developing a film industry, in the form of distribution and exhibition systems, in the first instance. We posit that the real birth year of a 'film industry' in Korea was 1916. This is the date by which formal and regularized distribution and exhibition systems had been estab-lished in Korea—albeit primarily through the local cinemas owned by major Japanese film companies (Nikkatsu and Tenkatsu), on the one hand, and other foreigners distributing films on behalf of various film compa-nies—Biograph, Edison Studios, Selig, Essannay, and Universal Pictures (Bluebird, Nester, Butterfly, Thanhouser) from the United States, and Pathé Frères, Bioscope, British and Colonial Cosmopolitan, Milano Films, Soci-età Anonima Ambrosio and Continental Kunstfilm GmbH from Europe —on the other hand. Contesting this foreign occupation of the market were only a few Korean businessmen who contributed to its growth. Hence, in 1919 there was already the core of a 'film industry' awaiting Korean par-ticipation when Korean filmmakers entered local production following the abortive March First 1919 Independence Movement.

In this early part of the colonial period—until the late 1930s—'going to the pictures' was a social, intellectual, and political activity, for at least three reasons. First, foreign films offered audiences an opportunity to escape from their austere physical surroundings and to lose themselves in the narratives they presented. Second, cinemas and other screening venues provided Koreans with the opportunity to mingle socially in un-Korean, that is, non-Confucian, and modern ways. Third, letting one's imagina-tion loose during the screening of a Korean film enabled viewers to re-live sentiments associated with the March First Independence Movement, even after all scenes explicitly referring to this event had been excised by the censors. In this way, audiences had the power to imagine the missing parts and to hold discussions about them in their daily lives. Although detailed records of every scene cut from every Korean, Japanese, and foreign film screened in Korea during this period no longer exist, we know what the censors were looking for, and we can imagine that filmmakers and others took a keen interest in the parts that were cut.

Developing these themes, chapter 3 makes the point that the developments in the 'film industry in Korea' after 1916, including Hollywood's first golden age in Korea between 1926 and 1936, enabled distribution, exhibition, *and* local production systems to expand, especially as they affected a local cinema-going culture that was accessible to millions of Koreans and a smaller number of Japanese and other expatriates. Between the mid-1920s and the mid-1930s, American films provided a powerful cultural distraction, a situation which, in our view, diluted Japan's hegemony over Korean culture—until the numbers of foreign films entering Korea were restricted as Japan increased its war-preparation efforts. Hence the development of a cinema culture had both a positive and a negative impact on Korean society, as well as a direct and an indirect effect on the 'film industry in Korea,' and then on the 'Korean cinema' after it was launched in 1919. After the early 1920s, Korean filmmakers, influenced by the flood of popular foreign films to which local audiences had been exposed, sought to create films that embodied particular aesthetics and that expressed empathetic sentiments in their characters and narratives.

Audiences—a group that has largely been overlooked in the history of cinema in Korea—demonstrated their agency in this process by choosing which films to see of the large and varied number on offer. The exhibition of this large quantity of imports was made possible by the Korean distributors who submitted hundreds of Hollywood (and a smaller number of Japanese) films to the censorship board for exhibition approval. As a result of this plethora of product, and the 160 cinemas and theaters exhibiting films, there was great choice in the marketplace—at least until the Korean Colonial Government began restricting the numbers of American, British, and European films from Allied countries entering Korea after 1937. After this time, American film companies lost both power and agency in Korea, signaling the end of Hollywood's first golden age in the peninsula.

Those who spoke before audiences at public (or private) film screenings were also in positions of power. Those *byeonsa* who developed a fan base commanded higher salaries because their popularity translated into selling more tickets. The power of their words—especially in place of scenes that had been cut by the censors—and their ability to improvise caused great concern among the police and censorship authorities—to such a great extent that, after 1926, all narration scripts had to be approved in advance of a live performance. As chapter 4 demonstrates, *byeonsa* remained under constant surveillance at their workplaces by police, who either sat in their permanently reserved seats or turned up at random, seeking to ensure that these live commentaries avoided even a hint of revolutionary ideas or encouraged independence from Japan in any way.

Chapter 5 shows how the Korean Colonial Government used film for three powerfully motivating purposes: as a propaganda tool to recruit young soldiers; to evoke in Koreans a sense of loyalty to the empire; and to remind Koreans and Japanese living in Korea (and in Japan) of the national assimilationist policy (*naeseon ilche*) and the Japanese government's views regarding national culture. This cultural ideology was asserted repeatedly in newspaper articles, formal government speeches, policy documents, and messages conveyed through military propaganda films co-produced by Korean and Japanese filmmakers. Yet, in reality, there was a power glitch in the system—the ideal of complete assimilation was unattainable because Koreans could never become equal to Japanese in all respects. Hence, there were two sides to the Japanese assimilationist policy that conflicted with each other in reality.

Both Korean and Japanese filmmakers experienced a loss of agency through their involvement in the production of military propaganda films between the late 1930s and 1945. During this time, and as a result of Japan's war priorities, filmmakers were restricted from making the types of narrative films that they had previously favored. While filmmakers from *both* countries shared misgivings about having to produce propaganda films, several of the Japanese filmmakers mentioned in chapter 5 looked forward to collaborating with their Korean counterparts, whose creativity was well known despite their limited opportunities.

As the war progressed, Koreans enjoyed less and less freedom of expression. Forced to apply their skills and expertise to the making of propaganda films, Korean filmmakers became central actors in executing the very national policy that maintained Korea's subservient role in Japan's empire. Whilst a number of the films made in this period could be called collaborative co-productions (made with both Korean and Japanese crews and actors), they failed to achieve the level of cultural diversity and mutual economic benefit that official co-production efforts embrace today. The overt foregrounding of propaganda and military recruitment messages in the feature films discussed in chapter 5 mirrored similar policies and strategies for controlling content seen in Japanese 'national policy' films. In other words, the Japanese Ministry of Home Affairs and the Korean Colonial Government coordinated efforts to increase their control over all film and media in order to actively promote a wartime ideology.

Nevertheless, multiple and shifting motives can be discerned in some of these propaganda and 'message' films as the Korean Colonial Government attempted to increase the scope and breadth of its administrative control over the colony. From the beginning, the *naeseon ilche* policy was never intended to create complete assimilation, and the reality that showed that Japan and

Korea were different was constantly threatening to break through the ideological veneer. As the film analyses in chapter 5 shows, the ideology of 'Japan and Korea as one body' was used as a convenient lure to recruit more Koreans to volunteer for the war. To turn this around, volunteering for the armed forces and fighting to the death for the empire were equated with becoming Japanese. In fact, dying as a soldier in the service of the Emperor was one of the highest honors admitted by the concept of *naeseon ilche*.

But no matter which of these filmmaking elements was embraced, at this time every film made was designed to encourage Koreans *en masse* to participate in the war—either as volunteer soldiers and pilots, unconditionally supportive parents and wives of young soldiers (or future soldiers), or schoolteachers training a new generation to make the ultimate sacrifice. Ideological constructs such as 'honor', 'loyalty', 'responsibility', 'sacrifice', 'pride', 'glory', and 'courage' formed the very backbone of all these wartime films. In other words, what it meant to be a 'good' loyal and subservient citizen of the empire was a core message in the films produced at this time.

If one wanted to remain in the film industry, one had no choice but to make films that prioritized these tropes. This dramatic shift reflected the influence on Korean filmmakers, and Korea in general, of Japan's so-called enlightenment (assimilation) policy. Turning Koreans into loyal members of the Japanese Empire was the main stimulus behind the Chosun Film Corporation's production of films such as *Angels on the Streets* (1941), *I am Going Now* (1942), *Look Up at the Blue Sky* (1943), *Straits of Chosun* (1943), *Portrait of Youth* (1943), *Dear Soldier* (1944), *Children of the Sun* (1944), and *Sons of the Sky* (1945). At the core of these narratives was the display of subservience and loyalty to the empire (mean and lustful record-company owners notwithstanding). In addition, films with 'co-production' status enabled them to enjoy special privileges such as exemption from censorship fees as well as increased chances of release in Japan and, possibly, Manchuria. It is no wonder, then, that Korean filmmakers were eager to cooperate with Japanese filmmakers and turn out propaganda films in order to enhance their position (and working conditions) within the industry.

Finally, as we show in chapter 6, after the Japanese colonial period ended, the USAMGIK used Hollywood films as a tool to undo whatever ties of loyalty had persisted over thirty-five years of Japanese occupation and a heavy diet of colonial propaganda films. In these ways, film became a powerful cultural tool used to indoctrinate (and un-indoctrinate) local audiences with specific themes and messages. That is not to say that after 1945 creativity was off limits to Korean filmmakers, who yearned for the opportunity to make their own films in their own ways. Indeed, in many cases, Koreans wrote scripts and directed films with experimentation in mind. As we can see today, particularly after the recent discovery of new colonial-era films, and the recent re-release of post-liberation films on DVD by KOFA, the films made during these periods embodied a wide array of narrative techniques, aesthetic styles, and genre conventions.

POSTSCRIPT

After the Korean War (1950–1953), efforts directed at social restoration took place in every sector of South Korean society. The conditions were ripe for the growth of a truly Korean cinema and national film industry. Signs of a recovery in the commercial market came with the introduction of an admission tax exemption for domestic films in 1954 and the huge success of Lee Gyu-hwan's *The Story of Chunhyang* (1955)—yet another remake of the traditional Korean love story. The ratio of domestic films to foreign imports increased, supporting the growth of the local production market. Between 1957 and 1958 the number of film companies in South Korea increased from twenty-six to seventy-one, illustrating the industry's sudden expansion. Industry growth and market expansion continued even after May 1961, when Major-General Park Chung Hee staged a coup, proclaimed martial law, and established a new military junta. Park's government accelerated economic growth, urbanization, and cultural Westernization, and the proliferation of Hollywood media culture was a key element. Modernization and industrialization forced enormous social and economic changes on Korea. Today, as we suggest in the introduction, the Korean cinema bears some of the fruits of this turbulent historical narrative.

Notes

NOTES TO THE INTRODUCTION

1. *Im Kwon-Taek* was the outcome of a 1996 retrospective conference held about the director at the University of Southern California. Though this is not the first book published in English on Korean film, it signaled a new beginning for Korean film history and collaborative scholarship between English- and Korean-speaking scholars.
2. Although the third edition of Bordwell and Thompson's *Film History: An Introduction* sheds light on the development of South Korea's contemporary cinema, including its key directors, it too has little to say about the rich and complex history of cinema in Korea.
3. Even Cumings (1997), one of the more thorough studies, lacks any discussion of the nation's encounter with film and entertainment culture.
4. See, for example, Jackson, Gibb, and White, eds. (2006); Gateward, ed. (2007); and Paquet (2009).
5. Before 1996, all domestic film scripts had to be approved in the preproduction stage and all foreign films had to be examined by the Performance Ethics Committee, which had maintained these powers since its formation in the late 1970s. It is no coincidence, then, that this date corresponds with the launching of the annual Pusan International Film Festival (PIFF), which has become a key networking hub for the Asian film and digital media industry and a major showcase for both South Korean and international films.
6. For a wider discussion of this Cinema Tiger, see Yecies (2010).
7. *Korean Cinema 2009*: 37–45.
8. *Korean Cinema 2000*: 265; *Korean Cinema 2006*: 495.
9. *Korean Cinema Today* July–August 2010: 5.
10. In July 2006, the SQS was reduced by half as part of free-trade agreement discussions with the United States—the result of four decades of relentless pressure from the Motion Picture Association of America.
11. *Korean Cinema 2004*: 297; *Korean Cinema 2009*: 42.
12. Segers 2000.
13. For a more detailed discussion of 'Planet Hallyuwood,' see Yecies 2009.
14. *Korean Cinema 2009*: 42; *Hanguk Yeonghwa* Vol. 1 (March 2010): 42; *Korean Cinema 2004*: 297.
15. H.I.J.M.'s Residency General 1908: 3
16. Anderson and Richie (1982), Gerow (2000), Makino (2001), Bernardi (2001), and High (2003).
17. Ho (2000), Lee (2004), Cho Jun-hyung (2005), and Chung (2007).

18. See, for instance, studies of the national cinemas of Spain (Triana-Toribio 2003), Germany (Hake 2002; Scharf 2010), China (Zhang 2004), Britain (Hanson 2007), Italy (Gennari 2008), and Japan and Hong Kong (Yau Shuk-ting 2009).
19. See Baskett (2008) and Kim (2009).
20. *The Second Annual Report*, 1908–9: 85.
21. *Maeil Shinbo* 13 Feb 1914: 3.
22. These include: Iwasaki (1937), Ichikawa (1941), Anderson and Richie (1982), Gerow (2000), Makino (2001), Bernardi (2001), High (2003), and Caprio (2009).
23. Shim Hun, the well-known Korean author of the novel *Evergreen Tree* (1935), described these early screenings years after the fact in the *Chosun Ilbo* (1 January 1929). In the early 1940s, Japanese scholars such as Ichikawa (1941) and Takashima (1943) also made similar claims. Over fifty years later, despite a continuing lack of evidence, Korean scholars such as Kim and Jeong (2001) and Kim Mee-hyun (2007: 17) still maintain that the first public film screenings were likely to have occurred in Korea in October 1897. These claims are thinly connected to evidence of early Kinetoscope screenings in Japan in November 1896 that are discussed in Makino (2001: 47), ease of travel between Korea and Japan in that period, and a mythical article in *The Times* of London supposedly published on 19 October 1897. To our knowledge, the veracity of these claims remains unproven.
24. The only news concerning Korea published around this time is a report on the king of Korea's proclamation that he would be enthroned as emperor in mid-October 1897 (*The Times*, 16 October 1987: 5). An exhaustive search in the 19th Century British Library Newspapers digital collection, which contains 48 national and regional newspapers, produced nothing relating to film screenings in Korea.
25. In 1898, in conjunction with the Seoul/Hansung Electric Company, the pair had gained contracts from King Gojong to electrify Seoul with public lighting. They were also later commissioned to develop an electric streetcar system for Seoul.
26. For instance, see Lee and Choe (1998), Lee (2000), Min, Joo, and Kwak (2003), Yi (2003), and Kim Mee-hyun (2007).

NOTES TO CHAPTER 1

1. Details of the trade mission appeared in the *New York Times*, 16 November 1883.
2. Nam 2000: 6.
3. *The Korea Review* September 1902.
4. Horace N. Allen (consulate-general of the United States) to William R. Day, assistant secretary of State, 15 February 1898. File Microcopies of Records in the National Archives: No. 167, Roll 1, Dispatches from United States Consuls in Seoul, 1886–1906, Vol. 1, 3 July 1886–21 December 1898.
5. *The Korea Review*, August 1901.
6. *The Korea Review*, August 1906.
7. *The Korea Review*, June 1903: 268.
8. Advertised in the *Hwangseong Shinmun* (23 June 1903). Details of this watershed event are also discussed in *Samcheolli* (May 1940: 227).
9. Kim Mee-hyun 2007.
10. Gunning 2004.
11. Musser 1990: 20–24.
12. Anderson 1992: 297; Gunning 2004.

13. *The Independent* (1896–1899) was a bi-daily and later daily newspaper published by American-educated Korean Christian Dr. Philip Jaisohn, which covered political, trade, literary, educational, and religious news from across the country. *The Morning Calm* (1890–1910) was a monthly gazette intended to facilitate communication between the British Anglican Church and Anglican missionaries in other countries—primarily in Korea. *The Korean Repository* (1882, 1885–1898), a scholarly journal, and *The Korea Review* (1901–1906), a Methodist monthly newspaper, were both published by American scholar Homer B. Hulbert, who came to Korea in 1886 to teach English to King Gojong and later became one of the king's advisors on educational issues and foreign affairs. *The Korea Methodist* (1901–1905), published by missionary George H. Jones, and *The Korea Field* (1901–1905), a Presbyterian monthly—which were combined in 1905 and renamed *The Korea Mission Field*—also aimed to introduce Korea to a Western audience.
14. *The Independent*, 2 October 1897.
15. May 1899.
16. August 1899.
17. According to Rick Altman (2001), who re-created this rowdy viewing atmosphere in his 'Living Nickelodeon' research project, nickelodeons were small store-front movie theaters that became popular around 1905 for showing short films.
18. Bernadou's exploits appear in an article in *The Washington Post*, 10 April 1890.
19. Webster 1900.
20. For a fascinating critique of advertising and consumer culture in colonial Korea, see Maliangkay 2010.
21. Barber 1993: 70.
22. Holmes 1953: 81–84.
23. The accession number for this item is 2005:0447:0009.
24. Available at: http://populargusts.blogspot.com/2006/09/film-of-seoul-in-1899.html. Accessed 3 March 2007.
25. Volume 10, 1901.
26. Depue 1947: 485.
27. Holmes 1901: 107.
28. 14 September 1901: 2.
29. Holmes 1901: 61–63.
30. Details of Thomas's exploits in Korea, although scanty in comparison to the thirty-odd years he dedicated to China, are held in archives at Duke University Library, NC. See China Through Western Eyes (hereafter CTWE), Reel 31, Box 1, Folders 1–3. Special Collections, Duke University Library.
31. "Report on the Commerce and Industries of Korea, 1903 to June 1904," p. 3. File Microcopies of Records in the National Archives: No. 167, Roll 2, Dispatches From United States Consuls in Seoul, 1886–1906, Vol. 2, 19 January 1899–5 July 1906.
32. Thomas 1931: 225–229.
33. Thomas 1931: 252.
34. The Admiral Cigarette brand was manufactured by the Louisville, Kentucky–based National Tobacco Company, which became part of the giant American Tobacco Company in the early 1890s.
35. See "Price List Catalogue [Fragment]", Edison, Thomas Alva, Maguire & Baucus, 1897 (http://hdl.rutgers.edu/1782.2/rucore00000001079. Book.16836); and "Lumière Films, Edison Films, International Films," Edison, Thomas Alva, Maguire & Baucus, Thomas A. Edison, Inc., Auguste & Louis Lumière, 1897 (http://hdl.rutgers.edu/1782.2/rucore00000001079.

Book.16837), Series One, Producers and Sales Agents Active Before 1900. Motion Picture Catalogs Collection, Rutgers, The State University of New Jersey. Accessed 12 January 2010.
36. Thomas 1931: 233.
37. Horace N. Allen to the U.S. assistant secretary of State, 15 March 1900. File Microcopies of Records in the National Archives: No. 167, Roll 2, Dispatches From United States Consuls in Seoul, 1886–1906, Vol. 2, 19 January 1899–5 July 1906.
38. Georgetown University Library Special Collections, C. F. Chase Papers, Box No. 1, Folder 67, "Typed Letter dated 2 March 1908 from C.F. Chase to A.R. Weigall, regarding lantern slides loaned to the East Gate Theater. Sent from Suan Mine"; and Box No. 1, Folder 112, "Typed Letter dated 10 August 1909 from C.F. Chase to Collbran & Bostwick Development Co., regarding return of his lantern slides."
39. Anderson and Richie 1982: 443.
40. Kirkpatrick 2007.

NOTES TO CHAPTER 2

1. A phrase borrowed from the title of the book *Americanizing the Movies and "Movie-Mad" Audiences, 1919–1914* by Richard Abel (2006).
2. Detailed overviews of the Press Law appear in H.I.J.M.'s Residency General 1908: 31–35; and H.I.J.M.'s Residency General 1909: 85–89.
3. For example, see Yi (1992), Lee (2004), Cho (2005), and Baskett (2008).
4. Anderson and Richie 1982: 28–29.
5. Merrit 1985: 83.
6. In the absence of surviving contracts as primary evidence, we are assuming that similar arrangements were obtained in Korea as in Japan.
7. Yu 1998: 22–23.
8. *Hwangseong Shinmun* 14 August 1906: 4.
9. *Hwangseong Shinmun* 4 June 1907: 4.
10. *Hwangseong Shinmun* 4 June 1907: 4.
11. *Hwangseong Shinmun* 20 February 1910: 3; *Maeil Shinbo* 2 February 1913: 3; *Maeil Shinbo* 15 March 1913: 3.
12. *Maeil Shinbo* 9 June 1914: 3; *Maeil Shinbo* 11 June 1914: 3.
13. Reflecting on the first three years of Japan's annexation of Korea, an article in *The Washington Post* on 11 January 1914 explained how the kinematograph had been used in 1908 by Japan's Prince Itō Hirobumi to seduce the Crown Prince of Korea while he was studying in Japan.
14. Anderson and Richie 1982: 32.
15. *Hwangseong Shinmun* 18 February 1910: 3.
16. Abel 1999: 63.
17. Hanson 2007: 16.
18. Bowser 1994; Abel 1999; and Hanson 2007.
19. *Hwangseong Shinmun* 9 April 1910: 2; *Daehan Maeil Shinbo* 10 April 1910: 2.
20. *Maeil Shinbo* 8 November 1912: 4; *Maeil Shinbo* 2 February 1913: 3.
21. *Maeil Shinbo* 2 Feb 1913: 3.
22. Rainey 1999: 1.
23. *Maeil Shinbo* 26 July 1912: 3.
24. *Maeil Shinbo* 30 May 1912: 3.
25. *Maeil Shinbo* 10 March 1911: 2.
26. *Maeil Shinbo* 1 January 1912: 16.

27. *Maeil Shinbo* 1 March 1912: 4.
28. *Maeil Shinbo* 27 July 1912: 3.
29. Kim 2004: 249.
30. *Maeil Shinbo* 16 August 1913: 3.
31. *Maeil Shinbo* 28 June 1916: 4.
32. *Maeil Shinbo* 17 December 1916: 4; *Maeil Shinbo* 1 January 1917: 3.
33. Singer 2001: 217.
34. Lee 2004: 76.
35. Kim 2006: 58.
36. Hayakawa's success is said to have inspired Park Seung-pil of the Danseongsa cinema to produce the feature film *Story of Janghwa and Hongryeon*, made with an all-Korean crew in 1924. See Ichikawa 1941: 100.
37. See Gerow 2000.
38. Gerow 2000.
39. This practice became so widespread throughout the 1920s and 1930s in the United States among the 'big five' vertically integrated studios (Loews [MGM], RKO, Paramount Pictures, Twentieth Century-Fox and Warner Bros.) that it was eventually banned by the United States Supreme Court under the 1948 Paramount Decree antitrust case (initiated in 1938).
40. Kim and Kim 2003b: 35.
41. Ichikawa 1941: 101–110.
42. Yu 1998: 74.
43. As chapter 5 explains, the Chosun Film Distribution Corporation and Chosun Film Production Corporation were formed in 1942 by consolidating all the existing film companies into single companies backed by the Korean Colonial Government.
44. *Maeil Shinbo* 19 April 1913: 1.
45. *Maeil Shinbo* 9 December 1914: 4; *Maeil Shinbo* 21 June 1916: 1.
46. *Maeil Shinbo* 17 July 1914: 4; *Maeil Shinbo* 23 July 1914: 1; *Maeil Shinbo* 25 July 1914: 3.
47. Koller 2002.
48. *Maeil Shinbo* 5 August 1915: 4.
49. Balio 1985: 109–110.
50. Bowser 1994: 127.
51. *Maeil Shinbo* 3 November 1914: 3; *Maeil Shinbo* 27 December 1914: 2.
52. *Maeil Shinbo* 16 November 1915: 4.
53. Lee 2003b: 241.
54. *Maeil Shinbo* 11 June 1912: 2 and *Maeil Shinbo* 3 July 1912: 2.
55. *Maeil Shinbo* 17 February 1912: 2; *Maeil Shinbo* 18 July 1912: 3; and *Maeil Shinbo* 24 July 1912: 3.
56. *Maeil Shinbo* 16 November 1915: 4.
57. *Maeil Shinbo* 25 April 1916: 2; *Maeil Shinbo* 25 May 1916: 3.
58. *Maeil Shinbo* 4 May 1916: 3.
59. *Maeil Shinbo* 9 February 1915: 3.
60. *Maeil Shinbo* 17 March 1915: 3; 24 August 1916: 3.
61. *Maeil Shinbo* 3 September 1915: 3.
62. Cinemas in some of the Southern states in the U.S. contained up to three different (race-specific) entrances (McKenna 2007: 48).
63. *Maeil Shinbo* 10 May 1913: 3; *Maeil Shinbo* 21 October 1913: 3.
64. This differed from those American cinemas that reserved balcony seats for 'colored' people under Jim Crow guidelines (Gaines 2007). Throughout the 1920s (and for decades after in Southern cities such as Atlanta), spatial separation of audiences was enforced along the racial lines drawn by the notorious Jim Crow laws (Allen 2007). This legal framework, enacted in 1876, mandated that all

public institutions and facilities employ racial segregation in order to 'protect' whites from mixing with African-Americans. Hence, racial segregation in the American South aimed to 'create the perfect illusion of two distinct societies' (Gains 2007: 68)—in which practice would follow the theory.

65. Caprio 2009.
66. Abel 2006.
67. *Hwangseong Shinmun* 13 April 1906: 3.
68. For audience habits elsewhere, see Gerow 2000, Hanson 2007, and Gains 2007.
69. Hanson 2007: 29.
70. *Maeil Shinbo* 1 April 1916: 3.
71. Kim and Kim 2003d: 195.
72. *Maeil Shinbo* 27 Feb 1914: 3.
73. 8 January 1916: 3.
74. *Maeil Shinbo* 3 September 1915: 3.
75. *Maeil Shinbo* 1 April 1916: 3.
76. *Maeil Shinbo* 4 September 1915: 4; *Maeil Shinbo* 9 September 1915: 3. As in the case of international expos and world's fairs today, the exposition aimed to develop a new, imagined national consciousness under Japanese occupation while also showing a lack of respect for Korea's royal family and Korean culture more generally because of its location at the Palace.
77. *Cinema Yearbook of Japan 1938*: 49. Details in Ichikawa (1941) and Ōta (1938) about the film industry in Korea also point to 1916 as a peak of production and exhibition.
78. *Maeil Shinbo* 20 July 1916: 3.
79. *Donga Ilbo* 29 March 1922: 3; and *Donga Ilbo* 18 April 1923: 3.
80. These Japanese film laws are discussed in Freiberg (2000).
81. In addition to gramophones and sewing machines, Morris also sold and repaired Overland touring cars and Indian motorcycles (*The Korea Magazine* January 1918).
82. Ichikawa 1941: 101; and Kim and Kim 2003b: 34.
83. Advertisements for the Victrola in *The Korea Magazine* (January 1918) picture the system in a wooden furniture cabinet containing a turntable and amplifying horn.
84. These statistics appear in the *Annual Report on Reforms and Progress in Chosen, 1921–1922*, 1923: 15.
85. *Maeil Shinbo* 15 July 1916: 3; *Maeil Shinbo* 16 July 1916: 3; *Maeil Shinbo* 19 July 1916: 3; *Maeil Shinbo* 20 July 1916: 3.
86. *Maeil Shinbo* 27 February 1916: 3.
87. *Maeil Shinbo* 19 March 1913: 5.

NOTES TO CHAPTER 3

1. An earlier version of this chapter was published in the *Journal of Korean Studies* Vol. 10, No. 1 (2005): 59–84; and in *Hanguk Mun Hak Yeon Gu (Studies in Korean Literature)* Vol. 29 (June 2006). Seoul: Dongguk University Institute of Korean Literature Studies. 203–237.
2. Ōta 1938; Ichikawa 1941.
3. Lee 2004: 76.
4. Kim 2006: 49.
5. Eckert et al. 1990: 282.
6. Eckert 1991: 236.
7. Cumings 1997: 154–155.

8. Robinson 1999: 63.
9. 'Kine-o-ramas'—as they were called in newspapers of the time, but called 'kino-dramas' elsewhere such as Lee (2000)—mixed live theater, filmed sequences on stage, and magic lantern slides of the type introduced by Christian missionaries in the early 1890s.
10. *Righteous Revenge* was inspired by Japanese *rensa-geki* (chain dramas, initially called 'cine-o-ramas' in Korean newspapers) that had been performed at multiple theatres in Seoul in early 1913 by the Japanese theatrical group Setonaikai (瀬戸内海). After watching the public presentations of *Hototogisu* (不如帰, Little Cuckoo) and *Ono ga tsumi* (己が罪), a small group of Koreans accompanied the troupe to Japan, where they became apprentices. Between 1913 and 1918 these Koreans, a group which probably included Kim Do-san—the director of *Righteous Revenge*—gained the experience necessary to make the first Korean kine-o-rama in 1919. Program advertisements for these indoor mixed-media theatrical events began appearing in the *Maeil Shinbo* 15 February 1913: 2; *Maeil Shinbo* 16 February 1913: 3; *Maeil Shinbo* 2 March 1913: 3. Reflections on these historical details appear in *Eiga Junpō* 11 July 1943: 16–19.
11. Government-General of Chosen 1936: 42.
12. See: DGGA, File# CJA0019728, Correspondence from the Chief of the Department of Home Affairs (Naimu Kyokuchō) to the head of each prefecture (Kaku Fuin dono), regarding: Motion picture distribution (Katsudō shashin eiga haifu kata no ken), "List of films in the custody of the Department of Home Affairs, Korean Colonial Government (Chōsen Sōtokufu Naimu kyoku hokan eiga mokuroku)", 2 June 1927.
13. KMPPC 1977: 46.
14. *Donga Ilbo* 19 November 1925.
15. See Lee 2000 and Kim Kyung Hyun 2002: 20.
16. Makino 2001: 64.
17. Makino 2001.
18. Salomon 2000: 148–149.
19. *Donga Ilbo* 24 April 1924: 2.
20. *Donga Ilbo* 30 June 1924: 2.
21. For a review of early Japanese film industry laws, see *Film Year Book 1922–1923;* Freiberg (2000); and Makino (2001).
22. Kim and Kim 2003c: 51; Kim and Kim 2003a: 187.
23. Mitchell 1976: 19.
24. Jung and Choi 2006: 130.
25. Kasza 1988.
26. H.I.J.M.'s Residency-General 1908: 31–35.
27. Makino 2001: 57.
28. Under Resident-General Itō Hirobumi, public gatherings were regulated by the 1907 Security Law, based on the Japanese Public Peace Police Law (1890). The advertising of specific films and the discussion of their reception in local newspapers was governed by the Newspaper Law of 1907, the Newspaper Regulations of 1908, and Publication Law of 1909, all of which were based on laws promulgated earlier in Japan. These and other regulations subjected the courts, prisons, and the police to micro-management and enabled the Japanese to assume widespread control throughout Korea. However, while the Security Law has been described as an instrument of 'domination over the soul' (Lee 1999: 45), the type of 'public disorder' fomented by cinemas caused the authorities additional concerns about the 'new thought trends such as socialism that challenged the socio-economic base on which the imperial order stood'—or so it seemed.

29. Kim et al. 2005: 532–533.
30. Lee Hwa-jin 2008: 420.
31. See "Future Outlook—Conditions in Oriental Territories," *Film Year Book 1925* (New York: Wid's Films and Film Folks, 1925), 663–666; and "The Foreign Market: Japan," *Film Year Book 1926* (New York: Wid's Films and Film Folks, 1926), 657, 820, 860.
32. The coalition included the Japan Moving Picture Producing Co., Shōchiku Cinema Co., Teikoku Cinema Co., and Makino Moving Picture Producing Co.
33. Thompson 1985.
34. Academy of the Motion Picture Arts and Sciences Library Archives (AMPAS), MPAA Censorship Regulations—Foreign, File #7, Censorship Reports: Japan. 501.
35. Freiberg 2000; *Film Year Book 1922–1923* (1923): 371.
36. *Film Year Book 1926* 1926: 820.
37. Government-General of Chosen 1927: 148.
38. As early as 1923, it was estimated that approximately 76,000 out of a total of 288,000 (26 percent) of the population in Seoul was Japanese. The southernmost port city of Busan included almost 44 percent Japanese among its 80,000 inhabitants. See *Annual Report on Administration of Chosen, 1922–23* 1924: 14–15.
39. For a discussion of the Korean business elite during the colonial era, see McNamara 1989 and Song 2003.
40. Architectural, electrical, and other pertinent documents can be found in "Motion Picture Film Censorship Building Re-construction Work" (Chōsen Sōtokufu; Katsudō shashin firumu kenetsujo shinchiku kōji), 1933 Financial Year (*Shōwa hachi nendo*), Government-General of Chōsen, File #CJA0012809, Ministry of Government Administration and Home Affairs, National Archives in Korea, Daejon, Korea (hereafter cited as Archives and Records Service).
41. See "Number 21 (*Nijūichi*), Motion Picture Film Censorship Situation" (Katsudō shashin firumu ken'etsu jōkyō), Sixty-ninth Imperial Parliament Document (Dairokujūkyūkai Teikoku Gikai Setsumei shiryō), Library Section of the Bureau of Police Affairs, Korean Colonial Government (Chōsen Sōtokufu Keimukyoku Toshōkan Teikoku Gikai Setsumei shiryō), 1935, File #CJA0002448, Archives and Records Service.
42. Censorship statistics cited in this chapter come from: "Table of Censored Motion Picture Films, 1 August 1926 to 31 March 1935" (Katsudō shashin [firumu] ken'etsu tōkeihyō, Taishō jūgonen hachigatsu tsuitachi kara Shōwa jūnen sangatsu sanjūichinichi made), Sixty-ninth Imperial Parliament Document (Dairokujūkyūkai Teikoku Gikai Setsumei shiryō), Library Section of the Bureau of Police Affairs, Korean Colonial Government (Chōsen Sōtokufu Keimukyoku Toshōkan Teikoku Gikai Setsumei shiryō), Serial# CJA0002448, File# 101-7-1-2, Archives and Records Service); and "Table of Censored Motion Picture Films, 1 April 1935 to 31 March 1936" (Katsudō shashin [firumu] ken'etsu tōkeihyō, Shōwa jūnen shigatsu tsuitachi kara Shōwa jūichinen sangatsu sanjūichinichi made), Sixty-ninth Imperial Parliament Document (Dairokujūkyūkai Teikoku Gikai Setsumei shiryō), Library Section of the Bureau of Police Affairs, Government-General of Chōsen, File #CJA0002471, Archives and Records Service.
43. Government-General of Chosen 1936: 47.
44. See "Number 21, Motion Picture Film Censorship Situation," File #CJA0002448, Archives and Records Service.
45. According to exchange rates published in July 1966 by the Bank of Japan, ¥100 traded for an average of $46.875 in New York in 1926 and $28.951 in 1936.

46. Foreign Market Reports, "Japan," *Film Year Book 1927* (New York: Wid's Films and Film Folks, 1927), 970–971; "Japan," *Film Daily Year Book 1928* (New York: J. W. Alicoate, 1928), 969; "Japan," *Film Daily Year Book 1929* (New York: J. W. Alicoate, 1929), 1033–1036; "Japan," *Film Daily Year Book of Motion Pictures 1933* (New York: Film Daily, 1933), 1003; and "Japan," *Film Daily Year Book of Motion Pictures 1934* (New York: Film Daily, 1934), 1037–1038.
47. *Donga Ilbo* 14 July 1926: 1.
48. Cho 2005: 79.
49. *Jungoi Ilbo* 23 August 1928: 2.
50. See Langdon "Chosen Motion Picture Notes" 31 March 1934.
51. *Film Daily Year Book of Motion Pictures 1939* (1939: 1174) and *Film Daily Year Book of Motion Pictures 1940* (1940: 1103–1104).
52. See Golden 1938: 1191–1193, and Langdon "Chosen Motion Picture Control Ordinance" 9 August 1934: 2.
53. Records from the Warner Bros. Archives at the School of Cinema-Television, University of Southern California, indicate that First National began distributing its films directly to the Korean market on January 1, 1928. See File: Japan #13101A.
54. Ōka's comments from 1933 have been translated into Korean and published in KOFA 2009: 324.
55. Mary Pickford both starred in and produced a number of films: *Tess of the Storm Country* (1914), directed by Edwin S. Porter, an 80-minute feature produced by the Famous Players Film Company (which eventually became Paramount Pictures); *Suds* (1920), directed by John Francis Dillon; *Polly-anna* (1920), *Little Lord Fauntleroy* (1921), and *Rosita* (1923), all directed by Ernst Lubitsch; *Through the Back Door* (1921); *Little Annie Rooney* (1925) and *Sparrows* (1926), directed by William Beaudine; *Dorothy Vernon of Haddon Hall* (1924), directed by Marshall Neilan; and, finally, *My Best Girl* (1927), a romantic comedy.
56. Douglas Fairbanks's movies included: *The Mark of Zorro* (1920); *When the Clouds Roll By* (1919), a romantic action comedy, and *The Mollycoddle* (1920), directed by Victor Fleming; *His Majesty, the American* (1919), directed by Joseph Henabery, another romantic comedy; *The Nut* (1921), and *The Gaucho* (1927), directed by F. Richard Jones, both with an uncredited appearance by Mary Pickford; *The Three Musketeers* (1921); *Robin Hood* (1922) and *The Iron Mask* (1929), both directed by Allan Dwan; *The Thief of Bagdad* (1924), a romantic family adventure fantasy, directed by Raoul Walsh; *Don Q Son of Zorro* (1925), directed by Donald Crisp; and, finally, *The Black Pirate* (1926), directed by Albert Parker, again with a cameo appearance by Mary Pickford.
57. Kim 2009: 18–19.
58. *Donga Ilbo* 13 November 1926.
59. See: United Artists Corporation. Series 5C: Foreign general ledgers [microform], 1929–1950. Reel 5. State Historical Society of Wisconsin. This collection contains financial information from United Artists' Japan foreign office, which also included Korea.
60. Balio 1985: 165–166.
61. See comments in "Number 21, Motion Picture Film Censorship Situation" ("Katsudō shashin firumu ken'etsu jōkyō"), Seventy-third Imperial Parliament Document (Dai nanajūsan kai Teikoku Gikai Setsumei shiryō), Bureau of Police Affairs (*Keimukyoku*), 1937, File #CJA0002471, Archives and Records Service.
62. According to archival documents relating to the Studio Relations Committee, a core American film industry advisory committee, MPPDA members shared

a regular flow of feedback from the New York, Pennsylvania, Maryland, Virginia, Ohio, and Kansas state censors. In turn, they used this intelligence as a guide for substituting 'objectionable' scenes with less objectionable material on a state-by-state (and country-by-country) basis. "Resume of Dinner-Meeting of the Studio Relations Committee," 19 April 1928. MPAA Censorship Reports. File# 10. Eliminations 1928-USA. AMPAS Library Archives.

63. Ōka 1931, translated into Korean and published in KOFA 2009: 320.
64. Bureau of Police Affairs 1931, translated into Korean and published in KOFA 2009: 222–229.
65. AMPAS Library Archives. MPAA Censorship Regulations—Foreign. File#7. Censorship Reports: Japan 500.
66. Lee 2004: 98.
67. Na November 1936, published in Kim Jong-wook 2002: 628.
68. See "Number 21, Motion Picture Film Censorship Situation," File #CJA0002448, Archives and Records Service.
69. See the discussion of KAPF in Yi 1994: 239–250; and Lee 2000: 25, 27–30, 38.
70. *Shinkō Eiga* March 1930: 112–114, 115–124.
71. Korean films such as Kim Yu-young's *Yurang* (Wandering, 1928) and *Honga* (The Imbecile Street, 1929) were made, but severely cut by the censors. The first roll of *Yurang* and 4 rolls (out of a total of 13) of *Honga* were cut by the censors, which ultimately made Kim Yu-young give up filmmaking *Shinkō Eiga* March 1930: 112–114.
72. See correspondence regarding "Motion Picture Distribution" (*Katsudō shashin eiga haifu kata no ken*) in "The List of Films in the Custody of the Government-General" (*Chōsen Sōtokufu naimukyoku hokan eiga mokuroku*), File #CJA0019728, Archives and Records Service. See *Jūroku miri Eiga sōmokuroku*, edited and published by the Section of Film Promotion, Fukada Ltd & Co. (*Henshū ken hakkōnin: Fukada Shōkai Eigabu Sendenka*), *Hakkōjo: Fukada Shōkai Eigabu Ōsaka sakai-suji Honchō kōsaten*), File #CJA0019728, Archives and Records Service.
73. Itagaki 1938: 44–46.
74. High 2003; Nornes 2003. Additional details regarding these film genres can be found in a 1937 16mm film library catalogue, which the Korean Colonial Government kept among its film distribution and exhibition records.
75. The *Donga Ilbo*, *Chosun Ilbo*, and *Maeil Shinbo* newspapers also carried film-related stories, editorials, photos of film people, and advertisements.
76. *Cinema Yearbook of Japan, 1936–1937* (1937): 7; Anderson and Richie 1982: 48, 315–318.
77. For more background details about these and other cases, see the double-volume reference book edited by Kim Jong-wook 2002.
78. Kim and Kim 2003b: 277–279.
79. Ho 2000: 39.
80. Lee 2009: 30
81. Ho 2000: 38.
82. Shin Chul, personal interview, Seoul, 17 December 2002.
83. Kim and Kim 2003b: 283.
84. Kim and Kim 2003b: 282–287.
85. This phrase is borrowed from the study of censorship in Imperial Japan by Mitchell (1983: 132).
86. Tani 1937: 1122–1123.
87. (1936): 1021–1123.
88. Anderson and Richie 1982: 69.
89. *Motion Picture Almanac 1935–1936* (1936): 1020.

90. United Artists collection, Series 1F Box 5–5, State Historical Society of Wisconsin.
91. "Chosen (Korea)," *Film Daily Year Book of Motion Pictures, 1938,* 1191–1193.
92. Rout 1932: 640.
93. Iwasaki 1940: 64–65.
94. These figures are derived from data in the *Cinema Yearbook of Japan* (1936–1937, 1938, and 1939), published in English by the Society for International Cultural Relations in Japan, and the Kim Jong-wook (2002) reference book.
95. Golden 1938: 1191–1193.
96. *Ōsaka Mainichi.* "Education by Movie Films." In *Japan Today and Tomorrow 1932–33,* 36–39. Ōsaka: Ōsaka Mainichi Publishing Co., 1933.
97. While this figure includes both types of films, an overwhelming majority were categorized in the censorship tables as for entertainment purposes.
98. (1936): 1189–1190.
99. AMPAS Library Archives, MPAA Censorship Regulations—Foreign, File #7, Censorship Reports: Japan. 506.
100. *Motion Picture Almanac* (1938): 1173–1175.
101. United Artists collection, Series 1F Box 5–4, State Historical Society of Wisconsin.
102. SCAP, *Summation No. 2,* November 1945: 174.

NOTES TO CHAPTER 4

1. 'Sound production' meant recording on either phonograph discs (sound-on-disc) or on the same filmstrip as the visual images (sound-on-film). 'Sound films' included a variety of forms: all-talkie, part-talkie, sound effects, asynchronous music, and synchronous music. Synchronization problems occurred with sound-on-disc pictures when discs skipped or parts of the film were cut due to damage, thus changing the alignment between the recorded sound and images.
2. Detailed conference minutes are held in the Academy of the Motion Picture Arts and Sciences Library Archives (hereafter cited as AMPAS) in the MPAA General Correspondence Files, MF Roll #1, 1929–30. Nowell-Smith and Ricci (1998) and Higson and Maltby (1999) also include extensive discussions of this American and European cartel.
3. Yecies 2005a; and Yecies 2007.
4. For a discussion of the rise and development of commerce in Korea, see Cumings 1997.
5. For more insight on the impact of Saitō's Cultural Policy reforms, see Eckert et al. 1990: 276–304.
6. One of the few comprehensive reports in English on the film industry in Korea can be found in Langdon (1934). In the early 1930s, William R. Langdon was the American Consul-General in Seoul. He regularly reported on film industry developments for the United States Department of State, which relayed this information to Hollywood studio executives and trade publications such as *Variety, Film Daily Year Book of Motion Pictures,* and Nathan D. Golden's film market reports for the United States Department of Commerce, Bureau of Foreign and Domestic Commerce.
7. *Film Daily Year Book 1937* (1938): 1230.
8. Ōta 1938: 49–50; Iwasaki 1939: 64. Both Ōta and Iwasaki were well-known Japanese film critics and members of the International Cinema Association of Japan. Iwasaki was also one of the editors of the *Cinema Year Book of Japan.*

9. Many were produced by the socialist Korean Artist Proletarian Federation (KAPF), whose films were made by Korean filmmakers with all-Korean crews. They were 'nationalistic' films stimulated by the appearance of *Arirang* (1926), the most famous silent (and possibly nationalistic) Korean film. Well-known KAPF films include: *Wandering* (Yurang, 1928); *Street of Darkness* (Honga, 1929); *The Dark Road* (Amno, 1929); *Underground Village* (Jihachon, 1931); and *Wheel of Fire* (1931).
10. Such as Lee (2000) and Min, Joo, and Kwak (2003).
11. These figures are compiled from Kim Jong-wook 2002.
12. This slogan is quoted from a speech given by Governor-General Ugaki at the Conference of Empire Middle School Principals in Seoul on September 11, 1934. See Ugaki (1934).
13. See, for example, Yi 1992; Ho 2000; Cho 2002b; and Kim Mee-hyun 2002.
14. See, for example, Lee 2000; James and Kim 2002; Min, Joo, and Kwak 2003; Kim Kyung Hyun 2004; McHugh and Abelmann 2005; and Shin and Stringer 2005.
15. See, for example, Richie 1971; Mellen 1976; Anderson and Richie 1982; Satō 1987; Nolletti and Desser 1992; and Bernardi 2001.
16. References to these screenings appear in: *Donga Ilbo* 16 January 1928: 3. Other details can be found in Yu (1997).
17. *Donga Ilbo* 20 May 1927: 3; *Donga Ilbo* 8 October 1927: 3; *Donga Ilbo* 9 October 1927: 3.
18. *Donga Ilbo* 16 January 1928: 3; *Donga Ilbo* 18 January 1928: 3; and *Donga Ilbo* 19 January 1928: 3.
19. In mid-1929 Shōchiku Studio, the largest of the 'big five' production and distribution companies in Japan, had ordered multiple Western Electric sound recording and projection systems. Shortly thereafter, the Western Electric Company Orient Ltd. opened regional offices in Tokyo, Ōsaka, Nagoya, Fukuoka, Sapporo, and Harbin and Darien (both in Manchuria), and in Seoul. A full set of Western Electric sound equipment, which included import duties and a compulsory ten-year service contract, cost theater owners and exhibitors up to approximately $55,000.
20. *Chosun Ilbo* 18 October 1931: 5.
21. *Chosun Ilbo* 3 August 1931: 3.
22. Ibid.
23. *Eiga Hyōron* December 1932: 113–114. See also Kim and Kim 2003b: 132–135.
24. His comments appear in a series of articles in: *Chosun Ilbo* 8 September 1931: 5; *Chosun Ilbo* 11 September 1931: 5; *Chosun Ilbo* 13 September 1931: 5; *Chosun Ilbo* 20 September 1931: 5; *Chosun Ilbo* 23 September 1931: 5.
25. According to Lee and Choe (1998: 60), Lee Gyu-hwan's ambition of studying directing in Hollywood was sparked by seeing Na Un-gyu's *Arirang*.
26. Lee 2000. New films from the colonial period continue to be unearthed. In mid-2007, 9 reels of Ahn Jong-hwa's *Cheongchun-ui Sipjaryo* (*Crossroads of Youth*, 1934) were discovered in Korea. After 8 months of restoration, a preview of this black-and-white silent movie was exhibited at the Korean Film Archive in March 2008.
27. According to the KOFA database, Lee Gyu-hwan's career spanned four decades. During this time he directed 22 films, wrote 16 screenplays, adaptations and novels, edited 12 films and produced or planned six productions. Given that he outlived the colonial era and civil war, it is easy to see why scholars such as Ho (2000), Lee and Choe (1998) consider Lee Gyu-hwan to be one of Korea's master filmmakers.

28. The average price of a Japanese sound projector such as the Nippon Sound System was between ¥3,000 and ¥5,500 (between approximately $860 and $1,570) in the early 1930s.
29. These types of films were officially classified as 'documentary films' in 1937 and 'cultural films' after 1938.
30. Yecies 2005b.
31. For instance, in late 1931, the Seoul-based distributor Kishin Yanghaeng acquired from Paramount's branch office in Japan dozens of sound-on-disc films for general exhibition, including *Paramount On Parade* (1930), *Charley's Aunt* (1930), *His Woman* (1931), *Rich Man's Folly* (1931), and *Newly Rich* (1931).
32. Anderson and Richie 1982; and Iwamoto 1992.
33. Documentary evidence describes *Secret Story* as involving a girl who becomes a *gisaeng* (*geisha*). She tries to keep her job a secret from her brother, who bursts into tears when he discovers the truth. See *Malmotal Sajeong*, catalogue entry #40205 (A-1, A-4), Korean Broadcasting System (KBS) Sound Archive, Seoul.
34. Maliangkay 2007: 57.
35. *Chosun Yeonghwa* No. 1 (October 1936): 60.
36. Maliangkay 2007: 57.
37. At one level, *Secret Story* was part of a scheme for generating new sources of Korean-language entertainment programs for the Gyeongseong Broadcasting Company (KBC), which was established in 1927. According to Robinson (1998), sales of radio receivers to Koreans were increasing significantly at this time. According to Maliangkay (2007), phonograph sales also experienced steady growth during the colonial period. A phonograph recording of *Secret Story* was in fact made and is still available as part of a compilation of Korean songs on a commercial CD.
38. Although Na Un-gyu made only a small number of sound films, many of the titles of the silent feature films which he directed and/or starred in were redolent of sound: *Samnyong the Mute* (1929); *Song for My Home Town* (1932); *Carmen* (1933); and *Sound of the Bullets* (1933).
39. See Na (September 1933).
40. Way 1930: 5.
41. Anderson and Richie 1982: 77; Kim and Kim 2003a: 244–249. Other material on Lee Pil-wu can be found in the personal interviews cited in Lee and Choe (1998).
42. Lee Pil-wu 1930: 4.
43. Yi 1996: 61.
44. Kim 2006: 50.
45. Lee 2004: 92.
46. Langdon 23 March 1934; Langdon 6 September 1934.
47. See Anderson 1992: 259–311.
48. Choe 1996: 222. For an earlier investigation into these complex issues, see Yecies and Shim 2003.
49. According to the *1937–38 Motion Picture Almanac* (1938: 1173–1175), since 1935 the Korean Colonial Government had been planning to formulate a 'cinema control plan,' which would increase the screening ratio of Japanese *and* Korean films to American films from one-third to more than half.
50. Lee and Choe 1998: 36.
51. These sentiments are expressed in Ahn Seok-yeong *Parts 1, 2 and 3* (1935).
52. Lee Myeong-wu 1936: 58.
53. Indol 11 October 1935: 3.
54. Shim Hun (1936: 82–86) believed that making talkies required precise scientific and technical know-how, skills he felt were lacking in Korean

screenwriters, cameramen, engineers, and actors. Essentially, he saw the Korean film community as a bunch of schoolchildren who, having just learned to read, could not wait to fulfill their childhood fantasy of reading adult books.

55. Kim Jong-wook 2002: 351–353.
56. See Kim Gwan (1936: 5). Kim was also displeased that foreign music—a symphony by Beethoven—was used in the soundtrack (instead of traditional Korean music); he believed this made the story harder for Koreans to follow and relate to.
57. Older Korean film scholars agree that a boom of silent films occurred between 1926 and 1934 (Lee 2004; Lee and Choe 1998; Ho 2000; Kim and Jeong 2001; and Yi 2002). This period is notable for the quantity and technical and artistic quality of films made and the proliferation of an estimated fifty film-production companies. According to Lee Young-il (1969: 84), about eighty films were produced between 1926 and 1935—over half of the total estimated productions made before liberation in 1945.
58. Government-General of Chosen 1936: 42. According to flow charts depicting the organization of the colonial government in the annual reports published by the Government-General of Chosen, the Central Council Investigation Section (after its Board of Information was amalgamated with the Statistics Section) was an affiliated department on the same level as the Communications Bureau, Railway Bureau, Monopoly Bureau, Customs House, and Law Courts.
59. Lee and Choe 1998.

NOTES TO CHAPTER 5

1. Lindstrom 1937.
2. Quoted from a speech by Governor-General Minami Jirō delivered to Korea's thirteen provincial governors in April 1937 (*Annual Report* 1938, 227).
3. Distributing free tickets to Koreans as a marketing strategy to increase their patronage of Japanese films was a practice that began around 1936 (*Eiga Hyōron* July 1941: 54–60). By this time and for a while after, Korean audiences were more attracted to Western films than Japanese films. Although fewer Western films were available to exhibit after 1937, the Korean Colonial Government still used promotional strategies such as this to increase the number of Koreans attending screenings of Japanese films.
4. Information based on a search of the Korean Movie Data Base (KMDB), available at www.koreafilm.org/database/database.asp.
5. *Annual Report 1938*: 227.
6. See Yu (1997), Kim and Jeong (2000), Lee (2004), and Lee (2005).
7. Kim 2006: 191.
8. See Kim (2006), Cho Jun-hyung (2006), and Yi (2008), for example.
9. For more details about Lee and the Goryeo Film Association, see Kim Hee-yoon 2007: 20–27. As discussed in chapter 2, collaborative projects involving Japanese and Korean filmmakers and business entrepreneurs had been happening since 1912, when the number of film distribution and exhibition initiatives began to rise. By 1916, Japanese companies Nikkatsu and Tenkatsu were running half of Seoul's six largest permanent indoor cinemas, often with the assistance of Korean personnel. Hayagawa Sōtarō scripted and directed *The Tale of Chunhyang* in 1923, with Japanese production funding under the umbrella of the Korean Donga Culture Association. This was a collaborative 'co-produced' project, which showcased the increasing number

of established Japanese film directors and actors who were participating in films produced in Korea.

10. This film, which seems to have appealed to working-class audiences in particular, depicts the mundane life of a struggling fish-market worker whose job keeps him away from his home and family. Returning to his hometown, he learns that his father has been murdered and the local barber is after his wife. In a fit of rage, the fisherman kills the barber and then turns himself in to the authorities, with his wife at his side.

11. Ōta 1938.

12. Oh 2007: 7.

13. *Samcheolli* June 1941: 220–221; Kim Hee-yoon 2007: 21.

14. This film, which used a screenplay by Yaki Yastaro and starred the famous Japanese theater actor Usuda Genji, was planned by Lee Chang-yong and directed by Jun Chang-keun.

15. During this period, Lee also produced *Suicide Squad of the Watchtower* (1943), *A Song of a Year of Abundance* (1942), and *Garden of Victory* (1940). According to KMDB, *Tuition* was Goryeo's second film and was based on an award-winning essay by a fourth-year primary school student telling the story of a poor student whose friends helped him to pay his tuition fees.

16. This organization was established in 1937 by the Manchurian government and the Manchurian Railroad Corporation with the aim of propagating Manchurian and Japanese national policy (Zhang 2004: 84).

17. Cho Jun-hyung 2006: 72.

18. Other films that fit the 'yellow' designation include *Light of the Sea* (1940), *Pure Heart* (1940), *Garden of Victory* (1940), and *Dawn of the Mountain Village* (1940).

19. The CFAA was absorbed into the Chosun Film Production Corporation in October 1943.

20. According to Ichikawa (1941: 112), these skills tests were administered by a committee that included public officials, film directors, actors, cameramen, and film scholars.

21. *Samcheolli* January 1941: 191.

22. Ibid.

23. *Samcheolli* January 1941: 161.

24. In the Korean version, the Japanese title of 'Minister' was exchanged for 'Governor-General.'

25. Nihon Eiga Zasshi Kyoukai Hen Eds. (Japanese Film Magazine Association) 1942: 7–14.

26. Cho Jun-hyung 2005: 86–92.

27. In a panel discussion hosted by *Eiga Junpō,* critic Iijima Tadashi, director Hazumi Tsuneo, and Korean Film Culture Research Center researcher Hirokawa Sōyō agreed that, in this collaborative relationship, the Koreans' main input should be to infuse productions with a sense of Korea's distinctive cultural identity (*Eiga Junpō* 1 November 1941: 15–22).

28. *Samcheolli* January 1941: 161.

29. The Japanese colonial authority's policy toward the Korean language changed eventually, and is well documented in Rhee (1992). The revised educational ordinance declared in 1938 intensified national language education for primary and secondary schools in Korea. Schools, like films, magazines, and newspapers, were required to accelerate the full implementation of the Japanese language in everyday learning and communication. It also became compulsory for individuals to adopt Japanese family names. In reality, a minimal use of the Korean language was still necessary to overcome literacy challenges and to provide a bridge for disseminating state

ideology—at least in the short term until all of Korea was proficient in the Japanese language.

30. This figure, which is cited faithfully, was a significant number given that the entire population of Korea, including foreign expatriates, was 24 million (*Samcheolli* January 1941: 163).

31. In 2008, *Volunteer* was released on DVD by the Korean Film Archive as part of its *Past Unearthed* collection of feature films from the colonial period. Other films in this boxed set include *Angles on the Streets* (1941), *Spring in the Korean Peninsula* (1941), and *Straits of Chosun* (1943).

32. Kim 2006: 276–282.

33. Tasaka was well-known, among other things, for co-writing and directing Nikkatsu's critically acclaimed *Five Scouts* (1938)—a drama exploring the friendship between five Japanese soldiers in Japan's 1930s war with China.

34. Baskett 2008: 23.

35. Baskett 2008: 87–88.

36. *Samcheolli* September 1941: 117.

37. Utsumi and Murai 1987, cited in High 2003: 308.

38. Yi 2008: 85–93.

39. Kim Shin-jae appeared in 20 colonial-era films, including *Sons of the Sky* (1945), *Vow of Love* (1945), *Children of the Sun* (1944), *Straits of Chosun* (1943), *Suicide Squad of the Watchtower* (1943), *Angels on the Streets* (1941), *You and I* (1941), *Tuition* (1940), and *The Story of Shim Cheong* (1937). Kim made nearly 200 films during her long career, which lasted until the late 1980s. *You and I* was Hwang's first film and she appeared in 366 subsequent films, working until the late 1980s.

40. Its production history is discussed in *Samcheolli* September 1941: 114–115.

41. Ho 2000: 71–72.

42. *Samcheolli* January 1942: 103. For a brief discussion of this film, see Anderson and Richie 1982: 124.

43. (1939: 21).

44. For example, see Yu (1997), Kim and Jeong (2000), Ho (2000), Lee (2004), and Kim (2006).

45. Lee 2004: 205.

46. High 2003: 308–314.

47. *Maeil Shinbo* 22 November: 4.

48. *Eiga Junpō* 21 October 1941: 31–35; and *Eiga Junpō* 11th December 1941: 35–36.

49. *Nihon Eiga* December 1941: 63 (cited in High 2003: 312).

50. Cited in High 2003: 313.

51. Said 1991: 49; Anderson and Richie 1982: 157. The dramatic story of Heo and his negotiation of three national identities is explored in South Korean filmmaker Kim Jae-bum's documentary *A Filmmaker with Three Names* (1997). Heo's comments on *You and I* appear in *Samcheolli* (September 1941: 114–115).

52. Sakuramoto 1983: 186.

53. High 2003: 307–308.

54. Sakuramoto 1983: 186.

55. Kim 2006: 233–237.

56. For instance, see Lee 2004: 202.

57. Choi In-gyu developed a reputation for his use of a realist aesthetic in his portrayal of contemporary life. After the colonial period, Choi made a major contribution to Korea's post-liberation cinema by directing such ultranationalist films as *Hurray for Freedom* (1946). His post-liberation work includes *An Innocent Criminal* (1948), *A National Referendum*

(1948), *The Night before Independence Day* (1948), *Dance of Jang Chu-hwa* (1948), and *The Town of Hope* (1948). Choi also trained directors such as Shin Sang-ok (1925–2006) and Han Hyung-mo (1917–1999), who also became masters of realism and leading filmmakers in South Korea's contemporary cinema.

58. Rookie director Lee Byeong-il had gained valuable experience working at the Nikkatsu Studios in Tokyo between 1934 and 1940. Returning to Korea, he created the Myeongbo Film Company; *Spring in the Korean Peninsula* was the company's first film. See Kim Jong-woon 2003: 456–457.

59. *Beautiful Sacrifice* was produced by the Manchurian Film Association and released in Korea in March 1941 (Kim 2006: 274).

60. Davis 1996: 130.

61. Anderson and Richie 1982: 141; High 2003: 268. The documentary footage also contains a rare shot of the cinema's display window featuring a mer-chandising tie-in campaign with Niyuutoni (a 'strong health tonic for a new generation'), revealing the type of promotional strategies that were popular in Korea at the time (see the middle-right image in Figure 5.2).

62. The many references to popular 1930s' French and German films include several portraits of Marlene Dietrich—on the walls of the producer's hospital room, in the home of the record company employee—revealing another facet of the diverse cinema cultures on display in colonial Korea.

63. Other films distributed following the formation of the CFDC included *Ōmura Masujirō*; *The Father*; Yutaka Abe's *South Seas Bouquet* (1942), a film that celebrated the bravery of the Japanese pilots who attacked Malaya in December 1941 and Singapore in February 1942; *Mother and Child*; Tetsu Taguchi's *Generals, Staff, and Soldiers*, made with the direct support of the military and shot on location near the fighting in North China; *The Day England Fell* (dir. Tanaka Shigeo); and *Flying South in his Plane*.

64. *Eiga Hyōron* July 1941: 54–60.

65. Anderson and Richie 1982: 130.

66. Sakuramoto 1983: 187.

67. See *Eiga Junpō* 1 November 1941: 15–22. The Chosun Film Culture Research Institution was run by Hirokawa Sōyō and published several film books including *Thirty Years of Chosun Film History* (1943) and *Korean Film Annual* (1943).

68. Tanaka Saburo owned 10,000 shares (or 25%) of the ¥2 million in shares behind the capitalization of the CFDC. Other chief shareholders included Kin Seikō, Toshiji Arai, Takeo Takai, Genroku Kobayashi, Teiichi Takagi, Miyasaku Kurokawa, and Takaaki Matsumoto.

69. Ichikawa 1941: 104.

70. Other companies included: the Korea Film Company (Chosun Yeonghwa Jusikhoesa); the Goryeo Film Association (Goryeo Yeonghwa Hyeo-phoe); the Korea Culture Film Association (Chosun Munhwa Yeonghwa Hyeophoe); Choi Nam-ju's Korea Film Company; Kim Gab-gi's Hanyang Film Company; Seo Hang-seok's Korean Entertainment Company; Lee Chang-geun's Dongyang Talkie Film Studio; the Kanyō Film Company; the Seoul Film Production Company (Gyeongseong Yeonghwa Jejakso); Lee Byeong-il's Myeongbo Film Company (Myeongbo Yeonghwa Hapja Hoesa); the Seoul Talkie Film Production Company (Gyeongseong Balseong Yeonghwa Jejakso); the Imperial Film Company (Hwangguk Yeonghwasa); the Dongyang Talkie Production Company; and the Korea and Manchuria Documentary Film Production Company (Seonman Girok Yeonghwa Jejakso).

71. Sakuramoto 1983: 188.

72. Some of the very few films exhibited in Korea at this time include the action and thriller genre pictures: Warner Bros.' *The Sea Hawk* (1940), starring Errol Flynn; Fox's *Little Old New York* (1940); *Destry Rides Again* (1939), starring Marlene Dietrich and James Stewart; and *Blackmail* (1939), starring Edward G. Robinson. These dramatic spectacle films, which foregrounded themes of romance, differed starkly from the military propaganda films being made and exhibited in Korea at this time (*Maeil Shinbo* 3 March 1941: 2; *Maeil Shinbo* 7 May 1941: 2; *Maeil Shinbo* 16 May 1941: 1). The 9 February 1940 Joe Louis fight against Chilean-born Arturo Godoy (aka *The Louis-Godoy Fight, Part 1*, 1940)—a 28-minute short (2-reel) film that was directed and filmed by Jack Rieger, and distributed by United Pictures—was also one of these thrilling American films shown at this time (*Chosun Ilbo* 21 July 1940: 2). This exciting heavyweight championship boxing match, which Louis won, lasted 15 rounds, leaving us to wonder how local (Korean and Japanese) audiences would have reacted to such a patriotic American film.
73. *Eiga Junpō* 11 July 1943: 8–9.
74. *Eiga Junpō* 11 July 1943: 9, 15.
75. *Eiga Hyōron*, July 1941: 47–49.
76. *Eiga Junpō* 11 July 1943: 10–15.
77. Sakuramoto 1983: 191.
78. Anderson and Richie 1982: 130.
79. High (2003: 439) describes this mob of bandits as 'Korean Communists,' but their clothing confirms their identity as Chinese. Furthermore, the identification of the insurgents as Korean would have potentially backfired on the CFPC (and the Korean Colonial Government) because it would have suggested to Korean audiences that there were resistance groups in Manchuria working for the independence of Korea.
80. Kim 2006: 309.
81. Sakuramoto 1983: 190.
82. Lee Myeong-wu directed Korea's first successful talkie, *The Story of Chunhyang* (1935), and was also the cinematographer for *Volunteer* (1941).
83. Yi 2008: 62.
84. Sakuramoto 1983: 190.
85. Sakuramoto 1983: 191.
86. *Eiga Junpō* 11 July 1943: 10–15. According to Sakuramoto (1983), Yamamoto Kajirō's *The War at Sea from Hawaii to Malaya* (*Hawai Marē oki kaisen*, Toho 1942), starring the popular Hara Setsuko as the heroine, was the most profitable film exhibited in Korea to date. This blockbuster film, made to celebrate the first anniversary of the attack on Pearl Harbor, earned ¥53,000 in Korea and an astounding ¥2,653,400 in Japan. Box-office revenues easily covered its expensive visual effects created by Tsuburaya Eiji, who was also responsible for the special effects for *Godzilla* in the 1950s.
87. *1944* featured cinematography by Korean Lee Myeong-wu (known as Seto Akira in Japanese), with music by Eizō Nakagawa.
88. *Samcheolli* January 1941: 162.
89. See the comments of Shimizu Shōzō, from the Film Censorship Section-Bureau of Police Affairs, in Takashima 1943: 283–288.
90. Kenez 1992: 34.
91. Sakuramoto 1983: 188.
92. Takashima 1943: 283.
93. Karashima's comments appear in *Eiga Junpō* 11 July 1943: 9, 15.
94. Ho 2000: 70.
95. *Kinema Junpō* 21 November 1939: 22–23.

NOTES TO CHAPTER 6

1. A slightly different version of this chapter appears in *The Asia-Pacific Journal*, 44–3–10, 1 November 2010 (available online at: http://japanfocus.org/-Brian-Yecies/3437).
2. *Pacific Stars and Stripes* 28 October 1950.
3. *Pacific Stars and Stripes* 28 August 1951: 10.
4. Self 1944: 6.
5. An insightful article about the USAMGIK by Lt. General Hodge appears in *National Geographic Magazine* June 1947: 829–840.
6. For example, see Cumings (1997), McCune (1947), Meade (1951), and Oh (2002).
7. The phrase 'Cannon and Camera!' appears above figure 6.1, which depicts film splicing equipment alongside its shadow that resembles a firing cannon. In addition to feature films, the OWI's domestic and overseas 'war films' campaign included victory films, the 'America Speaks' series, films for soldiers overseas and Red Cross hospitals, training films, orientation films, strategy films, 'good neighbor' films, newsreels, morale-boosting films, and United Nations films. See the table of contents and introduction to *Movies at War*, War Activities Committee, Motion Picture Industry, New York City, 1942. Records of the OWI, Records of the Historian Relating to the Domestic Branch, 1942–1945, RG 208, Box 1, Entry 6A, National Archives at College Park, Maryland (hereafter cited as NARAII).
8. See Lee and Choe (1998), Lee (2000), Kim Mee-hyun et al. (2002), Min, Joo, and Kwak (2003), Yi (2003), and Yi (2005).
9. This material is also contained in: Records of the OWI, Records of the Historian Relating to the Domestic Branch, 1942–1945, RG 208, Box 1, Entry 6A, NARAII.
10. Motion Picture Export Association of America (MPEAA) 1961, 'Japan Country Fact Book,' USC-Warner Bros. Archives, Japan File #16520B.
11. A few of the many films exhibited (released) in Korea during this time with one or more of these unedifying themes include: *Barbary Coast* (1935, released in 7/46, 8/46, 10/46, 11/46, and 5/47); *Tall in the Saddle* (1944, released in 9/46 and 1/47); *The Sea Hawk* (1940, released in 10/46); *Call of the Yukon* (1938, released in 12/46, 5/47, and 11/47); *Spawn of the North* (1938, released in 12/46, 1/47, and 5/47); and *Casablanca* (1942, released in 5/47).
12. Explicit details concerning these plans appear in: General Headquarters, Commander-in-Chief, United States Army Forces, Pacific, *Summation No. 11: United States Army Military Government Activities in Korea for the Month of August, 1946*: 12–13; and Records of the U.S. Department of State relating to the internal affairs of Korea, 1945–1949, Department of State, Decimal File 895, Reel 5, 'US role in Korea,' NARAII.
13. Copies of the OWI's *Government Information Manual* and other previously classified government and industry correspondence are available in: Records of the OWI, Records of the Historian Relating to the Overseas Branch, 1942–1945, RG 208, NARAII.
14. Barnes 1943: 34–45.
15. See 'Operational Guidelines for the Distribution of O.W.I. Documentaries and Industry Films in the Far East,' 22 December 1944, Records of the OWI, Records of the Historian Relating to the Overseas Branch, 1942–1945, RG 208, Box 2, Entry 6B, NARAII.
16. Department of State Decimal File 1945–1949, RG59, BOX 7398, 'Report of the Educational and Informational Survey Mission to Korea,' Seoul, Korea 20 June 1947, p30. NARAII.

17. Fay 2008: xix.
18. Lee 1946: 4.
19. *Missoulian* 13 March 1945.
20. "A Manual for Censors of the Motion Picture Department," RG331, Box 8603, Folder 7, SCAP Records, NARAII.
21. Report of the Educational and Informational Survey Mission to Korea, 20 July 1947, pp. 35–36. Dept of State, Decimal File 1945–49, RG59, Box 7398. NARAII.
22. See Hirano 1992; and Kitamura 2010.
23. Kitamura 2007.
24. See 'Memorandum,' from M. Bergher to the Chief of the C. I. & E., 12 April 1946. RG331, Box 5062, Folder 15, 'Motion Pictures, Sep 1946–Dec 1947,' and Box 1020, Folder 9, 'Central Motion Picture Exchange,' SCAP Records, NARAII.
25. *Jungoe Ilbo* 19 April 1946: 4.
26. Loew is quoted in Hicks 1947: 298–299.
27. Hicks 1947: 303.
28. For a thorough discussion of film policy in Japan during U.S. Occupation, see Hirano (1992) and Kitamura (2007, 2010).
29. Armstrong 2003: 82.
30. General Headquarters, SCAP, Commander in Chief, U.S. Army Forces, Pacific, 1946, 'Monthly Summation No. 8,' *U.S. Army Military Government Activities in Korea*, Tokyo, May, p. 88; and 1946, 'Monthly Summation No. 13,' October, p. 81.
31. Lee 1999: 42.
32. *Seoul Shinmun* 5 May 1946: 5.
33. *Jayu Shinmun* 5 May 1946: 3.
34. *Christian Science Monitor* 12 April 1946: 19.
35. RG331, Box 5062, Folder 15C "Motion Pictures, Sep 1946–Dec 1947," SCAP Records, NARAII.
36. See Kitamura 2007, 2010.
37. U.S. Embassy, Seoul 1950, 'Dispatch No. 657,' 2 January, U.S.-DOS, RG59, Decimal File 1945–49, Box 7398, NARAII.
38. Our understanding is that the exchange rate between the U.S. dollar and the Japanese Yen was set at ¥15 per $1 in the wake of war in September 1945, and the inflation of the early postwar economy led to a rate change to ¥50 per $1 in 1947. Eventually, this was capped at ¥360 per $1 in 1949.
39. General Headquarters, SCAP, Commander in Chief, U.S. Army Forces, Pacific, 1946, 'Monthly Summation No. 9,' *U.S. Army Military Government Activities in Korea* Tokyo, June, p. 79; and 1946, 'Monthly Summation No. 11,' August, p. 88.
40. *Donga Ilbo* 5 May 1946: 2.
41. Yecies 2005b.
42. Balio 1995: 180.
43. *Arirang* was screened multiple times, including at the Jeil Cinema (*Segye Ilbo* 9 April 1947, p. 2) and on 28 July 1948 at the Chosun Geukjang (*Jayu Shinmun* 28 July 1948).
44. Yoshimi 2003: 434.
45. Vieth 2002: 23–24.
46. *Chung Ang Shinmun* 31 March 1948.
47. This quote, an English translation of the original article, is contained in: 'Dispatch No. 80: Korean Opposition to American Motion Pictures,' 7 April 1948. Records of the U.S.-DOS relating to the internal affairs of Korea, 1945–1949, microfilm reel #7, Decimal File 895. NARAII.

48. Lee 1946: 4.
49. USAMGIK 1947, 'Report of the Educational and Informational Survey Mission to Korea,' 20 June, U.S.-DOS, RG59, Decimal File 1945–49, Box 7398, NARAII.
50. *Seoul Shinmun* 26 May 1946: 4.
51. *Seoul Shinmun* 26 May 1946: 4.
52. U.S. Embassy, Seoul 1949, 'Dispatch No. 247: South Korean Motion Pictures,' 4 May, RG59, U.S.-DOS Decimal File 1945–49, Box 7398, NARAII.
53. KMPPC 1976: 47.

Bibliography

ARCHIVAL SITES AND RECORDS IN THE UNITED STATES

Arts Special Collections, University of California, Los Angeles, California.

Cinema and Television Library, University of Southern California, Los Angeles.

David Allan Hubbard Library, Fuller Theological Seminary, Pasadena, California.

Duke University, Manuscript and Special Collections Library: James A. Thomas Papers; James B. Duke Papers.

George Eastman House, Rochester, NY.

Georgetown University Library, Special Collections, Washington DC.: C.F. Chase Papers.

Korean Heritage/East Asian Library University of Southern California, Los Angeles.

Manuscripts and Special Collections, Universal Studios, Los Angeles, California.

Margaret Herrick Library, Academy of Motion Picture Arts and Sciences, Los Angeles: Press Clippings, General Collections; Motion Picture Association of America Files, Special Collections; Production Code Administration Files, Special Collections.

National Archives and Records Administration, College Park, Maryland: General

Records of the Department of State, Record Group 59; Civil Affairs Division, Department of Army, Record Group 165; Records of the Office of War Information, Record Group 208; Records of the Supreme Commander of the Allied Powers, Record Group 331; Records of the U.S. Department of State Relating to the Internal Affairs of Korea, 1930–1939, Decimal File 895; Records of the U.S. Department of State Relating to the Internal Affairs of Korea, 1945–1949, Decimal File 895; Dispatches From United States Consuls in Seoul, 1886–1906.

New York Public Library, Manuscripts and Archives Division: Horace N. Allen Papers, 1883–1923.

Rutgers, The State University of New Jersey, AT&T Archives and History Center, Warren, NJ: Thomas A. Edison Files.

University of Iowa Library, Special Collections: Victor Animatograph Corp. Papers.

University of Maryland, College Park, Maryland: Gordon W. Prange Collection.

University of Michigan, Center for Japanese Studies, Prewar Proletarian Film Movements Collection.

Warner Bros. Archives, School of Cinematic Arts, University of Southern California, Los Angeles, California: Warner Bros. Collection.

Wisconsin Center for Film and Theater Research, Madison, Wisconsin: United Artists Collection.

ARCHIVAL SITES AND LIBRARIES IN SOUTH KOREA

KBS archive, Seoul
Korean Film Archive, Seoul
Korean Film Council, Seoul
Korea Press Foundation, Seoul
Lee Young-il archives, Korea National University of Arts, Seoul
Ministry of Government Administration and Home Affairs, Government Archives
    and Records Service, Daejon
National Assembly Library, Seoul
National Library, Seoul
Seoul National Library Digital Archives
Seoul National University Library: General Newspaper Collection, Seoul
Yonsei University Library: General Newspaper Collection, Seoul

LIBRARIES IN JAPAN

National Diet Library, Tokyo: General Newspaper Collection
Waseda University Library, Tokyo: General Newspaper Collection

NEWSPAPERS AND MAGAZINES (1880–1950)

Korean

Chosun Ilbo
Chosun Yeonghwa
Chung Ang Shinmun
Daejung Yeonghwa
Daidong Shinmun
Donga Ilbo
Hwangseong Shinmun
Jayu Shinmun
Jungoe Ilbo
Kyeongseong Ilbo
Kyunghyang Ilbo
Maeil Shinbo
Munye Yeonghwa
Nokseong
Samcheolli
Seoul Shinmun
Shin Chosun Bo
Shin Donga
Yeonghwa Sidae

English

Chicago Daily Tribune
Christian Science Monitor
Cinema Yearbook of Japan
Film Daily
Film Daily Yearbook
Foreign Commerce Weekly

Hollywood Reporter
The Independent
Korean Cinema
The Korea Field
The Korea Methodist
The Korea Mission Field
The Korean Repository
The Korea Review
London Times
Los Angeles Times
Missoulian
The Morning Calm
Motion Picture Almanac
Motion Picture Herald
MPEA Newsletter
National Geographic Magazine
New York Times
Pacific Stars and Stripes
Variety
Voice of Korea
Wall Street Journal
Washington Post
Wid's Year Book

Japanese

Kikan Sanzenri
Kinema Junpō
Eiga Hyōron
Eiga Junpō
Eiga Nenkan
Eiga no tomo
Nihon Eiga
Shin Eiga
Shinkō Eiga

FILM AND NEWSPAPER DATABASES

British Film Institute Film & TV Database. www.bfi.org.uk/filmtvinfo/ftvdb
Complete Index to World Film since 1895. www.citwf.com
The Internet Movie Database. www.imdb.com
Korean History Database. http://db.history.go.kr
Korean Movie Database. www.kmdb.or.kr
Korea Press Foundation Mediagaon. www.mediagaon.or.kr

GOVERNMENT PUBLICATIONS

General Headquarters, Commander-in-Chief, United States Army Forces, Pacific, *Summation No. 7: United States Army Military Government Activities in Korea for the Month of April, 1946*: 32–33.
———. *Summation No. 8: United States Army Military Government Activities in Korea for the Month of May, 1946*: 88–92.

————. *Summation No. 9: United States Army Military Government Activities in Korea for the Month of June, 1946:* 79–81.

————. *Summation No. 10: United States Army Military Government Activities in Korea for the Month of July, 1946:* 59–61.

————. *Summation No. 11: United States Army Military Government Activities in Korea for the Month of August, 1946:* 12–13, 87–92.

————. *Summation No. 12: United States Army Military Government Activities in Korea for the Month of September, 1946:* 74–78.

————. *Summation No. 13: United States Army Military Government Activities in Korea for the Month of October, 1946:* 81–85.

————. *Summation No. 14: United States Army Military Government Activities in Korea for the Month of November, 1946:* 79–82.

————. *Summation No. 15: United States Army Military Government Activities in Korea for the Month of December, 1946:* 75–78.

General Headquarters, Commander-in-Chief Far East, for the Allied Powers, *Summation No. 20: United States Army Military Government Activities in Korea for the Month of May, 1947:* 77–79.

Government-General of Chosen (Keijo (Seoul)). *Annual Report on Reforms and Progress in Chosen (Korea), 1910–11,* Tokyo: Tokyo Printing Co., December, 1911.

————. *Annual Report on Reforms and Progress in Chosen (Korea), 1911–12,* December, 1912.

————. *Annual Report on Reforms and Progress in Chosen (Korea), 1917–18.* July, 1920.

————. *Annual Report on Reforms and Progress in Chosen, 1918–21.* December, 1921.

————. *Annual Report on Reforms and Progress in Chosen, 1921–1922.* 1923.

————. *Annual Report on Administration of Chosen, 1923–24.* Keijo (Seoul): Chosen Book-Printing, Co., December 1925.

————. *Annual Report on Administration of Chosen, 1924–26.* Keijo (Seoul): Chosen Book-Printing, Co., December 1927.

————. *Annual Report on Administration of Chosen, 1935–36.* Keijo (Seoul), 1936.

Government-General of Tyosen (Chosen). *Annual Report on Administration of Tyosen, 1937–38.* Foreign Affairs Department (eds.) Tokyo: Toppau Printing Co., 1938.

H.I.J.M.'s Residency-General (Seoul). *Annual Report for 1907 on Reforms and Progress in Korea.* Tokyo: Japan Times, 1908.

————. *The Second Annual Report on Reforms and Progress in Korea (1908–9).* Tokyo: Japan Times, 1908.

Langdon, William. R. "Chosen (Korea) Motion Picture Notes," American Consulate-General, Seoul to U.S. Department of State. Records of the U.S. Department of State Relating to the Internal Affairs of Korea, 1930–1939, Motion Pictures/1, National Archives and Records Administration, File 895, Item 895.4061, 23 March 1934.

————. "Chosen Motion Picture Control Ordinance." American Consulate-General, Seoul to U.S. Department of State. Records of the U.S. Department of State Relating to the Internal Affairs of Korea, 1930–1939, Motion Pictures/2, National Archives and Records Administration, File 895, Item 895.4061, 6 September 1934.

United States Army Forces in Korea, *South Korea Interim Government Activities, No. 1: August, 1947:* 211–214.

Way, E. I. "Motion Pictures in China," edited by Department of Commerce, Bureau of Foreign and Domestic Commerce and U.S. Government Printing Office. Washington DC, 1930.

ARTICLES, BOOKS, AND BOOK CHAPTERS

"Catalogue of Magic Lanterns Stereopticons and Moving Picture Machines." Chicago: Montgomery Ward and Co., circa 1899. Available from the Internet Archive.

"Censorship—Japan." *Film Year Book 1926* (1926): 820.

"Chosen (Korea)." In *Film Daily Year Book of Motion Pictures 1940*. New York: Film Daily, 1940. 1103–1104.

"Discussing about the Entire Picture of Korean Films (Chōsen Eiga No Zenbō O Kataru)." *Eiga Hyōron* (July 1941).

"Film Review: The Rains Came/20th Century Fox (Yeonghwa Pyeong: Bineun Onda/20 Segi Poks Sa Jakpum)." *Joongoi Daily*, 9 May 1946.

"Foreign Market Reports, 'Chosen (Korea).'" In *Film Daily Year Book of Motion Pictures 1939*. New York: Film Daily, 1939. 1174.

"The Foreign Market—Tokio." *Wid's Year Book 1920–1921* (1921): 275.

"For Establishing the New System of Korean Films! (Chōsen Eiga Shin Taisei Juritsu No Tame Ni!)." *Eiga Junpō* (November 1941): 15–22.

"Japan Rules against Piracy." *Film Year Book 1922–1923* (1923): 371.

"Japan Rules against Piracy." In *Film Year Book 1922–1923*. New York: Wid's Films and Film Folks, 1923: 371.

Lee Young-Il's Korean Film History Lecture Notes (Lee Young-Il-Ui Hanguk Yeonghwasa Ganguirok). Edited by The Korean National Research Center for Arts, Korean Arts Archive Collections. Seoul: Sodo, 2002.

"Motion Picture Production in Korea 1938." *Cinema Yearbook of Japan*, 1939. Tokyo: Kokusai Bunka Shinkokai, 1939. 49–50.

"Panel Discussion About *You and I* (Geudaewa Na-Reul Malhaneun Jwadamhoe)." *Samcheolli* 13, no. 9 (September 1941).

"The Peculiarity of Korean Films (Chōsen Eiga No Tokushusei)." *Eiga Junpō* (July 1943): 10–15.

"You and Me (Kimi to Boku) in Symposium." *Eiga Junpō* (October 1941): 31–35.

"Your Military Training Plans for Girls' High School (Agyo-Ui Nyeohaksaeng Gunsa Gyoryeon-an)." *Samcheolli* 14, no. 1 (January 1942): 102–105.

Abel, Richard. *Americanizing the Movies And "Movie-Mad" Audiences, 1910–1914*. Berkeley: University of California Press, 2006.

Affairs, Bureau of Police. *Overview of Film Censorship (Hwaldong Sajin Pileum Geomyeol Gaeyo)* Seoul, 1931 (translated into Korean and published in KOFA 2009: 153–290).

Ahn Jong-hwa. *Stories Behind the Korean Cinema (Hanguk Yeonghwa Cheungmyeon Bisa)*. 2nd ed. (originally published in 1962). Seoul: Chunchugak, 1998.

Ahn Seok-yeong. "After Watching the Korean Talkie Chunhyangjeon: Talking about the Future of the Korean Film Community—Part 1." *Chosun Ilbo* 11 October 1935: 4.

———. "After Watching the Korean Talkie Chunhyangjeon: Talking about the Future of the Korean Film Community—Part 2." *Chosun Ilbo* 12 October 1935: 4.

———. "After Watching the Korean Talkie Chunhyangjeon: Talking about the Future of the Korean Film Community—Part 3." *Chosun Ilbo* 13 October 1935: 5.

Altman, Rick. "The Living Nickelodeon." In *The Sounds of Early Cinema*, edited by Richard Abel and Rick Altman, 232–240. Bloomington: Indiana University Press, 2001.

Anderson, Joseph L. "Spoken Silents in the Japanese Cinema; or, Talking to Pictures: Essaying the Katsuben, Contextualizing the Texts." In *Reframing*

Japanese Cinema, edited by David Desser and Arthur Nolletti Jr., 259–311. Bloomington: Indiana University Press, 1992.

Anderson, Joseph L., and Donald Richie. *The Japanese Film: Art and Industry*. Expanded edition. Preston: Princeton University Press, 1982.

Armstrong, Charles K. "The Origins of North Korean Cinema: Art and Propaganda in the Democratic People's Republic." *Acta Koreana* 5, no. 1 (January 2002): 1–19.

———. "The Cultural Cold War in Korea, 1945–1950." *The Journal of Asian Studies* 62, no. 1 (Feb. 2003): 71–99.

Bacon, Elizabeth M. "Marketing Sewing Machines in the Post-Civil War Years." *Bulletin of the Business Historical Society*, no. 3 (June 1946): 90–94.

Balio, Tino. "Struggles for Control, 1908–1930." In *The American Film Industry*, edited by Tino Balio, 103–132. Madison: The University of Wisconsin Press, 1985.

———. "Stars in Business: The Founding of United Artists." In *The American Film Industry*, edited by Tino Balio, 153–172. Madison: The University of Wisconsin Press, 1985.

———. *Grand Design: Hollywood as a Modern Business Enterprise, 1930–1939*. Vol. 5, History of American Cinema Series. Los Angeles: University of California Press, 1995.

Barber, X. Theodore. "The Roots of Travel Cinema. John L. Stoddard, E. Burton Holmes and the Nineteenth-Century Illustrated Travel Lecture." *Film History* 5, no. 3 (1993): 68–84.

Barnes, Joseph. "Fighting with Information: OWI Overseas." *The Public Opinion Quarterly* 7, no. 1 (1943): 34–45.

Baskett, Michael. *Attractive Empire: Transnational Film Culture in Imperial Japan*. Honolulu: University of Hawaii Press, 2008.

Benham, Albert. "The 'Movie' as an Agency for Peace or War." *Journal of Educational Sociology* 12, no. 7 (1939): 410–417.

Bernadou, J. B. "Korea and Koreans." *National Geographic Magazine* 2, no. 4 (1890): 231–242.

Bernardi, Joanne. *Writing in Light: The Silent Scenario and the Japanese Pure Film Movement*. Detroit, MI: Wayne State University Press, 2001.

Bowser, Eileen. *History of American Cinema Volume 2: 1907–1915*. Berkeley and Los Angeles: University of California Press, 1994.

Caprio, Mark. *Japanese Assimilation Policies in Colonial Korea, 1910–1945*. Seattle: University of Washington Press, 2009.

Cheong Seong-hwa, and Robert Neff. *Foreigners Living in Chosun (Seoyangin-Ui Chosunsari)*. Seoul: Pureun Yeoksa, 2008.

Cinema Yearbook of Japan, 1936–1937. Tokyo: Sanseido, 1937.

Cinema Yearbook of Japan, 1938. Tokyo: Kokusai Bunka Shinkokai, 1938.

Cinema Yearbook of Japan, 1939. Tokyo: Kokusai Bunka Shinkokai, 1939.

Cho Hee-moon. "Movie Theatres—Another History of Korean Movie (1)." *Journal of Film & Culture*, no. 21 (Autumn 2001).

———. "Reflection from the Silent Film Era—Byeonsa, the Narrator." Paper presented at the FIAF Fifty-eighth Congress Seoul 2002: Asian Cinema—Yesterday, Today and Tomorrow. Seoul: 2002a.

———. *Debates in Korean Film 1 (Hanguk Yeonghwa-Ui Jaengjeom)*. Seoul: Jimmundang, 2002b.

Cho Jun-hyung. "Film Policy under the Japanese Colonial Rule, 1903–1945 (Ilje Gangjeomggi Yeonghwa Jeongchaek, 1903–1945 Nyeon)." In *A History of Korean Film Policy (Hanguk Yeonghwa Jeongchaeksa)*, 45–106. Seoul: Nanam Publishing, 2005.

———. "Chosun Film Scene since the Mid-1930s: Generation Shift-Incorporation-System of Control." In *The Time of Change and Choice: Discovery of Films from Japanese Colonial Period*, 66–88. Pusan: PIFF, 2006.

Cho Poong-yeon. *Encyclopedia of Trivial Things of Seoul (Seoul Jabhak Sajeon)*. Seoul: Jeongdong Chulpansa, 1989.

Cho Seong-un. "Overview: Japan's Assimilation Policy in the 1910s and *Maeil Shinbo* (Chongnon: 1910 Nyeondae Ilje-Ui Donghwa Jeongchaek-Gwa *Maeil Shinbo*)." In *Japan's Colonial Policy and Maeil Shinbo in the 1910s (Ilje-Ui Singminji Jibae Jeongchaek-Gwa Maeil Shinbo 1910 Nyeondae)*, 9–26. Seoul: Duri Media, 2005.

Cho Young-jung. "Korean Cinema Retrospective, Discovery 1: Films from Japanese Colonial Period." In *11th Pusan International Film Festival Catalogue*, edited by Eunah Kim, 114–123. Pusan: Pusan International Film Festival, 2006.

Choe Young-chol. "Film Policy under Japanese Colonization (Ilje Singminjiha-Ui Yeonghwa Jeongchaek) " In *Understanding Korean Cinema: From Arirang to Silver Stallion (Hanguk Yoeonghwa-Ui Ihae: Arirang-Eso Eunmaneun Oji Anneundaggaji)*, 217–242. Seoul: Yenni, 1992.

Choi Chuck-ho. *North Korean Film History (Bukan Yeonghwasa)*. Seoul: Jimmundang, 2000.

Chosun Film Company. *Korean Cinema Vol. 1 (Chosun Yeonghwa Je 1jip)*. Seoul, October 1936.

Chung Jong-hwa. *A History of Korean Cinema: 100 Years of Korean Movies in One Book (Hanguk Yeonghwasa: Han Gwon-Euro Ingneun Yeonghwa 100 Nyeon)*. Edited by Korean Film Archive, Film Story Collection 01. Seoul: Korean Film Archive, 2007.

Chung, Youn-tae. "Refracted Modernity and the Issue of Pro-Japanese Collaborators in Korea." *Korea Journal* 42, no. 3 (Autumn 2002): 18–53.

Cook, David A. *A History of Narrative Film*. 4th ed. New York: W. W. Norton, 2004.

Cule, Nicholas J., David Culbert, and David Welch. *Propaganda and Mass Persuasion: A Historical Encyclopedia: 1500 to the Present*. Oxford: ABC CLIO, 2003.

Cumings, Bruce. *Korea's Place in the Sun: A Modern History*. New York: W.W. Norton, 1997.

Davis, Darrell William. *Picturing Japaneseness: Monumental Style, National Identity, Japanese Film*. New York: Columbia University Press, 1996.

De Ceuster, Koen. "The Nation Exorcised: The Historiography of Collaboration in South Korea." *Korean Studies* 25, no. 2 (2002): 207–242.

Depue, Oscar B. "My First Fifty Years in Motion Pictures." *Journal of the Society of Motion Picture Engineers* 49, no. 6 (1947): 481–493.

Eckert, Carter J. *Offspring of Empire: The Koch'ang Kims and the Colonial Origins of Korean Capitalism, 1876–1945*. Seattle: University of Washington Press, 1991.

Eckert, Carter, Ki-Baik Lee, Young Lew, Michael Robinson, and Edward W. Wagner. *Korea Old and New: A History*. Seoul: Published for the Korea Institute, Harvard University by Ilchokak, 1990.

Eiga Nenkan (Film Yearbook). Tokyo: Nihon Eiga Zasshi Kyoukai (Japanese Film Magazine Association), 1942.

Eom Seong-hee. "Ceramic Policy of the Central Test Center Noticed in *Maeil Shinbo* in the 1910s (Maeil Shinbo-Eh Natanan Chungang Siheomso-Ui Yoeop Jeongchaek)." In *Japan's Colonial Policy and Maeil Shinbo in the 1910s (Ilje-Ui Singminji Jibae Jeongchaek-Gwa Maeil Shinbo 1910 Nyeondae)*, 229–268. Seoul: Duri Media, 2005.

Farhi, Paul. "Seoul's Movie Theaters: Real Snake Pits?" *The Washington Post*, 17 September 1988.

Fay, Jennifer. *Theaters of Occupation: Hollywood and the Reeducation of Postwar Germany*. Minneapolis: University of Minnesota Press, 2008.

Freiberg, Freda. "The Transition to Sound in Japan." In *History on/and/in Film: Proceedings of the 3rd History and Film Conference*, edited by Tom O'Regan and Brian Shoesmith. Perth, 1985.

———. "Comprehensive Connections: The Film Industry, the Theatre and the State in the Early Japanese Cinema." *Screening the Past: An Online Journal of Media and History*, no. 10 (2000): 1–23.

Fujiwara, Chris. "Pusan 2006: A Desolate Flute Is Heard: Korean Films from the Japanese Colonial Period." Fédération Internationale de la Presse Cinématographique (aka FIPRESCI, International Federation of Film Critics), http://www.fipresci.org/festivals/archive/2006/pusan/pusan_fujiwara.htm

Gaines, Jane M. "The White in the Race Movie Audience." In *Going to the Movies: Hollywood and the Social Experience of Cinema*, edited by Richard Maltby, Melvyn Stokes, and Robert C. Allen, 60–75 (notes 402–405). Exeter, UK: University of Exeter Press, 2007.

Gennari, Daniela Treveri. *Post-War Italian Cinema: American Intervention, Vatican Interests*. London: Routledge, 2008.

Gerow, Aaron. "One Print in the Age of Mechanical Reproduction: Film Industry and Culture in 1910s Japan." *Screening the Past: An Online Journal of Media and History*, no. 11 (2000), www.latrobe.edu.au/screeningthepast/firstrelease/fr1100/agfr11e.htm.

Gleason, Abbott, Peter Kenez, and Richard Stites, eds. *Bolshevik Culture: Experiment and Order in the Russian Revolution*. Bloomington and Indianapolis: Indiana University Press, 1989.

Golden, Nathan D. "Review of Foreign Film Markets During 1937—Chosen (Korea)." In *Film Daily Year Book of Motion Pictures 1938*. New York: Film Daily, 1938: 1191–1193.

Gunning, Tom. "Illusions Past and Future: The Phantasmagoria and Its Specters." *Refresh! Programmatic Key Texts* (2004), http://hdl.handle.net/10002/296

Hake, Sabine. *German National Cinema*. London: Routledge, 2002.

Hannavy, John. *Encyclopedia of Nineteenth-Century Photography*. New York: Routledge, 2008.

Hanson, Stuart. *From Silent Screen to Multi-Screen: A History of Cinema Exhibition in Britain since 1896*. Manchester: Manchester University Press, 2007.

Harrington, Fred H. *God, Mammon and the Japanese: Dr. Horace N. Allen and Korean-American Relations, 1884–1905*. Madison: University of Wisconsin Press, 1944.

Hazumi Tsuneo. "Manchuria and the Korean Film Industry (Manshū Oyobi Chōsen No Eigakai)." *Kinema Junpō* (November 1939): 22–23.

Hicks, O. H. "American Films Abroad." *Journal of the Society of Motion Picture Engineers* 49, no. 4 (October 1947): 298–299.

High, Peter B. *The Imperial Screen: Japanese Film Culture in the Fifteen Years' War, 1931–1945*. Madison: University of Wisconsin Press, 2003.

Higson, Andrew, and Richard Maltby, eds. *"Film Europe" and "Film America": Cinema, Commerce, and Cultural Exchange, 1920–1939*. Exeter, UK: University of Exeter Press, 1999.

Hinatsu Eitarō. "Interchange of Korean Film Industry (Naisen Eiga Kai No Kōryū Ni Tsuite)." *Eiga Hyōron* (July 1941): 49–51.

Hirano, Kyoko. *Mr. Smith Goes to Tokyo: Japanese Cinema under the American Occupation, 1945–1952*. Washington DC: Smithsonian Institute Press, 1992.

Hodge, General. "With the U. S. Army in Korea " *National Geographic Magazine*, June 1947, 829–840.

Hollinger, Hy. "5-Day Event: Afma Planning S. Korea Minimart." *Variety* 6 April 1988.

Holmes, E. Burton. *The Burton Holmes Lectures.* 10 vols. Vol. 10. Battle Creek: The Little-Preston Co., 1901.

———. *The World Is Mine.* Culver City, CA: Murray & Gee, 1953.

Ichikawa Sai. *The Creation and Development of the Motion Pictures in Asia (Asiano Eiga Souzou Oyobi Kensetsu).* Republished (original 1941) ed, A Period of Film Control on the War Period 10 (Senjikano Eiga Touseiki 10). Tokyo: Yumani Shobo, 2003.

Iizima, Tadasi (aka Iijima Tadashi). "Documentary Films." In *Cinema Yearbook of Japan, 1936–1937.* Tokyo: Sanseido, 1937: 58–60.

Indol. "After Watching the First Korean Talkie Chunhyangeon—1 (Chosun Choecho-Ui Balseong Yeonghwa Chunhyangjeon-Eul Bogo Sang)." *Donga Ilbo* 11 October 1935: 3.

———. "After Watching the First Korean Talkie Chunhyangeon—2 (Chosun Choecho-Ui Balseong Yeonghwa Chunhyangjeon-Eul Bogo Jung)." *Donga Ilbo* 12 October 1935: 3.

———. "After Watching the First Korean Talkie Chunhyangeon—3 (Chosun Choecho-Ui Balseong Yeonghwa Chunhyangjeon-Eul Bogo Ha)." *Donga Ilbo* 16 October 1935: 3.

Itagaki, Takao. "Cultural Films." In *Cinema Yearbook of Japan, 1938.* Tokyo: Kokusai Bunka Shinkokai, 1938. 44–46.

Iwamoto, Kenji. "Sound in the Early Japanese Talkies." In *Reframing Japanese Cinema: Authorship, Genre, History,* edited by Arthur Nolletti Jr. and David Desser, 312–327. Bloomington: Indiana University Press, 1992.

Iwasaki, Akira. "An Outline History of the Japanese Cinema." In *Cinema Year Book of Japan 1936–1937,* edited by Tadasi Iizima, Akira Iwasaki, and Kisao Uchida. Tokyo: The International Cinema Association of Japan, 1937, 1–13.

———. "The Korean Film." In *Cinema Year Book of Japan 1939.* Tokyo: International Cinema Association of Japan and the Society for International Cultural Relations, 1939, 64–65.

Johnston, R. J. H. "Japanese Put out of Korea Rapidly." *New York Times* 10 October 1945: 7.

Ju Seong-won. "The Best Sori-Man the Late Park Dong-Jin's Devoted Life (Isidae Choego-Ui Soriggun Go Park Dong-Jin Myeongchang-Ui Oegil Insaeng)." *Shin Donga,* no. 527 (August 2003): 528–535.

Jung Jong-hwa. *Korean Cinema History Seen through Evidences 1–2 (Jaryoro Bon Hanguk Yeonghwasa 1–2).* Seoul: Yeolhwadang, 1997.

Jung Keun-sik. "Censorship Apparatus and Censors in Colonial Korea." In *Association for Asian Studies Annual Meeting.* Chicago, 2005.

———. *Top Secret: Press Censorship and Control by the Government-General of Chosun (Geukbi: Chosun Chongdokbu-Ui Eollon Geomyeolgwa Tanap).* Seoul: Communication Books, 2007.

Jung Keun-sik, and Choi Kyeong-hee. "The Book Department and the Systemization of Japan's Publication Police in Korea, 1926–1929." *The Studies in Korean Literature (Hanguk Munhak Yeongu)* 30 (June 2006): 103–170.

Kal, Hong. "Modeling the West, Returning to Asia; Shifting Identities in Japanese Colonial Expositions in Korea." *Comparative Studies in Society and History* 47, no. 3 (July 2005): 507–531.

Karashima Takeshi. "Korea and Films." *Eiga Junpō* (11 July 1943): 9, 15.

Kasza, Gregory J. *The State and Mass Media in Japan, 1918–1945.* Berkeley: University of California Press, 1988.

Kenez, Peter. *Cinema and Soviet Society, 1917–1953.* Cambridge: Cambridge University Press, 1992.

Kim Dong-ho et al. *A History of Korean Film Policy (Hanguk Yeonghwa Jeongchaeksa)*. Seoul: Nanam Publishing, 2005.

Kim, Choong Soon. *A Korean Nationalist Entrepreneur: A Life of Kim Songsu, 1891–1955*. Albany, NY: State University of New York Press, 1998.

Kim Chun-mi, and Kim So-hee, eds. *Testimonies for Korean Film History Collected by Lee Young-Il: Yu Jang-San, Lee Gyeong-Soon, Lee Pil-Wu and Lee Chang-Geun (Lee Young-Il-Ui Hanguk Yeoghwasa-Reul Wihan Jeungeollok: Yu Jang-San, Lee Gyeong-Soon, Lee Pil-Wu, Lee Chang-Geun Pyeon)*. Seoul: Sodo, 2003a.

———, eds. *Testimonies for Korean Film History Collected by Kim Seong-Chun, Bok Hye-Sook and Lee Gu-Young (Lee Young-Il-Ui Hanguk Yeonghwasa-Reul Wihan Jeungeollok: Kim Seong-Chun, Bok Hye-Sook, Lee Gu-Young Pyeon)*. Seoul: Sodo, 2003b.

———, eds. *Testimonies for Korean Film History Collected by Lee Young-Il: Seong Dong-Ho, Lee Gyu-Hwan and Choi Geum-Dong (Lee Young-Il-Ui Hanguk Yeonghwasa-Reul Wihan Jeungeollok: Seong Dong-Ho, Lee Gyu-Hwan, Choi Geum-Dong Pyeon)*. Seoul: Sodo, 2003c.

Kim, Dong Hoon. "Segregated Cinemas, Intertwined Histories: The Ethnically Segregated Film Cultures in 1920s Korea under Japanese Colonial Rule." *Journal of Japanese and Korean Cinema* 1, no. 1 (2009): 7–25.

Kim Hee-yoon. "History of Goryeo Film Association (Goryeo Yeonghwa Hyeophoe-Ui Yeoksa)." In *Koryo Film Association and New Film System: 1936–1941 (Goryeo Yeonghwa Hyeophoe-Wa Yeonghwa Sincheje: 1936–1941)*, edited by KOFA, 20–27. Seoul: KOFA, 2007.

Kim Hwa. *Korean Film History (Saero Sseun Hanguk Yeonghwa Jeonsa)*. Seoul: Dain Media, 2003.

Kim, Hyae-joon. "South Korea: The Politics of Memory." In *Being & Becoming: The Cinemas of Asia*, edited by Aruna Vasudev, Latika Padgaonkar, and Rashmi Doraiswamy, 281–300. Delhi: Macmillan India, 2002.

Kim Jeong-hyeok. "The Objective of Developing Korean Cinema, toward Realization of Pure Filmmaking Spirit (Chosun Yeonghwa Jinheung-Ui Mokpyo, Jinsilhan Yeonghwa Jeongsin-Ui Suribeul Wihaya)." *Samcheolli* 13, no. 1 (January 1941): 160–165.

Kim Jong-won. *The Dictionary of Korean Film Directors (Hanguk Yeon ghwa Gamdok Sajeon)*. Seoul: Kookhak Jaryowon, 2003.

Kim Jong-won, and Jeong Joong-heon. *100 Years of Our Film (Uri Yeonghwa 100 Nyeon)*. Seoul: Hyonam Publishing, 2001.

Kim Jong-wook, ed. *Korean Cinema Collection Part 1: 1903–August 1945 (Sillok Hanguk Yeonghwa Chongseo Sang Je 1 Jip: 1903–1945.8)*. Seoul: Kookkhak Jaryowon, 2002.

———, ed. *Korean Cinema Collection Part 2: 1903–August 1945 (Sillok Hanguk Yeonghwa Chongseo Sang Je 2 Jip: 1903–1945.8)*. Seoul: Kookkhak Jaryowon, 2002.

———, ed. *Chunsa Na Un-Gyu's Complete Works (Chunsa Na Un-Gyu Yeonghwa Jeonjakjip)*. Seoul: Kookhak Jaryowon, 2002.

———. *The Dictionary of Korean Film Directors (Hanguk Yeonghwa Gamdok Sajeon)*. Seoul: Korean Studies Research Center (Kookhak Jaryowon), 2004.

———. "Exhibition of Moving Pictures." In *Korean Cinema: From Origin to Renaissance*, 22–23. Seoul: Communication Books, 2007.

Kim Gwan. "New Film Review: After Watching Honggildong-Jeon Part 2." *Chosun Ilbo* 25 June 1936: 5.

Kim, Kyung Hyun. *The Remasculinization of Korean Cinema*. Durham, NC: Duke University Press, 2004.

Kim, Mee-hyun, ed. *Korean Cinema: From Origins to Renaissance*. Seoul: Communication Books, 2007.

Kim Mee-hyun, Chung Jong-hwa, and Jang Seong-ho. *History of Korean Film Technology (Hanguk Yeonghwa Gisulsa)*. Seoul: KOFIC, 2002.

———. *Study on History of Motion Picture Distribution in Korea (Hanguk Yeonghwa Baegeupsa Yeongu)*. Seoul: KOFIC, 2003.

Kim Ryeo-shil. *Projecting Empire Mirrored Colony: Rethinking Korea's Film History 1901–1945 (Tusahaneun Jeguk Tuyeonghaneun Singminji: 1901–1945 Nyeonui Hanguk Yeonghwa-Reul Doejipda)*. Seoul: Samin, 2006.

Kim Soyoung. *Phantom of Modernity: Fantastic Korean Cinema (Geundaesong-Ui Yuryeongdeul: Fantastic Hanguk Yeonghwa)*. Seoul: Ssiaseul Ppurineun Saramdeul, 2000.

Kim Su-nam. *Korean Film Directors 1: 12 Colonial Directors (Hanguk Yeonghwa Gamdongnon 1: Haebang-Jeon Hanguk Yeonghwa Jakga 12 in.)* Seoul: Jisiksaneop Publisher, 2002.

———. *Korean Film Directors 2: 14 Korean Directors from the Immediate Post Liberation Time Period to 1970s (Hanguk Yeonghwa Gamdongnon 2: Haebang Dwieseo 1970 Nyeondaeggaji Hanguk Yeonghwa Jakga 14 in)*. Seoul: Jisiksaneop Publisher, 2003.

———. *Korean Film Directors 3: Korean Film Movement by 14 Korean Directors in the 1980–90s (Hanguk Yeonghwa Gamdongnon 3: 1980–90 Nyeondae Yeonghwa Gamdok 14 in-Ui Hanguk Yeonghwa Undongsa)*. Seoul: Jisiksaneop Publisher, 2005.

Kim Su-yong. *My Love Cinema (Naui Sarang Cinema)*. Seoul: Cine21, 2005.

Kirihara, Donald. *Patterns of Time: Mizoguchi and the 1930s*. Madison: University of Wisconsin Press, 1992.

Kirkpatrick, Peter. "Hunting the Wild Reciter: Elocution and the Art of Recitation." In *Talking and Listening in the Age of Modernity*, edited by J. Damousi and D. Deacon. Canberra: ANU ePress, 2007: 27–39.

Kitamura, Hiroshi. "Exhibition and Entertainment: Hollywood and the American Reconstruction of Defeated Japan." In *Local Consequences of the Global Cold War*, edited by Jeffrey A. Engel, 33–56. Washington DC: Stanford University Press, 2007.

———. "Screening Enlightenment: Hollywood and the Cultural Reconstruction of Defeated Japan." Ithaca.: Cornell University Press, 2010.

KMPPC. *Korean Film Data Collection: From Beginning to 1976 (Hanguk Yeonghwa Jaryo Pyeollam: Chochanggi–1976 Nyeon)*. Edited by KMPPC. Seoul: KMPPC, 1977.

———. *Korean Film Annual Book (Hanguk Yeonghwa Yeongam)*. Edited by KMPPC. Seoul: KMPPC, 1977.

———. *Looking at Korean Cinema 60 Years through Pictures (Sajineuro Bon Hanguk Yeonghwa 60 Nyeon)*. Seoul: Gyoyuk Gwahak Publishing, 1980.

———. *200 Representative Films from 70 Years of Korean Cinema (Hanguk Yeonghwa 70 Nyeon Daepyojak 200 Seon)*. Seoul: KMPPC, 1989.

———. *Korean Film Index 1919–1989 (Hanguk Yeonghwa Jakpum Saegin 1919–1989)*. Seoul: KMPPC, 1990.

KOFA. "News: Acquired 35mm Korean Travelogue by Elias Burton Holmes (Elias Burton Holmes-Ui Hanguk Gihaeng Girok Yeonghwa 35mm Film Sujib)." *KOFA Newsletter*, no. 001 (7 September 2004), http://www.koreafilm.or.kr/newsletter/news_letter_001.html

———. *Korean Cinema in Newspaper Articles: 1945–1957 (Sinmungisaro Bon Hanguk Yeonghwa: 1945–1957)*. Seoul: Gonggan Gwa Saramdeul, 2004.

———, ed. *Speaking of Korean Cinema: Korean Cinema Renaissance 1 (Hanguk Yeonghwa-Reul Malhanda: Hanguk Yeonghwa-Ui Renaissance 1)*. Seoul: Yiche, 2005.

———, ed. *Speaking of Korean Cinema: Korean Cinema Renaissance 2 (Hanguk Yeonghwa-Reeul Malhanda: Hanguk Yonghwa-Ui Renaissance 2)*. Seoul: Yiche, 2006.

————, ed. *Koryo Film Association and New Film System: 1936–1941 (Goryeo Yeonghwa Hyeophoe-wa Yeonghwa Sincheje: 1936–1941).* Seoul: KOFA, 2007.

————, ed. *Chosun Cinema in Newspaper Articles 1911–1917 (Shinmun Gisaro-Boneun Joseon Yeonghwa 1911–1917).* Edited by Korean Film Research Institute, Film Data Collection from Japanese Colonial Periods-01 (Iljegangjeomgi Yeonghwajaryo Chongseo-01). Seoul: KOFA, 2008.

————, ed. *Film Censorship under the Colonial Rule: 1910–1934 (Singminji Sidae-Ui Yeonghwa Geomyeol: 1910–1934),* Korean Film Research Material Collection (Hanguk Yeonghwa Yeongu Jaryo Chongseo). Seoul: KOFA, 2009.

————, ed. *Chosun Cinema in Newspaper Articles 1918–1920 (Shinmun Gisaro-Boneun Joseon Yeonghwa 1918–1920).* Edited by Korean Film Research Institute, Film Data Collection from Japanese Colonial Periods-02 (Iljegangjeomgi Yeonghwajaryo Chongseo-02). Seoul: KOFA, 2009.

Koller, Michael. "Cinémathèque Annotations on Film, Kitsch, Sensation—Kultur Und Film: Die Spinnen." *Senses of Cinema* (2002), http://archive.sensesofcinema.com/contents/cteq/02/21/spinnen.html

Koppes, Clayton R., and Gregory D. Black. *Hollywood Goes to War: How Politics, Profits and Propaganda Shaped World War II Movies.* Berkeley: University of California Press, 1987.

Korean Film Commission. *Korean Cinema 1989.* Seoul: Korean Film Commission, 1989.

Korean Film Council. *Korean Cinema 2005.* Seoul: Korean Film Council, 2005.

————. *Korean Cinema 2007.* Seoul: Korean Film Council, 2007.

————. *Korean Cinema 2009.* Seoul: Korean Film Council, 2009.

Korean Film Support Union. *Korean Film Collection (Hanguk Yeonghwa Chongseo).* Seoul: Korean Film Support Union, 1972.

Korean Film Culture Research Institution. "The Thirty Year History of Korean Films." *Eiga Junpō* (11 July 1943): 16–19.

Kuhn, Annette, and Richard Abel. "The Rise of the American Film Industry." In *The Cinema Book,* edited by Pam Cook, 12–18. London: British Film Institute, 2007.

Kuramochi Shūzō. "The Request to Korean Films (Chōsen Eiga Eno Kibō)." *Eiga Junpō* (11 July 1943): 8–9.

Kuroda Shōzō. "Various Impressions about Korean Film (Chōsen Eiga Zakkan)." *Eiga Hyōron* (July 1941): 47–49.

Lee, Chulwoo. "Modernity, Legality, and Power in Korea under Japanese Rule." In *Colonial Modernity in Korea,* edited by Gi-Wook Shin and Michael Robinson, 21–51. London: Harvard University Asia Center, 1999.

Lee Chung-gi. "Prehistory and Birth of Korean Cinema and Its Characteristics 1 (Hanguk Yeonghwa-Ui Jeonsa Sidae Mit Balsaenggi-Ui Seonggyeog-E Gwanhan Yeongu Sang)." *Collection of Art Papers* 5 (1966): 192–210.

————. "Prehistory and Birth of Korean Cinema and Its Characteristics 2 (Hanguk Yeonghwa-Ui Jeonsa Sidae Mit Balsaenggi-Ui Seonggyeok-E Gwanhan Yeongu Ha)." *Collection of Art Papers* 6 (September 1967): 229–248.

Lee, Hyangjin. *Contemporary Korean Cinema: Identity, Culture, Politics.* Manchester, UK: Manchester UP, 2000.

Lee Hwa-jin. *Chosun Cinema: From Coming of Sound to Pro-Japanese Films (Chosun Yeonghwa: Sori-Ui Doibesobuteo Chinil Yeonghwaggaji).* Seoul: Chaeksesang, 2005.

————. "The Development of the Film Censorship During Colonial Period in Korea (Singminsigi Yeonghwa Geomyeor-Ui Jeongae-Wa Jihyang)." *Hanguk Munhak Yeonggu (Studies in Korean Literature)* 35 (December 2008): 417–456.

Lee Jung-geo. "The Role of Japanese and Japanese Capital in Colonial Cinema Industry in Korea (Iljeha Hanguk Yeonghwa-E Iseoseo-Ui Ilbonin Mit Ilbon Jabon-Ui Yeokhal-Eh Gwanhan Yeongu)." In *Understanding Korean Cinema: From Arirang to Silver Stallion (Hanguk Yeonghwa-Ui Ihae: Arirang-Eso Eunmaneun Oji Anneundaggaji)*, edited by Shin Eun-soo, 111–133. Seoul: Yenni, 1992.

———. "The Study of Korea Film History (Hanguk Eonghwa-Sa Yeongu)." In *Understanding Korean Cinema: From Arirang to the Silver Stallion (Hanguk Yeonghwa-Ui Ihae: Arirang-Eseo Eeonmaeun Oji Anneunda)* edited by Shin Eun-soo, 13–70. Seoul: Yenni, 1996.

Lee Myeong-wu. "The Making of Chunhyangjeon (Chunhyangjeon-Eul Jejakhal Ttae)." *Chosun Yeonghwa (Korean Film)* October 1936, 58.

Lee Pil-wu. "Regarding Talkies: The Making of Secret Story." *Chosun Ilbo* 17–18 April 1930: 4.

Lee Soon-jin. "Miles Away from Happiness (Bokji Malli)." In *Goryeo Film Association and New Film System: 1936–1941 (Goryeo Yeonghwa Hyeophoe-Wa Yeonghwa Shincheje: 1936–1941)*, edited by Oh Sung-ji, 165–166. Seoul: KOFA, 2006.

———. "Spring of Korean Peninsula." In *The Past Unearthed: Feature Film Collection of the Japanese Colonial Period*, 53–56. Seoul: KOFA, 2008.

———. "Straits of Joseon." In *The Past Unearthed: Feature Film Collection of the Japanese Colonial Period*, 63–60. Seoul: KOFA, 2008.

Lee Tae-woo. "Future Direction of Korean Cinema (Hanguk Yeonghwa-Ui Jillo)." *Shin Gyeonghyang (New Trend)* 2, no. 3 (March 1950): 57–59.

———. "How Are We Going to Watch US Films (Miguk Yeonghwa-Reul Eoteoke Bol Geosinga)." *Kyunghyang Ilbo*, 31 October 1946: 4.

Lee Woo-seok. "Film Policy in Post-Liberation Era: 1945–1960 (Gwangbok-Eseo 1960 Nyeonggajiui Yeonghwa Jeongchaek: 1945–1960)." In *A History of Korean Film Policy (Hanguk Yeonghwa Jeongchaeksa)*, 107–188. Seoul: Nanam Publishing, 2005.

Lee Young-il. *History of Korean Cinema (Hanguk Yeonghwa Jeonsa)*. Seoul: Samesa, 1969.

———. *History of Korean Cinema*, 2nd edition *(Hanguk Yeonghwa Jeonsa)*. Seoul: Sodo, 2004.

Lee, Young il, and Young-chol Choe. *The History of Korean Cinema*. Translated by Richard Lynn Greever. Korean Studies Series. Seoul: Jimoondang, 1998.

Lindstrom, S.F. "Nationalism Reported Making Japan Tight Market for Films." *Motion Picture Herald* 16 January 1937: 33.

Litman, Barry R. *The Motion Picture Mega-Industry*. Boston: Allyn & Bacon, 1998.

Lukes, Steven. *Power: A Radical View*. 2nd ed. New York: Palgrave Macmillan, 2005.

Makino Mamoru. "On the Conditions of Film Censorship in Japan before Its Systematization." In *In Praise of Film Studies: Essays in Honor of Makino Mamoru*, edited by Aaron Gerow and Abé Mark Nornes, 46–67. Victoria, BC: Kinema Club in cooperation with Trafford Publishing, 2001.

Maliangkay, Roald. "Their Masters' Voice: Korean Traditional Music Sps (Standard Play Records) under Japanese Colonial Rule." *The World of Music* 49, no. 3—Music and Politics on the Korean Peninsula (2007): 53–74.

———. "New Symbolism and Retail Therapy: Advertising Novelties in Korea's Colonial Period." *East Asian History*, no. 36 (2010): 45–70.

McCune, George M. "Post-War Government and Politics of Korea." *The Journal of Politics* 9, no. 4 (November 1947): 605–623.

McHugh, Kathleen, and Nancy Abelmann, eds. *South Korean Golden Age Melodrama: Gender, Genre, and National Cinema*. Detroit: Wayne State University Press, 2005.

McKenna, Christopher J. "Tri-Racial Theaters in Robeson County, North Carolina, 1896–1940." In *Going to the Movies: Hollywood and the Social Experience of Cinema*, edited by Richard Maltby, Melvyn Stokes, and Robert C. Allen, 45–59 (notes 399–402). Exeter, UK: University of Exeter Press, 2007.

McNamara, Dennis. "The Keishō and the Korean Business Elite." *Journal of Asian Studies* 48, no. 2 (May 1989): 310–323.

Meade, E. Grant. *American Military Government in Korea*. New York: King's Crown Press, 1951.

Mellen, Joan. *The Waves at Genji's Door: Japan through Its Cinema*. New York: Pantheon, 1976.

Merritt, Russell. "Nickelodeon Theaters, 1904–1905: Building an Audience for the Movies." In *The American Film Industry*, edited by Tino Balio, 83–102. Madison: The University of Wisconsin Press, 1985.

Min, Eungjun, Jinsook Joo, and Han Ju Kwak. *Korean Film: History, Resistance, and Democratic Imagination*. Westport, CT: Praeger, 2003.

Mitchell, Richard H. *Thought Control in Prewar Japan*. Ithaca and London: Cornell University Press, 1976.

———. *Censorship in Imperial Japan*. Princeton, NJ: Princeton University Press, 1983.

Mori Hiroshi. "About the Films in Korea (Chōsen Ni Okeru Eiga Nit Suite)." *Eiga Junpō* (11 July 1943): 4–5.

Musser, Charles. *The Emergence of Cinema: The American Screen to 1907*. Edited by Charles Harpole. Vol. 1, History of the American Cinema. Berkeley: University of California Press, 1990.

———. "Passions and the Passion Play: Theater, Film, and Religion in America, 1880–1900." In *Movie Censorship and American Culture*, edited by Francis G. Couvares, 43–72. Washington DC: Smithsonian Institution Press, 1996.

Na Un-gyu. "Making Arirang: Difficulty of Being a Korean Director (Arirang-Eul Mandeulttae: Chosun Yeonghwa Gamdok Gosimdam)." *Chosun Yeonghwa* no. 1 (November 1936. Republished in Kim Jong-wook (2002: 627–630).

———. "*Arirang*, Company and Me (Arirang-Gwa Hoesa-Wa Na)." *Samcheolli* (September 1930): 53–54.

Nagai Reiko. "Thoughts on Korean Films (Chōsen Eiga Zuisō)." *Shin Eiga* (November 1942): 90–94.

Nahm, Andrew. "Korea under Japanese Colonial Rule." In *Korea Tradition and Transformation: A History of the Korean People*, 223–260. Elizabeth, NJ: Hollym, 1996.

Nam In-young. "Film (Yeonghwa)." In *Korean Modern Art History I: Times of Liberation and Separation (Hanguk Hyeondae Yesulsa Daegye I: Haebang-Gwa Bundan Gochak Sigi)*, edited by The Korean National Research Center for Arts, 191–232. Seoul: Sigongsa, 1999.

Nam, Moon-Hyon. "Early History of Electrical Engineering in Korea: Edison and First Electric Lighting in the Kingdom of Corea." In *Singapore 2000: Promoting the History of EE Jan 23–26, 2000*, 1–9. Singapore, 2000.

Noble, Harold J. "The Korean Special Mission to the United States in 1883." *Transactions of the Korea Branch of the Royal Asiatic Society* 48, no. 18 (1929): 1–21.

Nolletti, Arthur Jr., and David Desser. *Reframing Japanese Cinema: Authorship, Genre, History*. Bloomington: Indiana University Press, 1992.

Nornes, Abé Mark. *Japanese Documentary Film: From the Meiji Era to Hiroshima*. Minneapolis: Minnesota University Press, 2003.

Nowell-Smith, Geoffrey, ed. *The Oxford History of World Cinema: The Definitive History of Cinema Worldwide*. Oxford: Oxford University Press, 1996.

Nowell-Smith, Geoffrey, and Stephen Ricci, eds. *Hollywood and Europe: Economics, Culture, National Identity 1945–95*. London: BFI Publishing, 1998.

Oh, Bonnie B. C., ed. *Korea under the American Military Government, 1945–1948*. Westport, CT.: Praeger, 2002.

Oh Seong-ji. "Preface (Seomun)." In *Goryeo Film Association and New System for Film Industry: 1936–1941 (Goryeo Yeonghwa Hyeophoi-Wa Yeonghwa Sincheje: 1936–1941)*, edited by KOFA, 6–9. Seoul: KOFA, 2007.

Ōka Shigematsu. "Many Thoughts on Film Censorship (Yeonghwa Geomyeol Jabgam)." *Chosun and Manchuria* (Chosun geup manju), no. 305 (April 1933, translated into Korean and published in KOFA 2009: 324–327).

———. "Regarding Film Censorship in Korea (Chosuneseo Ui Yeonghwa Geomyeol Eh Daehayeo)." *Chosun* (Chosun), no. 190 (March 1931, translated into Korean and published in KOFA 2009: 314–323).

Ōsaka Mainichi. "Education by Movie Films." In *Japan Today and Tomorrow 1932–33*, 36–39. Ōsaka: Ōsaka Mainichi Publishing Co., 1933.

Ōta Tuneya. "The Prospect of the Korean Film Industry (Chōsen Eigakai No Tenbō)." *Kinema Junpō* (May 1938): 12–13.

Paik, L. George. *The History of Protestant Missions in Korea, 1832–1910*. 4th ed, A Series of Reprints of Western Books on Korea. Seoul: Yonsei University Press, 1987.

Pugach, Noel H. "Second Career: James A. Thomas and the Chinese American Bank of Commerce." *The Pacific Historical Review* 56, no. 2 (1987): 195–229.

Rhee, M. J. "Language Planning in Korea under the Japanese Colonial Administration, 1910–1945." *Language, Culture and Curriculum* 5, no. 2 (1992): 87–97.

Richie, Donald. *Japanese Cinema: Film Style and National Character*. New York: Anchor, 1971.

———. *A Hundred Years of Japanese Film: A Concise History, with a Selective Guide to DVDs and Videos*. Tokyo: Kodansha International, 2001.

Roan, Jeanette. "Exotic Explorations: Travels to Asia and the Pacific in Early Cinema." In *Re/Collecting: Early Asian America*, edited by Imogene L. Lim, Josephine Lee, and Yuko Matsukawa, 187–199. Philadelphia: Temple University, 2002.

Robinson, Michael E. "Colonial Publication Policy and the Korean Nationalist Movement." In *The Japanese Colonial Empire, 1895–1945*, edited by Ramon H. Myers and Mark R. Peattie, 312–343. Princeton, NJ: Princeton University Press, 1984.

———. "Broadcasting, Cultural Hegemony, and Colonial Modernity in Korea, 1924–1945." In *Colonial Modernity in Korea*, edited by Gi-wook Shim and Michael Robinson, 52–69. Cambridge and London: Harvard University Asia Center, 1999.

———. *Cultural Nationalism in Colonial Korea, 1920–1925*. Seattle: University of Washington Press, 1988.

Rout, Marcel. "The Motion Picture Industry in Japan." *Journal of the Society of Motion Picture Engineers* 18, no. 5 (May 1932): 628–642.

Said, Salim. *Shadows on the Silver Screen: A Social History of Indonesian Film*. Translated by Toenggoel P. Siagian. Edited by John H. McGlynn and Janet P. Boileau. Jakarta Lontar Foundation, 1991.

Sakuramoto Tomio. "Korean Film During the 15 Year War—Korea in a Transparent Body." *Kikan Sanzenri* 34 (1983): 184–191.

Satō, Tadao. *Currents in Japanese Cinema: Essays by Tadao Sato*. Translated by Gregory Barrett. Tokyo: Kodansha International, 1987.

Scharf, Inga. *Nation and Identity in the New German Cinema: Homeless at Home*. London: Routledge, 2010.

Schnitman, Jorge A. *Film Industries in Latin America: Dependency and Development*. Norwood, NJ: Ablex, 1984.

Scott, Martin G. "Japan (1914–15; 1921)." In *1922–23 Film Year Book*, 423. New York: Wid's Film and Film Folks, 1923.

Segers, Frank. "Seoul Train: S. Korea Drives World Cinema." *Hollywood Reporter* 18–24 April 2000, 14–16.

Segrave, Kerry. *American Films Abroad: Hollywood's Domination of the World's Movie Screens*. London: McFarland, 1997.

Self, S. B. "Movie Diplomacy: 'Propaganda' Value of Films Perils Hollywood's Rich Markets Abroad." *Wall Street Journal* 16 August 1944: 6.

Shim Hun. "Too Early for Talkies in Korea." *Chosun Yeonghwa* October 1936 82–86.

Shin Chul (Byeonsa). Personal Interview. Seoul, 17 December 2002.

Shin Myeong-jik. *Modern Boy Strolling in Seoul (Modern Boy Gyeongseong-Eul Geonilda)*. Seoul: Hyeonsil Munhwa Yeongu, 2003.

Song, Changzoo. "Business Elite and the Construction of National Identity in Korea." *Acta Koreana* 6, no. 2 (July 2003): 55–86.

Takashima Kinji. *The History of the Film Control System for Korea (Chōsen Eiga Tōsei Shi)*. Seoul: Chōsen Eiga Bunka Kenkyūjo, 1943.

Tani, Chikushi. "Chosen (Korea)." In *Motion Picture Almanac 1936–37*. New York: Quigley Publishing Co., 1937, 1122–1123.

Thomas, James A. *A Pioneer Tobacco Merchant in the Orient*. Durham, NC: Duke University Press, 1928.

———. *Trailing Trade a Million Miles*. Durham, NC: Duke University Press, 1931.

Thompson, Kristin. *Exporting Entertainment: America in the World Film Market 1907–34*. London: British Film Institute, 1985.

Thompson, Kristin, and David Bordwell. *Film History: An Introduction*. 2nd ed. New York: McGraw Hill, 2003.

Triana-Toribio, Nuria. *Spanish National Cinema*. London: Routledge, 2003.

Ugaki Kazushige (Governor-General of Chōsen). "Speech on the Future of Chōsen in Thriving Chosen: A Survey of Twenty-Five Years' Administration." In *Conference of Empire Middle School Principals (11 September 1934)*, 79–93. Seoul, October 1935.

Utsumi Aiko, and Murai Yoshinori. *Shineasuto Kyo Ei no "Shōwa."* Tokyo: Gaifusha, 1987.

Vieth, Eva. "A Glamorous, Untouchable Elsewhere: Europe's American Dream in World War II and Beyond." *International Journal of Cultural Studies* 5, no. 1 (2002): 21–44.

War Activities Committee, Motion Picture Industry. "Movies at War, Volume 1." New York, 1942.

———. "Movies at War, Volume 2." New York, 1943.

———. "Movies at War, Volume 3." New York, 1944.

———. "Movies at War, Volume 4." New York, 1945.

Webster, Harrie. "Korea—the Hermit Nation." *National Geographic Magazine* 11 (1900): 145–155.

Yau Shuk-ting, Kinnia. *Japanese and Hong Kong Film Industries: Understanding the Origins of East Asian Film Networks*. London: Routledge, 2009.

Yecies, Brian. "Transformative Soundscapes: Innovating De Forest Phonofilms Talkies in Australia." *Scope: An Online Journal of Film Studies* no. 1 (2005a), www.nottingham.ac.uk/film/journal

———. "Systematization of Film Censorship in Colonial Korea: Profiteering from Hollywood's First Golden Age, 1926–1936." *Journal of Korean Studies* 10, no. 1 (2005b): 59–84.

———. "Talking Salvation for the Silent Majority: Projecting New Possibilities of Modernity in the Australian Cinema, 1929–33." In *Talking and Listening in the Age of Modernity*, edited by J. Damousi and D. Deacon. Canberra: ANU ePress, 2007.

———. "Sounds of Celluloid Dreams: Coming of the Talkies to Cinema in Colonial Korea." *Korea Journal* 48, no. 1 (2008): 16–97.

Yecies, Brian, and Ae-Gyung Shim. "Lost Memories of Korean Cinema: Film Policies During Japanese Colonial Rule, 1919–1937." *Asian Cinema* 14, no. 2 (Fall/Winter) (2003): 75–90.

———. "Disarming Japan's Cannons with Hollywood's Cameras: Cinema in Korea under U.S. Occupation, 1945–1948 " *The Asia-Pacific Journal* (November 1 2010), http://www.japanfocus.org/-Brian-Yecies/3437

Yi Hyoin. *Korean Film History Lecture 1 (Hanguk Yeoksa Gangui 1)*. Seoul: Irongwa Silchon, 1992.

———. "The Korean Film Community and Film Movements During the Post-Liberation Era." In *Traces of Korean Cinema from 1945 to 1959*, 11–89. Seoul: KOFA, 2003.

———. "The Korean Film Community and Film Movements During the Post-Liberation Era." In *A History of Korean Cinema: From Liberation through the 1960s*, 6–29. Seoul: KOFA, 2005.

Yi Hyoin, Oh Gi-seong, and Yu Young-il. *50 North Korean Films for Unified Koreans (Tongil Hangugin-I Boayahal Bukan Yeonghwa 50 Seon)*. Seoul: Korean Film Council, 2002.

Yi, Hyo-in, Jong-hwa Jung, and Ji-yeon Park. *A History of Korean Cinema: From Liberation through the 1960s*, Korean Film History Review Vol. 1. Seoul: KOFA, 2005.

Yi Hyo-in, and Yi Jung-ha. *Cinema on the Road (Ssitgim)*. Seoul: Yeolin Chaekdeul, 1995.

Yi Young-jae. *Japanese Empire and Chosun Cinema: Korean Peninsular at the End of Colonial Rule—Sentiment of Collaboration, Policy and Logic (Jeguk Ilbon-Ui Chosun Yeonghwa: Singminji Mal-Ui Bando—Hyeomnyeog-Ui Simjeong, Jedo, Nolli)*. Seoul: Hyunshil Book, 2008.

Yoshimi, Shunya. "'America' as Desire and Violence: Americanization in Postwar Japan and Asia During the Cold War." *Inter-Asia Cultural Studies* 4, no. 3 (2003): 433–450.

Yu Hyun-mok. *History of Korean Film Development (Hanguk Yeonghwa Baldalsa)*. Seoul: Hanjin Publishing, 1997.

Yu Min-young. *Korea's Modern Theater History (Hanguk Geundae Geukjang Byeoncheonsa)*. Seoul: Taehak Publishing, 1998.

Zhang, Yingjin. *Chinese National Cinema*. New York and London: Routledge, 2004.

Index

46; number of, 2; number of
screens, 2; seating, 44–45, 46,
59–60; as subversive locations,
61; ticket sales, 3. *See also* audiences, segregation
cinematographers: fascination with
'native' subjects, 16, 20; early,
19, 20
Civilization, 70
Colbert, Claudette, 154
Collaboration. *See* cooperation with
occupying power
Collbran, Henry, 12, 18, 19, 21, 31, 34,
36, 37, 44
Columbia Pictures, 80
comedies/comedy films, 54, 70, 106, 153;
action-comedy, 177; comedy-mysteries, 157; musical comedy, 159;
romantic comedy, 177
Commissioner Tanaka [Saburo]'s
Speech, 132
communications infrastructure, development of, 17–18
communist films, 159
CMPE. *See* Central Motion Picture
Exchange
Confucian traditions, 44; Hollywood
movies and, 146–147; impact of
foreign films on, 41, 43–44, 162,
163; impact of cinema culture
on, 60–61; moral panics and, 60;
U.S. disregard for, 15, 146–147,
157–158. *See also* Hollywood
consolidation of film distribution and
production, 114, 118, 130–140,
114
Continental Kunstfilm, 54, 163
cooperation with occupying power:
audiences 5; entrepreneurs 5;
filmmakers 5, 14
co-productions 5, 14, 69, 86, 90, 96,
97, 117, 133, 165; under Korean
Film Law, 119, 120, 133. *See
also* cooperation with occupying
power
Corfe, Bishop C. J., 22, 24
Crosby, Bing, 154
cross-cultural media flows, 20
Crossroads of Youth, 151
Crowd Roars, 90
Crowd, A, 29
cultural films, 132, 139. *See also* propaganda films
Cunard, Grace, 81

D
Daejeonggwan Cinema, 46, 55; Daejeonggwan I, 47, 54; Daejeonggwan II, 50, 54, 56, 57; special
license arrangements, 52
Daejung Yeonghwa magazine, 103, 104
Daiei studio, 131, 132, 137
Danish Painter's Dream, 56
Danseongsa Cinema, 46, 50, 52, 53,
59, 81, 87, 104, 109, 111; renovations, 67–68
Dark Light, see Make-up of God
de Banos, Richard, 56
de Chomón, Segundo, 56
De Forest Phonofilms, 98
de Forest, Lee, 99
Dear Soldier, 138, 166
Declaration of Independence, The, 57
DeMille, Cecil. B., 153
democratic ideals: U.S. promotion of,
145, 146
Department of Home Affairs, 92; *see
also* censorship
Depue, Oscar B., 28, 43
Desperate Desmond, 66
Destry Rides Again, 186. See also
Dietrich, Marlene; and Stewart,
James
Devil and Daniel Webster, The, 157
Devil Doll, The, 153
Dietrich, Marlene, 185; starring in
Destry Rides Again, 186,
diplomatic relations: early, 4, 17; with
France, 17; with Japan, 17;
Japanese control over, 42; with
United States, 17
Disney animations, 141
Dix, Richard, 154
documentaries, 19, 49, 52, 54, 55, 58,
59, 67, 68, 69, 75, 79, 86, 91,
98, 101, 106, 129, 133, 134,
139, 152, 153, 160. *See also
actualité* films
Dok Eun-gi, 136
Donga Cultural Association, 51
Donga Ilbo, 8, 71, 98, 110
Dongyang Film Company, 106
Dr. Gar-el-hama, 66
Dracula, 106
Duvivier, Julien, 129, 150

E
Earth, 131
economic growth, 167